6/15/11
45.00

THE BULLY PULPIT AND THE MELTING POT

THE BULLY PULPIT AND THE MELTING POT

American Presidents and the Immigrant, 1897–1933

Hans P. Vought

MERCER UNIVERSITY PRESS
Macon, Georgia
25th Anniversary

ISBN 0-86554-887-0
MUP/H659

First Edition.

∞The paper used in this publication meets the minimum requirements of American National Standard for Information Sciences—Permanence of Paper for Printed Library Materials, ANSI Z39.48-1992.

Library of Congress Cataloging-in-Publication Data
Vought, Hans P.
 The bully pulpit and the melting pot : American presidents and the immigrant, 1897/1933 / by Hans P. Vought.— 1st ed..
     p. cm.
 Includes bibliographical references and index.
 ISBN 0-86554-887-0 (hardcover : alk. paper)
 1. United States—Emigration and immigration—
Government policy—History. 2. Presidents—
United States—History. I. Title.
 JV6483.V68 2004
 325.73'09'041—dc22
                                        2004020511

CONTENTS

I suppose my critics will call that preaching,

but I have got such a bully pulpit!

—*Theodore Roosevelt*

America is God's crucible, the great Melting-Pot where all of the races of Europe are melting and re-forming! Here you stand, good folk, think I, when I see them at Ellis Island, here you stand in your fifty groups, with your fifty languages and histories, and your fifty blood hatreds and rivalries. But you won't be long like that, brothers, for these are the fires of God you've come to–these are the fires of God. A fig for your feuds and vendettas! Germans and Frenchmen, Irishmen and Englishmen, Jews and Russians–into the Crucible with you all! God is making the American.

—Israel Zangwill, *The Melting Pot*

PREFACE

In the last three decades, the number of immigrants entering the United States has rivaled the historic peak of 1890-1920, although the foreign-born do not constitute as great a percentage of the population now as they did then. According to the 2000 census, there were over thirty-one million foreign-born residents, representing eleven percent of the population.[1] This resurgence of immigration has brought renewed attention to the ongoing debate between those who emphasize America's cultural pluralism and those who stress the need for national unity. In particular, the arrival of millions of Asian and Hispanic immigrants since the passage of the 1965 Immigration Act has led many to reexamine what it means to be an American and to weigh the costs and benefits of immigration. Groups like the Center for Immigration Studies and the Federation for American Immigration Reform (FAIR) warn of the negative consequences resulting from a rapidly rising population and the influx of low-skilled workers who compete with America's existing underclass. Other groups, such as the National Immigration Forum and the American Civil Liberties Union, see such concerns as simply a recrudescence of nativism and racism, particularly since they come in response to the arrival of groups historically discriminated against.

Political leaders, especially presidents, play a key role mediating this public debate. Since the states which receive the most immigrants—California, Texas, Florida, New York, New Jersey and Illinois—are also key battlegrounds in national elections, presidents and their challengers need to take seriously the attitudes of voters in those states who feel overwhelmed by the growing burden immigrants place on their taxes and social services.

---

[1] Actually, 31,098,945, of whom an estimated 8,705,419 entered the country illegally. J. Gregory Robinson, *ESCAP II: Demographic Analysis Reports: Executive Steering Committee for A.C.E. Policy Report No. 1* (Washington DC: U.S. Census Bureau, 2001) A–5.

The presidents represent the whole nation, however, and therefore they are also under considerable pressure to celebrate its racial, ethnic and cultural diversity. The concept of the United States as a melting pot, which recognizes both America's diversity and Americans' desire for unity, offers a constructive way to resolve this dilemma.

This use of the melting pot concept dates back to the Progressive Era, the first two-to-three decades of the twentieth century. All the presidents from 1897 to 1933 proclaimed that the United States was a melting pot, offering asylum to freedom-loving immigrants and assimilating them into American social and political life. In doing so, the chief executives called for the creation of a singular national identity based upon American political ideals. Supporters of the melting pot concept set minimal criteria for assimilation of the foreign-born, assuming that the process was both inevitable and desirable. Immigrants were welcomed into American society as long as they embraced democratic political ideals and capitalist economic principles, and conducted their public and private affairs with a sense of civic responsibility. They also had to show their commitment to their new country by becoming citizens, learning English, and abandoning any allegiance (but not emotional or cultural attachment) to their old homelands. To the presidents, this simply meant that immigrants had to take advantage of the freedom and opportunity the United States offered to them.[2]

The metaphor of a melting pot, conjuring an image of the large blast furnaces in which iron ore was purified and formed into iron or steel, was appropriate to the industrializing America most immigrants entered in the nineteenth and early twentieth centuries. British Jewish immigrant Israel Zangwill popularized the term in the United States. His 1908 play, *The Melting Pot*, which was dedicated to President Theodore Roosevelt, portrayed the United States as God's crucible, in which he was creating a new race of supermen.[3] The underlying concept dated back to the agrarian

---

[2] Philip Gleason, "American Identity and Americanization," *Harvard Encyclopedia of American Ethnic Groups*, ed. Stephan Thernstrom, (Cambridge: Harvard University Press, 1980) 32–33, 38–39; Peter D. Salins, *Assimilation, American Style* (New York: Basic Books, 1997) 43–59.

[3] Philip Gleason, *Speaking of Diversity: Language and Ethnicity in Twentieth-Century America* (Baltimore: Johns Hopkins University Press, 1992) 5–11, 35. The metaphor had long been used in Great Britain to describe any process of change.

republic of 1782, however, when Michael-Guillaume Jean de Crèvecoeur wrote that America was an asylum where individuals from all races were melted into a new race of men.[4] This result implied intermarriage and thus raised fears of miscegenation, which was the main reason why African and Asian Americans were not considered to be assimilable. European immigrants, however, were mostly seen as assets in the early and mid-nineteenth century, helping to build the nation and settle its frontier. Their assimilation was taken for granted, and seemed compatible with racialist thinking that celebrated the ability of the "Anglo-Saxon race" to assimilate other European races, and Darwinism that suggested mixed strains were hardier than pure breeds.[5]

The easy confidence of the early nineteenth century gave way to greater demands for social control in the Gilded Age of the late nineteenth century and the Progressive Era of the early twentieth century. Nativism, which arose out of mutually-reinforcing traditions of anti-Catholicism, anti-radicalism, and the championing of a superior "Anglo-Saxon" culture, began to challenge the traditional faith in the melting pot concept. Proponents of immigration restriction asserted that only Protestants from Northern and Western Europe could be assimilated, and even they had to abandon completely their old languages and cultures. Catholic immigrants from Germany and Ireland were targeted by the American Protective Association in the 1890s. Likewise, in the late nineteenth century the new immigrants from Austria-Hungary, Italy, and Russia were anathematized because of alleged racial and religious inferiority, and their lack of an understanding of and commitment to democracy and capitalism.[6]

Nativists contrasted the old immigrants from Northern and Western Europe with the new immigrants from Southern and Eastern Europe. They argued that the former had come to the United States as farmers or skilled workers, brought their families and settled permanently in smaller cities or in the countryside, and quickly adopted the language, culture, and political

---

[4] Ibid., 5–11; see also Gleason, "American Identity," 32–33.

[5] Gleason, "American Identity," 38–39. The exception, of course, was the short-lived "Know-Nothing" movement of the 1850s.

[6] Ibid., 39–41; and John Higham, *Strangers in the Land: Patterns of American Nativism, 1860–1925,* 2d ed. (New Brunswick: Rutgers University Press, 1988).

ideals of America. The latter, however, were unskilled factory workers, men who came without their families and stayed only briefly, living in filthy tenements, never learning English, and spreading radical political doctrines like anarchism and communism. Nativists alleged that the rate of naturalization among the new immigrants, which compared unfavorably to that of the old immigrants, and the crime rate for the new immigrants, which was higher than that of the native-born, showed that the newcomers were undesirable. The new immigrants' support for the corrupt urban political machines and their failure to learn English were further proof that they had not assimilated and did not accept American ideals. Eugenicists, scientists who studied human genetics with the goal of breeding a better race, explained that Southern and Eastern Europeans had biologically inherited character flaws which were immutable and rendered them unassimilable.

Liberal progressives countered these nativist arguments by redefining the melting pot concept in subtle ways. They acknowledged the need for more careful management of the assimilation process, and supported screening immigrants for physical and mental defects and barring Asians. They also agreed that learning the English language was a prerequisite for fully embracing American ideals, and thus they supported the 1906 Naturalization Act that made English literacy a requirement for gaining citizenship. Nevertheless, they continued to believe that the new European immigrants would eventually assimilate just like the old ones. Liberal progressives denied that the foreign-born had to abandon their old cultures completely and conform to an "Anglo-Saxon" model. Instead, they celebrated the contributions that European immigrants made to American culture as part of the melting process. They also emphasized the responsibility of native-born Americans to provide a supportive environment and economic opportunities for immigrants in order to eliminate the appeal of socialism and communism.

While rejecting nativism and eugenics, liberal progressives also opposed the cultural pluralists who viewed the melting pot as a tool to coerce immigrants into submitting to the dominant "Anglo-Saxon" culture. Pluralists insisted that a true democracy would not force immigrants to give up their deeply ingrained racial or ethnic identities. They wanted each racial and ethnic group to retain its own language and customs, but use English as the *lingua franca*. Liberal progressives rejected cultural pluralism because they firmly believed that the United States needed to create a common culture and national identity. They promoted, however, the potential contributions of various European ethnic groups to that common culture and identity.[7]

The progressive revision of the melting pot concept steered a middle path between the extremes of nativism and cultural pluralism, and so it was consistently upheld by the presidents from William McKinley to Herbert Hoover. They used the prestige of the office (which Theodore Roosevelt called "a bully pulpit") to shape public opinion, denying the claims of nativists that racially and culturally inferior immigrants threatened the health and strength of the nation.[8] At the same time, they called on the foreign-born to join wholeheartedly in upholding American political and economic ideals, contributing their gifts to strengthen the United States. The result was a civic nationalism that embodied the motto, "*E pluribus, unum*" ("Out of many, one"), leaving individuals free to express their cultural heritages as long as they were devoted to their new country. There were racial limits to this nationalism, however, as the presidents continued to exclude African and Asian Americans from their vision of the melting pot.[9]

The presidents' position as head of state made them the focal point of American nationalism. Taking advantage of this position, each one tried to embody and articulate the national identity and the ideals to which citizens aspired. This gave them a unique opportunity to set the limits of citizenship, defining who was acceptable as an American. Such definition was subject to conflicting pressures. The president was the only elected official in the

---

[7] Nathan Glazer, "Is Assimilation Dead?" *The Annals of the American Academy of Political and Social Science,* 530 (November 1993): 123 30; Gleason, *Speaking of Diversity,* 14–20; John Higham, *Send These To Me: Jews and Other Immigrants in Urban America,* 2d ed. (Baltimore: Johns Hopkins University Press, 1984) 200, 203–08, 212; and Rivka Shpak Lissak, *Pluralism and Progressives: Hull House and the New Immigrants, 1890–1919* (Chicago: University of Chicago Press, 1989) 25–33, 143–54.

[8] Roosevelt's phrase is quoted in Lyman Abbott, "A Review of President Roosevelt's Administration, IV: It's Influence on Patriotism and Public Service," *The Outlook* 91 (27 February 1909): 430.

[9] The intertwining strains of civic and racial nationalism are discussed in Gary Gerstle, *American Crucible: Race and Nation in the Twentieth Century* (Princeton: Princeton University Press, 2001).

federal government who could not be an immigrant and each incumbent had a natural tendency to define the ideal American in his own image. As leaders of their political parties, however, presidents had to appeal to the greatest possible number of voters nationwide. Consequently, they could not risk offending ethnic groups.

United States presidents from 1897–1933 were caught in the middle of a fierce debate over immigration and assimilation. As all politicians do, they sought to lead without getting too far ahead of public opinion. By upholding the progressive melting pot concept against the racially exclusive model championed by nativists and eugenicists, William McKinley, Theodore Roosevelt, William Howard Taft and Woodrow Wilson resisted race-based restriction until World War I and the Red Scare raised fears of unassimilable immigrants that resulted in an overwhelming demand for the exclusion of certain classes of newcomers to America. Warren Harding, Calvin Coolidge and Herbert Hoover softened the blow of the restrictive National Origins quotas in the 1920s by salvaging the progressive version of the melting pot from the coercive Americanization campaigns spawned by the war, while rejecting cultural pluralism. In doing so, they laid the groundwork for the New Deal's ethnic, working-class coalition and maintained the universalist ideals that would be called upon in World War II and the civil rights movement.

The progressive concept of the melting pot never fully resembled the model attacked by the new ethnicity scholars of the 1960s and 1970s, who defined assimilation as complete conformity to White, Anglo-Saxon, Protestant culture and then belabored the obvious point that such Americanization had not happened.[10] The progressive legacy is worth reexamining because scholars are once again considering the topics of nationalism, immigration and assimilation. Historians have observed that the melting pot concept did not necessarily mean adopting a clearly defined, unchangeable, core group culture. Most recent scholarship has focused on

---

[10] See, e.g., Nathan Glazer and Daniel P. Moynihan, *Beyond the Melting Pot: The Negroes, Puerto Ricans, Jews, Italians and Irish of New York City,* 2d ed. (Cambridge: Massachusetts Institute of Technology Press, 1970); Andrew M. Greeley, *Why Can't They Be Like Us?: America's White Ethnic Groups* (New York: E. P. Dutton & Co., 1971); and Michael Novak, *The Rise of the Unmeltable Ethnics* (New York: Macmillan Company, 1972).

the various ways in which the extent and meaning of assimilation were contested by different immigrants and ethnic groups. Historian John Bodnar has shown that rather than accepting or rejecting assimilation outright, immigrants kept the Old World traditions that were in their best self-interest, creating a "culture of everyday life" that centered around the family unit rather than the ethnic group.[11] Scholar Lawrence Fuchs points out that immigrants could choose to be both Americans (by embracing civic ideals) and ethnic group members (by retaining some or all of their culture).[12] Immigrants in labor unions also co-opted the rhetoric of Americanization and used it to advance their own agenda in a process of "Americanization from the bottom up."[13]

This book complements recent scholarship by reexamining immigration and assimilation from the top down, through the perspective of the presidents. Those scholars who deny that assimilation occurred, or that it was even desirable, correctly point out that most immigrants never became "100 percent Americans." They misunderstand, however, the nature of the progressive melting pot concept. The presidents welcomed newcomers on the basis of shared ideals rather than shared genes, believing that diversity did not preclude national unity. They did not deny that individual citizens had the freedom to choose what customs to keep; they merely insisted that their primary group loyalty be to America, not to a class or race. The presidents' prejudice, shared by most White Americans, excluded Asian Americans from immigration and naturalization, and limited the number of Southern and Eastern Europeans admitted to the United States. Nevertheless, the melting pot concept was a noble ideal, one worth reviving today without the barriers of bigotry which accompanied it in the past.

---

[11] John Bodnar, *The Transplanted: A History of Immigrants in Urban America* (Bloomington: Indiana University Press, 1985) 206–16.

[12] Lawrence H. Fuchs, *The American Kaleidoscope: Race, Ethnicity, and the Civic Culture* (Hanover NH: University Press of New England; Middletown CT: Wesleyan University Press, 1990) 1–69.

[13] James R. Barrett, "Americanization from the Bottom Up: Immigration and the Remaking of the Working Class in the United States, 1880–1930," *Journal of American History* 79/3 (December 1992): 996–1020; and Gary Gerstle, *Working-Class Americanism: The Politics of Labor in a Textile City, 1914–1960* (Cambridge: Cambridge University Press, 1989).

The value of the progressive melting pot concept lies in the fact that it offers a middle path between the extremes of nativism and pluralism, the latter better known today as multiculturalism. As historian David Hollinger has pointed out, multiculturalism offers no place for national identity, and thus provides no certain means to hold together the democratic nation-state that remains the dominant power structure in society. Furthermore, the inaccurate ethno-racial classifications employed by the government to chart diversity and punish discrimination oversimplify complex identities and ironically reinforce racialist notions that an earlier generation of liberals labored mightily to banish from the national discourse.[14] One of those liberals, historian Arthur Schlesinger, Jr., has rightly criticized this separatism because it "nourishes prejudices, magnifies differences and stirs antagonisms," leading to "the fragmentation, resegregation, and tribalization of American life."[15] Although the United States and its presidents have frequently confused civic nationalism with racial nationalism, to trade the latter for the former is to make a bad bargain.

While some scholars dismiss the melting pot concept as a false and even insidious myth, I contend that the progressive model of the melting pot championed by the presidents of the early twentieth century offers a paradigm of civic nationalism that, when broadened to include all racial, ethnic and religious groups, combines a respect for America's diversity with an appreciation of and commitment to the best of the nation's ideals. It presents a path to follow in the early twenty-first century, as the United States once again attracts millions of immigrants. In the light of the World War I experience and the current situation in the United States, it seems obvious that the true alternative to the melting pot concept is not multiculturalism, but rather an intolerant, xenophobic nationalism that rejects racial or religious minorities as un-American and seeks to curtail their civil liberties. In such circumstances, I would argue that the melting pot concept, which includes the ideal that equal rights must be enjoyed by all citizens, is the only sensible choice to make.

---

[14] David A. Hollinger, *Postethnic America: Beyond Multiculturalism* (New York: Basic Books, 1995).

[15] Arthur M. Schlesinger, Jr., *The Disuniting of America: Reflections on a Multicultural Society* (New York: W. W. Norton & Co., 1992) 17–18.

A note on terminology is in order here. For the sake of historical clarity, I use the term Indian rather than Native American in this book. In the late nineteenth century and early twentieth century, the term Native American referred to native-born citizens (and usually, albeit implicitly, those of European origin) rather than the original inhabitants of North America. In the documents that I quote the words "native" and "Native American" have this meaning. As I wish to allow historical actors to speak for themselves in their own words, I have not altered such passages, but I intend no offense. Instead, I will follow their usage in my own text, as well, to remain true to the time period and avoid confusion.

This book is a revised version of my Ph.D. dissertation for the University of Connecticut. Careful reading by A. William Hoglund, Ralph Fierro, R. Kent Newmyer, Jeffrey Ogbar, Thomas Price, Bruce Stave, Edmund Wehrle and the anonymous readers for Mercer University Press has improved my work in many ways, though I have persisted, no doubt, in several errors. I am grateful to Ronald Bayor, editor of the *Journal of American Ethnic History*, for generously allowing the reuse of portions of an earlier article.[16] I also want to thank the many people who assisted me in my research, particularly Dwight Miller and the staff of the Herbert Hoover Presidential Library in West Branch, Iowa, who made my time there both productive and enjoyable; the staff of the Ohio Historical Society in Columbus, Ohio, who helped me locate relevant materials in the Warren G. Harding Papers; and the Interlibrary Loan staff at the Homer Babbidge Library of the University of Connecticut, who secured many reels of microfilm for me. Financial support from the University of Connecticut and the Herbert Hoover Presidential Library enabled me to complete my research. Above all, I thank my wife and family for their endless patience, support and love, and I dedicate this book to them.

---

[16] Hans P. Vought, "Division and Reunion: Woodrow Wilson, Immigration, and the Myth of American Unity," *Journal of American Ethnic History* 13/3 (Spring 1994): 24–48.

CHAPTER 1

SETTING THE PARAMETERS OF CITIZENSHIP

Many Americans describe the United States as a melting pot where people from different lands come together to form one nation. Americans have always struggled, however, to define exactly which immigrants were welcome to take part in the amalgamation. The nation's presidents have played a unique role in shaping public opinion on this matter. According to the Constitution, the presidency is the only office which cannot be assumed by an immigrant, ensuring that the chief executive of the nation will always be native-born. The president is also the only elected official whose constituency is the entire nation, and thus office-holders must appeal to the largest possible number of Americans in order to retain the presidency. The president shapes public discourse on immigration in two ways: by using the powerfully symbolic role as head of state, or what Theodore Roosevelt termed the "bully pulpit," to define the nature and responsibilities of American citizenship; and by administering the laws on immigration.

The egalitarian principles which define, in theory, American citizenship are the twin ideals of assimilation and asylum. This theory, formed during the American Revolution, was defined in ideological rather than racial or ethnic terms. Although a majority of the White population was British in background, they could not explicitly base their national identity on a common cultural heritage because they were attempting to throw off British rule and needed the help of German, Dutch, and other colonists to do so. Instead, the revolutionaries made adherence to their republican ideology the criterion for citizenship. This ideology was built on the radical Whig political tradition of Great Britain, but it emphasized the idea that America was a "new world" emerging from the ruins of the old.[1] The Puritan belief

---

[1] Philip Gleason, "American Identity and Americanization," *Harvard Encyclopedia of American Ethnic Groups*, ed. Stephan Thernstrom, (Cambridge: Harvard University Press, 1980) 31–33. On the revolutionaries' republican ideology, see Bernard Bailyn, *The*

that America would be a "city on a hill" was thus secularized and made universal: the United States would be a political rather than spiritual example to the rest of the world.

From the very beginning, however, the universality of American national identity was belied by racist realities. The egalitarian principles of the American Revolution have been in constant conflict with the racist attitudes of many Americans. For example, when Thomas Jefferson wrote that "all men are created equal," one-fifth of the population in the thirteen American colonies was held in perpetual slavery. Although some of his fellow founders were moved to free their slaves and so avoid hypocrisy, none of them seriously objected to the exclusion of Indians from the new nation's citizenry. The city on a hill was a *herrenvolk* democracy, limited to White European males and their descendants.

Nevertheless, within those European limits, the two essential components of an inclusive definition of citizenship remained the ideals of assimilation and asylum. Although the revolutionaries could not exclusively identify themselves with their British heritage, they never disowned it. The founders spoke the English language, they believed in English political ideals, and they expected those of different nationality to do the same. Because assimilation had long been under way in the colonies, they had no reason to believe that it would not continue. This confidence in what would later be termed the "melting pot" was best expressed by the French-American writer, Michael-Guillaume Jean de Crèvecoeur, in his famous description of Americans: "They are a mixture of English, Scotch, Irish, French, Dutch, Germans, and Swedes. From this promiscuous breed, that new race now called Americans have arisen." Assimilation eliminated all differences, whether racial or religious, in the process of forming a new culture. *"He* is an American, who, leaving behind him all his ancient prejudices and manners, receives new ones from the new mode of life he has embraced, the new government he obeys, and the new rank he holds," Crèvecoeur explained. He celebrated "this great American asylum" as a place where "individuals of all races are melted into a new race of men, whose labours and posterity will one day cause great changes in the world."

Ideological Origins of the American Revolution, enlarged ed. (Cambridge: Harvard University Press, 1992); and Gordon S. Wood, *The Radicalism of the American Revolution* (New York: Alfred A. Knopf, 1992).

The hyperbole of "all races," however, was modified by his definition of an American as "either a European, or a descendant of an European."[2]

The concept of America as an asylum for the oppressed of Europe was dependent on the belief in assimilation. There was no point in being a "city on a hill" if no one was attracted to come and live there. Americans, however, worried about attracting those who would mar the purity of the city.[3] Americans would only celebrate their nation as an asylum as long as they were confident that the refugees who came could successfully be assimilated. On the other hand, the noble ideal of providing asylum lent a moral purpose to assimilation: immigrants, like religious converts, had to be catechized in the faith. The concept of asylum also helped to distinguish the new world from the old, including Great Britain. In the Revolutionary classic, *Common Sense*, Thomas Paine refuted the notion that Great Britain was the "mother country" to which obedience and respect was due. He wrote that "Europe, and not England, is the parent country of America. This new world hath been the asylum for the persecuted lovers of civil and religious liberty from *every part* of Europe."[4]

Throughout the first hundred years of the nation's existence, confidence in the United States as an asylum and melting pot remained high. As a result, the federal government paid scant attention to immigration issues, and there were no serious movements to limit immigration, other than the anti-Catholic hysteria of the "Know-Nothing" movement in the early 1850s. The United States was so decentralized that a weak, ideologically-based national identity made more sense than a strong, ethnically-defined one. Furthermore, the Christian belief in the brotherhood of man and the Lockean emphasis on environment created confidence in America's ability to create a unified national character. Blacks and Indians remained troubling

---

[2] J. Hector St. John Crèvecoeur, *Letters from an American Farmer. Describing Certain Provincial Situations, Manners, and Customs, Not Generally Known; and Conveying Some Idea of the Late and Present Interior Circumstances of the British Colonies in North America, Written for the Information of a Friend in England* (London: Thomas Davies, 1782; reprint, New York: Fox, Duffield & Co., 1904) 39–44. The metaphor of the melting pot comes from British Jew Israel Zangwill's 1908 play of the same name. See Philip Gleason, *Speaking of Diversity: Language and Ethnicity in Twentieth-Century America* (Baltimore: Johns Hopkins University Press, 1992) 5–11.

[3] John Higham, "Integrating America: The Problem of Assimilation in the Nineteenth Century," *Journal of American Ethnic History* 1/1 (Fall 1981): 15–18.

[4] Thomas Paine, *Common Sense* (Philadelphia: W. & T. Bradford, 1776) 29.

exceptions, however, and the South began to embrace racial determinism in justifying slavery.[5]

Although Article I, Section 9 of the United States Constitution gives to Congress the power to regulate immigration, the federal government proved reluctant to exercise it until the 1870s. That reluctance was intertwined with an unwillingness to regulate the domestic slave trade. Other than outlawing the international slave trade in 1808, Congress largely avoided dealing with the potentially explosive issue during the first 90 years of national life. In addition, immigration contributed to America's growth and development: westward expansion offered seemingly limitless room for a burgeoning population, and the growing industries of the northeast welcomed an inexpensive labor supply.

Despite such reluctance, the first congressional attempt to regulate immigration was based on the belief that the assimilation of immigrants was essential to national unity. The Federalists, alarmed by fears of immigrant disloyalty during an undeclared naval war with France, passed the Alien Act and the Alien Enemy Act in 1798. The Alien Act, which gave the president the power to deport aliens who were "dangerous to the peace and safety of the United States," expired by its own terms two years later. The Alien Enemy Act, applicable only in wartime allowed the government to detain or deport male enemy aliens.[6] remained forgotten on the books until even more hysterical fears of immigrant disloyalty during World War I prompted Woodrow Wilson to use it and Congress to strengthen it. While the Alien and Sedition Acts represented only a momentary surge of panic, they showed that national unity is of most importance during wartime. World War I led not only to the drastic curtailment of civil liberties for immigrants, but also to the postwar decision to close the nation's gates to them.

The Alien and Sedition Acts aside, federal naturalization laws rested on an easy confidence in the assimilation of immigrants. The process of becoming a citizen was not difficult, but it was limited to Whites. Congress established only a two-year waiting period in 1790. In 1795 the waiting period was increased to five years, and the new law required a declaration of intent to seek citizenship ("first papers") three years prior to naturalization.

---

[5] Gleason, "American Identity," 33–36; Higham, "Integrating America," 10–14; and Oscar Handlin, *Race and Nationality in American Life* (Boston: Little, Brown & Co., 1957) 29–50.

[6] Edward P. Hutchinson, *Legislative History of American Immigration Policy, 1798–1965* (Philadelphia: University of Pennsylvania Press, 1981) 12–16.

Although the waiting period was briefly raised to fourteen years by the Naturalization Act of 1798, it was lowered once again to five years in 1802. Thomas Jefferson requested it on the basis of asylum, asking, "shall we refuse to the unhappy fugitives from distress that hospitality which the savages of the wilderness extended to our fathers arriving in this land? Shall oppressed humanity find no asylum in this globe?" The Naturalization Act of 1824 simplified the process further and decreased the waiting period between declaration and naturalization to two years. In 1855, derivative citizenship was granted to foreign-born wives and children of US citizens.[7] Many states even allowed aliens who had taken out their "first papers" to vote in elections.[8]

The confidence in assimilation expressed in the naturalization laws was matched by confidence in America's ability to welcome all Europeans to the asylum of the frontier. President John Tyler's 1841 annual message to Congress noted the vast amount of unpopulated land in the territories and said, "We hold out to the peoples of other countries an invitation to come and settle among us as members of our rapidly growing family." Two years later, he praised the "emigrants from all parts of the civilized world, who come among us to partake of the blessings of our free institutions, and to aid by their labor to swell the current of our wealth and power."[9] Tyler celebrated America's role as an asylum, but his welcome was limited to "the civilized world" of Europe.

Antebellum confidence in assimilation was reflected in the lack of federal laws restricting immigration. In the first half of the nineteenth century, Congress acted mostly to protect immigrants from the hazards of the journey to the United States. The Passenger Act of 1819 set a limit of two passengers for every five tons of vessel burden (crew excepted), and required a list of all passengers with basic information about them (name, sex, occupation, and nationality). In 1847, a new Passenger Act required fourteen square feet of clear deck space per passenger (twenty if the ship passed through the tropics) to improve the health of passengers. Two hundred passengers on ships arriving at New York had died the previous winter, many of them victims of the Irish Potato Famine. Amendments in 1848 and 1849 set ventilation, sanitation, and nutrition standards for all ships

---

[7] Ibid., 11–17, 23, 40.

[8] Gerald L. Neuman, *Strangers to the Constitution: Immigrants, Borders, and Fundamental Law* (Princeton: Princeton University Press, 1996) 63–71.

[9] Hutchinson, *Legislative History*, 30–31.

with fifty or more steerage passengers, and applied the regulations to Pacific ocean vessels for the first time. The 1855 Passenger Act limited ships to one passenger for every two tons, with children under eight counted as one-half.[10]

Other than these shipboard regulations, the control of immigration was left to state governments. State regulation of immigration was really a continuation of colonial policy. Several of the colonial governments had passed laws barring Catholics, Quakers, paupers, and criminals, and requiring passenger lists. In the early national period New York and Massachusetts, the states which received most of the immigrants, took the lead in regulating immigration. In addition to refusing paupers and criminals, they passed laws calling for the inspection of all arrivals and barring the physically disabled and diseased. An 1837 Massachusetts statute excluded all aliens found to be "lunatic, idiot, maimed, aged or infirm persons incompetent in the opinion of the officer so examining, to maintain themselves, or who have been paupers in any other country." Ten years later, a New York law similarly excluded those who were "lunatic, idiot, deaf and dumb, blind or infirm…and who, from attending circumstances, are likely to become permanently a public charge." The United States Supreme Court allowed states to exclude immigrants or require a bond from the ship captains who brought them. The head tax on each arrival, however, used by the states to fund their inspections, was struck down by the Supreme Court in the 1849 *Passenger Cases* and again in *Henderson v. Mayor of New York* in 1876 as an unconstitutional infringement on the federal government's authority to regulate immigration.[11]

Senators and representatives from New York, Massachusetts and other seaboard states occasionally pressed Congress to fulfill its responsibility to regulate. In 1836 the Senate passed a resolution requesting the US Secretary of the Treasury to investigate European countries' dumping of paupers in the United States, but he found little evidence of such practices. Two years later, a House Select Committee on Immigration sent questionnaires to the mayors of the principal coastal cities, as well as the restrictionist Native American

---

[10] Ibid., 21–22, 35–39. Steerage refers to the inferior accommodations given to those passengers paying the lowest fares.

[11] Patricia Russell Evans, "'Likely to Become a Public Charge': Immigration in the Backwaters of Administrative Law, 1882–1933" (Ph.D. diss., George Washington University, 1987) 52–53, 78–83, 86–87; Hutchinson, *Legislative History*, 388–404; and Neuman, *Strangers to the Constitution*, 21–34.

Association, and incorporated the responses into a bill which would have fined or imprisoned ships captains importing convicts, idiots, lunatics, maniacs, the incurably diseased, or those unable to support themselves. The House, however, did not pass the bill.[12] Nativism—a hostile attitude toward immigrants based on their presumed inferiority—made little headway against the confidence and optimism of the antebellum era.

Despite this optimism, there were many Americans who were worried about the deleterious effects of immigration on the nation's economic and cultural well-being, particularly as several hundred thousand Irish and Germans came to the United States in the 1840s and 1850s. Nativism was characterized by three major strains in the nineteenth century: fear of different religions (especially Roman Catholics and Jews), fear of radicalism, and fear of ethnic groups other than Anglo-Saxon. All three strains represented uncertainty about the limits of assimilation and asylum. Catholics were believed to be subservient to the tyranny of an ecclesiastical hierarchy, and thus unable to embrace the republican ideology that was the prerequisite for American citizenship. Devotion to a foreign monarch (the Pope) allegedly compromised their loyalty to the United States. Radicals, particularly socialists and anarchists, were likewise seen as a threat to the republican ideology, because they refused to accept American concepts of individual and property rights and the capitalist economy. Finally, Anglo-Saxon racism led many old-stock Americans to question whether those of different races (including what would be called ethnic groups today) could truly appreciate and conform to the Anglo-American standards of political action.[13]

The American Party of the mid-1850s (identified by the moniker "Know-Nothings") represented the strongest form of antebellum nativism. Largely directed against Irish Catholics, who were seen as both racially and religiously inferior, the party included many foreign-born Protestants. The Know-Nothings called for a twenty-one year waiting period for naturalization and the denial of voting rights and public offices to aliens. They did not, however, formally endorse immigration restriction, and even the lengthy waiting period simply indicated a belief that assimilation took longer than five years. The American Party elected five senators and forty-three representatives to Congress in 1854, and helped many other Democrats and Whigs gain office. Their numbers dwindled quickly when the party split

---

[12] Hutchinson, *Legislative History*, 26, 28–29.

[13] John Higham, *Strangers in the Land: Patterns of American Nativism, 1860–1925*, 2nd ed. (New Brunswick: Rutgers University Press, 1988) 3–11.

over slavery in 1856.[14] The Know-Nothing movement reflected evangelical Protestant bigotry as well as anxiety over the changes wrought by industrialization, but its concerns were overshadowed by the larger sectional crisis besetting the union.

The Civil War marked the high point of acceptance for immigrants. Because the enemy was internal, disloyalty could not be associated only with those from foreign lands. Instead, the Republican party adopted a policy of actively encouraging immigration to meet wartime labor shortages. The Homestead Act of 1862 offered the same generous terms to immigrants as to natives in order to hasten the settlement of the western territories and remove any danger of slavery's spread. Abraham Lincoln's annual message of 1863 urged Congress to create a system to encourage immigration. Congress responded by passing an act that permitted laborers to pledge up to one year's worth of wages to their employer in exchange for passage to the United States, with the understanding that such contracts did not involve the kind of involuntary servitude that Union armies were fighting to abolish in the South. The act also created a Commissioner of Immigration in the State Department and a Superintendent of Immigration in New York to disseminate information to the immigrants and assist them in reaching their final destinations. Lincoln signed the bill into law on 4 July 1864. The following December he asked Congress to amend the act to prevent frauds against immigrants, and declared that he regarded immigration "as one of the principal replenishing streams which are appointed by Providence to repair the ravages of internal war, and its waste of national strength and wealth."[15]

The enthusiasm for immigration did not long endure following Lincoln's abbreviated presidency. In 1866 President Andrew Johnson signed a joint congressional resolution protesting the dumping of convicts from foreign countries in America. In 1868 the contract labor law passed four years earlier was quietly repealed by an amendment to a diplomatic and consular appropriations bill. The 1864 and 1868 Republican party platforms proclaimed "that foreign immigration, which in the past has added so much to the wealth, development of resources, and increase of power to the nation—the asylum of the oppressed of all nations—should be fostered and

---

[14] Roger Daniels, *Coming to America: A History of Immigration and Ethnicity in American Life* (New York: HarperCollins, 1990) 269–70; Higham, *Strangers in the Land*, 4–7, 12–13; and Hutchinson, *Legislative History*, 622. See also Ray Allen Billington, *The Protestant Crusade, 1800–1860* (New York: Macmillan, 1938).

[15] Hutchinson, *Legislative History*, 48–50.

encouraged by a liberal and just policy."[16] When Radical Republicans extended the benefits of citizenship to African Americans, Charles Sumner pressed unsuccessfully to amend the 1870 Naturalization law to remove all racial limitations.[17] The defeat of his motion marked the limit of egalitarian citizenship. From that point on, the tide began to turn.

The tide turned first against Asian immigrants. President Ulysses S. Grant asked Congress in December 1869 for "such legislation as will forever preclude the enslavement of the Chinese upon our soil under the name of coolies, and also prevent American vessels from engaging in the transportation of coolies." Grant's annual message of 1874 requested legislation to prohibit the importation of Asians and prostitutes, and Congress responded by passing the 1875 Page Act, which prohibited the importation of Chinese "without their free and voluntary consent," prostitutes, and those convicted of crimes other than purely political offenses.[18] Neither Grant nor the West Coast politicians were satisfied with that measure. In his last annual message Grant once again requested that Congress address the issues of Chinese immigration and prostitution. A joint congressional committee set up to investigate Chinese immigration recommended modifying the Burlingame Treaty with China to permit the exclusion of Chinese laborers on the grounds that they impeded White migration to the West Coast, they did not come to settle permanently and become citizens, and their morals and sanitary habits were unacceptable.[19]

The need to carry the Pacific states in the close elections of the late 1870s and 1880s led candidates for Congress and the presidency to cater to anti-Asian racism in California.[20] While both major party platforms said nothing about immigration in 1872, four years later both were calling for

---

[16] Ibid., 623.

[17] Ibid., 51, 57–58.

[18] Ibid., 56, 61, 65–66; and Sucheng Chan, ed., "The Exclusion of Chinese Women, 1870–1943," in *Entry Denied: Exclusion and the Chinese Community in America, 1882–1943* (Philadelphia: Temple University Press, 1991) 105–09.

[19] Hutchinson, *Legislative History*, 68–70. Of course, the Chinese were not allowed to become citizens.

[20] On the anti-Chinese movement in California, see Raymond Lou, "Chinese-American Agricultural Workers and the Anti-Chinese Movement in Los Angeles, 1870–1940," in Robert Asher and Charles Stephenson, eds., *Labor Divided: Race and Ethnicity in United States Labor Struggles* (Albany: SUNY Press, 1990) 49–62; and Alexander Saxton, *The Indispensable Enemy: Labor and the Anti-Chinese Movement in California* (Berkeley: University of California Press, 1971).

restriction of Chinese immigration. In 1879 Congress passed a bill restricting all Chinese immigration, but President Rutherford B. Hayes vetoed it on the ground that Congress had no right to abrogate a treaty. In any case, the Chinese were willing to negotiate a new treaty. The Angell Treaty of 1880 allowed the United States to "regulate, limit, or suspend," but not "absolutely prohibit," the immigration of Chinese laborers. Only Senator George F. Hoar of Massachusetts spoke out against ratification of the treaty in 1881. Both parties trumpeted their support for Chinese exclusion in the 1880 campaign. Republican candidate James Garfield lost support when a forged letter purporting to show him secretly favoring the importation of "coolies" was published by the Democrats.[21]

The 1882 Chinese Exclusion Act was the first to prohibit immigration by race and class and provide for the deportation of illegal aliens. It suspended for ten years the immigration of all working-class Chinese, but allowed merchants, professionals, students, and travelers to continue to come to the United States. The law permitted the deportation of "any Chinese person found unlawfully within the United States." It forbade state and federal courts from naturalizing them. In his 1881 annual message, President Chester Arthur had asked Congress to be considerate of the Chinese government in modifying the immigration laws. He vetoed the initial 1882 act because its twenty-year suspension was too long. Congressional support for Chinese exclusion was strong, however, as the revised act later passed the House 201 to 37 and the Senate 32 to 15. In his annual message of 1883, Arthur warned that Chinese officials were falsely certifying laborers as members of the exempt classes. Congress amended the law the following year to require an immigrant's proof of status as a merchant, professional, or student, and to apply the act to all Chinese, rather than just citizens of China (as the courts had interpreted the law). The suspension was renewed for another ten years by the 1892 Geary Act, which also added the requirement that all Chinese laborers in the United States must obtain a certificate of residence, backed by the testimony of "at least one credible white witness." As the last requirement shows, "Jim Crow" was easily adapted to Asian Americans.[22]

---

[21] Andrew Gyory, *Closing the Gate: Race, Politics, and the Chinese Exclusion Act* (Chapel Hill: University of North Carolina Press, 1998) 136–218; and Hutchinson, *Legislative History*, 73, 76–77.

[22] Gyory, *Closing the Gate*, 225–259; and Hutchinson, *Legislative History*, 81–82, 85–86, 104. On the enforcement of the law, see Lucy E. Salyer, *Laws Harsh as Tigers:*

The year 1882 also marked the beginning of restriction for European immigration. In his 1881 message to Congress, Chester Arthur called for the supervision and transitory care of immigrants at the port of entry. As a former customs collector at the port of New York, he was familiar with some of the abuses of immigrants that occurred there. His political mentor, New York Senator Roscoe Conkling, had been lobbying the federal government to take over the regulation of immigration after the Supreme Court had again struck down New York's head tax in 1876. In response, Congress passed the Immigration Act of 1882. It followed the model of the earlier state laws, barring entry to lunatics, idiots, and persons likely to become a public charge, imposing a fifty-cent head tax on all immigrants. The Secretary of the Treasury was to supervise immigration matters, but administration of the law was left to state authorities.[23]

In 1885 Congress completely reversed the Republican policy of the Civil War years by passing the Foran Alien Contract Labor Act, which forbade all contracts to prepay or assist immigrants' passage to the United States. Professional artists, actors, lecturers, domestic servants and skilled laborers were exempted, and Americans were still allowed to help their relatives or personal friends in emigrating from Europe. The Homestead Act was likewise reversed in 1887; the Payson Act barred aliens who had not declared their intent to naturalize from owning land in the territories. Although trade unions, including the Knights of Labor, pushed Congress to outlaw contract labor, they were still unwilling to embrace general restriction. Not only did it violate their belief in internationalism and individualism, it threatened the status of their foreign-born members.[24]

President Grover Cleveland, who took office in 1885, showed sympathy for the immigrants coming in increasing numbers during the 1880s. As Governor of New York in 1883, Cleveland called the administration of the state's immigrant receiving station at Castle Garden "a scandal and a reproach to civilization."[25] He was also concerned about the growing

---

Chinese Immigrants and the Shaping of Modern Immigration Law (Chapel Hill: University of North Carolina Press, 1995). "Jim Crow" refers to the post-reconstruction system of racial segregation and discrimination in the South. Courts frequently would not accept the testimony of Blacks unless corroborated by White witnesses.

[23] Hutchinson, *Legislative History*, 77–80.

[24] Ibid., 87–89, 91–92; and Higham, *Strangers in the Land*, 48–50. In 1887 the Foran Act was amended to give the Secretary of the Treasury the power to enforce it by sending back contract laborers upon arrival.

[25] Evans, "Likely to Become a Public Charge," 100.

nativism and racism which inspired the restriction laws. Cleveland's 1886 annual message to Congress stated, "In opening our vast domains to alien elements, the purpose of our law-givers was to invite assimilation, and not to provide an arena for endless antagonisms." He denounced recent mob violence against the Chinese in the West: "The paramount duty of maintaining public order and defending the interests of our own people may require the adoption of measures of restriction, but they should not tolerate the oppression of individuals of a special race."[26] He accepted restriction, but rejected the racist motivation behind it, especially when it manifested itself in lynching. He actually called for religious restriction in 1885 when he asked Congress to exclude Mormons, which it did in the 1891 Immigration Act.[27]

Meanwhile the momentum for further restriction continued to build in Congress. In 1888 the House of Representatives established a select committee to investigate immigration. The committee was chaired by Melbourne H. Ford of Michigan and included William C. Oates of Alabama, Francis B. Spinola of New York, Richard B. Guenther of Wisconsin, and William W. Morrow of California. Its 1889 report said that the facilities and staff at the ports were inadequate to inspect immigrants properly. Further, it noted that no inspection took place whatsoever on the land borders. The committee found evidence of assisted immigration for paupers and convicts, and claimed that the contract labor law was easily evaded. More importantly, they warned that the current immigrants did not measure up to earlier ones, and called for the exclusion of anarchists and seasonal migrant workers ("birds of passage"). The committee concluded, "the time has come when immigration should be more effectively regulated, that persons who immigrate to the United States should at least be composed of those who in good faith desire to become citizens and are worthy to be such." While the accompanying bill was not acted upon, both the House and Senate established standing committees on immigration for the first time in December 1889.[28]

---

[26] Hutchinson, *Legislative History*, 90–91.

[27] Ibid., 89. The act did not name the Church of Jesus of Latter-Day Saints, but it excluded all who believed in and practiced polygamy.

[28] Ibid., 95–98; and United States Immigration Commission, *Reports of the Immigration Commission*, 42 vols., *Immigration Legislation,* 61st Cong., 3d sess., S. Doc. 758, serial 5879 (Washington: Government Printing Office, 1911) 39:37–38.

The report marks the first time that Congress distinguished between the "old immigrants" of Northern and Western Europe and the "new immigrants" of Southern and Eastern Europe. This spurious dichotomy was to become the focal point of the debate over restriction for the next forty years. In general, the old immigrants were hailed as pioneers who settled as families on the land, supported themselves as farmers, became citizens and rapidly assimilated. The new immigrants, by contrast, were mostly single men, many of whom came as temporary "birds of passage." Instead of being pioneering farmers, they worked in factories and crowded together in vile slums. They were viewed as being dirtier, more immoral, less intelligent, and in general more degenerate than their predecessors. Prejudice grossly distorted reality: very few of the old immigrants were pioneer farmers, and the unhealthy living and working conditions of the new immigrants were the responsibility of the tenement and factory owners.

In essence, the "new immigrants" were being blamed for the problems of a rapidly industrializing society. The labor unrest of the late 1880s, including the Haymarket bombing of 1886, prompted the creation of several nativist organizations, of which the Junior Order United American Mechanics and the American Protective Association were the most prominent. The depression of the 1890s further fueled xenophobia. In 1891, eleven Italian-Americans were lynched in New Orleans, prompting a brief threat of war with Italy until President Benjamin Harrison agreed to pay an indemnity.[29]

It took a while for the differences between the old and new immigration to be attributed to race. While racism against Blacks, Indians, and Asians had a long history in America, it was generally assumed that all Europeans were members of the "White race." As a consequence, early restriction efforts focused on the specific problems identified with the new immigrants: their alleged mental and physical defects, criminal tendencies, and lack of intelligence. The Immigration Act of 1891 added persons likely to become a public charge or suffering from a loathsome or contagious disease and polygamists to the excludable list, and provided for the deportation of aliens who entered illegally or became public charges within one year of their

---

[29] Higham, *Strangers in the Land*, 53–95; and Maldwyn Allen Jones, *American Immigration*, 2nd ed. (Chicago: University of Chicago Press, 1992) 215–19.

arrival. Poverty, ill health and bad morals were grounds for exclusion; race (except for the Chinese) was not.[30]

The 1891 Immigration Act created the administrative apparatus of the Bureau of Immigration. The office of Superintendent of Immigration (renamed Commissioner-General in 1895) was created within the Treasury Department to oversee the inspection of immigrants, and new federal facilities—including the one at Ellis Island—were constructed. Until 1892 the state of New York inspected immigrants at Castle Garden at the southern tip of Manhattan. The facility, a former fort, was grossly inadequate for the purpose, however, and federal officials sought a new location that would be more spacious and more removed from the swindlers who crowded around the Battery to take advantage of the new arrivals. Treasury Secretary William Windom suggested Bedloe's (Liberty) Island as the site for the new federal immigrant receiving station, but the New York *World* launched a campaign to prevent the Statue of Liberty from being "converted instead into a Babel." Attention then turned to nearby Ellis Island, which was occupied by a small battery and a naval powder magazine until 1891. The original Bureau of Immigration facility opened 1 January 1892, but the wooden structure burned down 14 June 1897. The brick buildings still present to-date opened 17 December 1900.[31]

The 1891 law gave the sole power to review decisions on admissions and deportations to the Superintendent and the Secretary of the Treasury. The Supreme Court ruled in the 1892 case, *Nishimura Ekiu v. United States*, that courts could not review inspectors' findings of fact but only their interpretations of the laws. The following year the Court ruled in *Fong Yue Ting v. United States* that Congress had the "inherent sovereign power" to deport aliens, and that Constitutional guarantees of due process of law did not apply to deportation hearings because they were not criminal proceedings. The American Bar Association's Committee on International Law called the ruling "very extreme." Nevertheless, the Court's decision allowed the Bureau of Immigration great latitude in setting its own standards

---

[30] Hutchinson, *Legislative History*, 98–103; and U. S. Immigration Commission, *Reports*, 39:39–40.

[31] Hutchinson, *Legislative History*, 98–103; and Thomas M. Pitkin, *Keepers of the Gate: A History of Ellis Island* (New York: New York University Press, 1975) 4–12, 19–21, 32–33.

for fairness, which were called into question in the Palmer Raids during the Red Scare of 1919–1920.[32]

Following the establishment of the federal Bureau of Immigration in 1891, inspection became the focus of immigration restriction. Nativists hoped that federal officials would bar most new immigrants on the basis of disease or other defects, thus avoiding the appearance of racism. In 1893 Congress passed an act requiring the commanding officers of sea-going vessels to conduct a preliminary investigation of all passengers and report the findings to the immigration officials upon arrival. Boards of review were created to rule on doubtful cases, but they were not required to follow judicial procedure. An 1894 act raised the head tax to one dollar to defray the increased expense of inspection. Further, it expanded the size and scope of the Bureau of Immigration, assigning commissioners to each major port to oversee inspection. The House of Representatives passed a bill that year to require inspection of would-be immigrants by US consuls in European ports prior to embarkation, but at the urging of the Secretary of the Treasury, the Senate instead proposed immigration officials perform the inspections abroad. Although the two chambers could not agree to whom the responsibility should fall, inspection abroad remained one of the key goals of restrictionists for the next three decades. They realized press reports from Ellis Island and other stations created public sympathy for immigrants, sentiment that hindered strict enforcement of the laws.[33]

These early attempts at restriction failed to stop or even slow the flood tide of immigration, so nativists called for more overtly racist strategies. The literacy test was the bridge between restriction based on immigrants' health and character and that based on race. Such tests were being introduced in the Southern states as one way to exclude African Americans from voting. Progressive economist Edward W. Bemis first proposed a literacy test in 1887 as a means of keeping out cheap foreign labor. In two *Andover Review*

---

[32] *Nishimura Ekiu v. United States*, 142 US 651 (1892); *Fong Yue Ting v. United States*, 149 US 698 (1893); Evans, "Likely to Become a Public Charge," 125–27; Salyer, *Laws Harsh as Tigers*, 26–32, 46–55; and William Preston, Jr., *Aliens and Dissenters: Federal Suppression of Radicals, 1903–1933* (Cambridge: Harvard University Press, 1963; reprint, New York: Harper & Row, 1966) 11–13. The Court thus contradicted its unanimous ruling in an 1886 case that the Fourteenth Amendment protected "all persons...without regard to any differences of race, of color, or of nationality." *Yick Wo v. Hopkins*, 118 US 356, 369 (1886); and Neuman, *Strangers to the Constitution*, 62.

[33] Hutchinson, *Legislative History*, 105–108, 111–13; Pitkin, *Keepers of the Gate*, 23–24; and US Immigration Commission, *Reports*, 39:41–45.

articles (1888) he distinguished between the old and new immigrants, claiming that the latter were disproportionately criminals, paupers, insane, immoral, slum-dwellers, and anarchists. The literacy test would keep out most of these undesirable immigrants.[34] Richmond Mayo Smith, a professor of political economy at Columbia University, wrote in 1890 that the illiteracy of Italian, Hungarian and French Canadian immigrants carried into the second generation and retarded the vital process of assimilation.[35]

Massachusetts Congressman Henry Cabot Lodge seized on the idea and argued for the literacy test bill almost as soon as he was elected to the US House of Representatives in 1890. He focused, however, not on the labor but the racial aspect. As a US Senator in 1896, Lodge recommended the literacy test to his colleagues because it would discriminate against undesirable "new" immigrants like the Italians, Poles, Hungarians, Greeks, and Asians, while allowing the "old" British, German, Scandinavian, and French immigrants to enter. He argued that the test would provide a racial qualification while avoiding outright discrimination, just as it did in the South, because "illiteracy runs parallel with the slum population, with criminals, paupers, juvenile delinquents of foreign birth or parentage," and because "those who bring the least money to the country…come most quickly upon private or public charity for support." The new immigrants who did work only drove down wages and the standard of living for native workers. Furthermore, Lodge warned, the new immigrants were dangerous because they were "changing the quality of our race and citizenship through the wholesale infusion of races whose traditions and inheritances, whose thoughts and whose beliefs are wholly alien to ours." He accepted the French eugenicist Gustave Le Bon's argument that "If a lower race mixes with a higher in sufficient numbers, history teaches us that the lower race will prevail." While Lodge did not completely reject the old ideal of the melting pot, he warned that "there is a limit to the capacity of any race for assimilating and elevating an inferior race."[36]

Lodge introduced Congress to the emerging pseudo-science of eugenics. The "Linnaean Web" trapped nineteenth and early twentieth-

---

[34] Higham, *Strangers in the Land*, 101; and Robert Fredric Zeidel, "The Literacy Test for Immigrants: A Question of Progress" (Ph.D. diss., Marquette University, 1986) 9–11.

[35] Richmond Mayo Smith, *Emigration and Immigration* (New York: Charles Scribner's Sons, 1890) 161–65; and Zeidel, "Literacy Test," 21–24.

[36] Henry Cabot Lodge, *Speeches and Addresses, 1884–1909* (Boston/New York: Houghton Mifflin, 1909), 246–50, 259–66.

century scientists into trying to categorize and classify various human races. Charles Darwin's theory of evolution broke the general dominence of the biblical idea of a homogenous human race uniquely created by God. In Darwin's wake, scientists tried to construct several human races by reading their stereotypes and prejudices into language, skin color and skull size. Francis Galton, Darwin's cousin, coined the phrase "eugenics" to describe the study of human heredity with the goal of scientifically breeding a better race.[37]

In the United States, eugenics had its main period of influence from 1905 to 1930, when it was used to buttress arguments for immigration restriction. Eugenics appealed to middle-class ideologues as a "scientific" explanation for the incorrigibility of the poor and delinquent. In part, it reflected middle-class resentment of their growing tax burden to pay for the housing and care of paupers, criminals, and the mentally and physically disabled.[38] In 1904 Charles Davenport, a descendant of the Puritan founder of New Haven colony who was a biology professor at the University of Chicago, became director of the Carnegie Institute's Station for Experimental Evolution at Cold Spring Harbor, New York. In 1910 he convinced Mary A. Harriman, wife of railroad tycoon Edward H. Harriman, to donate money to set up a Eugenics Record Office there. Davenport and his assistant, Harry H. Laughlin, a former biology teacher at the North Missouri Normal School, began to collect data on how various characteristics were transmitted from generation to generation. Davenport was also secretary of the American Breeders' Association's Committee on Eugenics. He created subcommittees on related topics, including one on immigration in 1911, chaired by Prescott Farnsworth Hall and Robert DeCourcy Ward of the Immigration Restriction League.[39]

---

[37] Handlin, *Race and Nationality*, 71–92. On eugenics, see Mark Haller, *Eugenics: Hereditarian Attitudes in American Thought* (New Brunswick: Rutgers University Press, 1963); Daniel J. Kevles, *In the Name of Eugenics: Genetics and the Uses of Human Heredity* (New York: Alfred A. Knopf, 1985); Kenneth M. Ludmerer, *Genetics and American Society: A Historical Appraisal* (Baltimore: Johns Hopkins University Press, 1972); and Donald K. Pickens, *Eugenics and the Progressives* (Nashville: Vanderbilt University Press, 1968).

[38] Haller, *Hereditarian Attitudes*, 6–7, 76–94, 144–59, 163–75; Kevles, *Name of Eugenics*, 51–73; and Pickens, *Eugenics*, 119–30.

[39] Haller, *Hereditarian Attitudes*, 63–75; Pickens, *Eugenics*, 56–59, 65; and Rachel Leah Hershfield, "The Immigration Restriction League: A Study of the League's Impact

Hall and Ward founded the Immigration Restriction League in 1894. The following year, the members of its executive committee administered their own literacy test to one thousand immigrants, and found a "close connection between illiteracy and undesirability."[40] From 1902 to 1910, Hall also served as an advisor to the nativist Junior Order United American Mechanics. Sometimes working together, sometimes separately, the Immigration Restriction League and the Eugenics Record Office spearheaded the drive for restriction in the first three decades of the twentieth century. Lodge did not join the League as a matter of principle, but he worked closely with Hall and Ward to enact the literacy test and other restrictive legislation.[41]

Lodge introduced a literacy test bill in the US Senate in 1896. It was modeled on the voting laws of the South, consisting of twenty-five-word sections of the Constitution. It applied to all immigrants over the age of fourteen (except for aged parents and grandparents), and was limited to English or the language of the immigrants' native country (thus excluding Hebrew—not yet revived as a modern language as it would be in the mid-twentieth century—or Yiddish, the dialect spoken by many working-class Eastern European Jews.) Senator Charles H. Gibson of Maryland blasted the "pestilential intolerance" of the Immigration Restriction League, which supplied the research Lodge submitted along with the bill, and he declared that the literacy test was "undemocratic, unrepublican, and un-American."[42] Despite such vehement opposition, the Senate passed the bill and forwarded it to the House of Representatives.

The House Immigration Committee, chaired by German-American Richard Bartholdt of Missouri, limited the requirement to males between the ages of sixteen and sixty, declaring that there was a shortage of White female servants. Bartholdt, although ostensibly in favor of the literacy test, repeatedly damned it with faint praise or outright scorn. He had argued against restriction in the 1890 hearings conducted by Senate Immigration

---

on American Immigration Policy, 1899–1924" (M.A. thesis, University of Calgary, April 1993) 109.

[40] Hershfield, "Immigration Restriction League," 24–25; and Barbara Miller Solomon, *Ancestors and Immigrants: A Changing New England Tradition* (New York: John Wiley & Sons, 1956) 116–17.

[41] Zeidel, "Literacy Test," 29–30.

[42] *Congressional Record*, 54th Cong., 1st sess., 1896, 5214–215; and Zeidel, "Literacy Test," 68–71, 76–80.

Committee chairman William Chandler of New Hampshire. Bartholdt seems to have been trying to sabotage the literacy test bill in 1896.[43]

In the final version produced by the conference committee in the "lame duck" session of 1896–1897, the literacy test consisted of twenty to twenty-five words from the Constitution in "the English language or some other language," and applied to males and females over sixteen years of age. In the Senate, Roger Q. Mills of Texas opposed the literacy test because it violated America's traditional offer of asylum to the oppressed of Europe. When Chandler explicitly compared it to the Southern voting laws, Mills responded that he opposed those laws, too.[44] In the House, Bartholdt argued against the use of the Constitution, maintaining that its arcane legal language would be impossible to decipher. "You might as well hand the immigrant…a stone with Assyrian cuneals or Egyptian hieroglyphics upon it," he declared. He pointedly suggested that Congress substitute Psalm 146:9: "The Lord preserveth the stranger."[45] Nevertheless, the bill passed the House overwhelmingly, 217 to 36 (125 not voting), but barely passed the Senate, 34 to 31 (25 not voting).[46]

Ellis Island Commissioner Joseph H. Senner, formerly on the editorial board of a German-American newspaper, the New York *Staats-Zeitung*, and Commissioner-General Herman Stump both wrote to Treasury Secretary John G. Carlisle, urging that the president veto the bill.[47] Grover Cleveland did so, calling the literacy test a "radical departure" from the longstanding tradition of America as an asylum for the oppressed of Europe. "A century's stupendous growth, largely due to the assimilation and thrift of millions of sturdy and patriotic adopted citizens, attests the success of this generous and free-handed policy," he insisted. The only restrictions necessary to guard the people's interests were those that ascertained the immigrants' "physical and moral soundness" and their "willingness and ability to work." To those who claimed that "the quality of recent immigration is undesirable," he retorted,

---

[43] Zeidel, "Literacy Test," 84–91. Zeidel suggests that Bartholdt acted at the behest of the North German Lloyd and Hamburg-America steamship lines, which had granted numerous favors to him in the past. However, the evidence is only circumstantial.

[44] *Congressional Record*, 54th Cong., 2d sess., 1896, 241; Zeidel, "Literacy Test," 105–106.

[45] *Congressional Record*, 54th Congress, 2d sess., 1897, 1223; Zeidel, "Literacy Test," 111–14.

[46] Hutchinson, *Legislative History*, 116–21; US Immigration Commission, *Reports*, 39:46–50; and Zeidel, "Literacy Test," 106–126.

[47] Zeidel, "Literacy Test," 143, 146.

"The time is within quite recent memory when the same thing was said of immigrants who, with their descendants, are now numbered among our best citizens." Besides, he added, it was hypocritical to pretend that a racial restriction was merely an educational one. He also objected to the exclusion of "birds of passage." The House voted to override the veto, 193 to 37. The Senate took no action, however, since the close margin of passage for the bill made a two-thirds vote in its favor improbable.[48] Cleveland's veto message stood as a ringing defense of the old ideals of the melting pot and asylum. It would be upheld by two more presidents before the literacy test finally became law in 1917.

William McKinley took office on the heels of Cleveland's veto. McKinley, like his mentor Mark Hanna, was Scots-Irish and grew up in a family of devout Methodists and staunch abolitionists. He was active in the Methodist church and the Young Men's Christian Association, as well as the Ancient Free and Accepted Masons. As a Congressman from Ohio, he supported immigration restriction and voted for the Chinese Exclusion Act, believing that it would benefit labor.[49] McKinley also argued that immigration restriction was necessary to promote good citizenship.

In a campaign speech in Dayton in 1887, he quoted from the platform of the Ohio Republican party, which he called "fearless and outspoken" on the subject of immigration. The plank praised the historic contributions of immigrants and welcomed "the well-disposed and industrious immigrant who contributes by his energy and intelligence to the cause of free government," but viewed "with alarm unrestricted immigration from foreign lands as dangerous to the peace and good order of the country and the integrity and character of its citizenship." McKinley urged Congress to pass laws excluding "the anarchist, the communist, the polygamist, the fugitive from justice, the insane, the dependent pauper, the vicious and criminal classes, contract labor in every form," as well as those "who acknowledge no allegiance to our laws, no sympathy with our aims and institutions, but

---

[48] Hutchinson, *Legislative History*, 120–21; US Immigration Commission, *Reports*, 39:48–49, 127–29; and Zeidel, "Literacy Test," 150–58.

[49] H. Wayne Morgan, *William McKinley and His America* (Syracuse: Syracuse University Press, 1963) 2–4, 12–13, 34, 39–40, 57, 71–72. Hanna joked that McKinley got the Scotch and he got the Irish. Hanna was a businessman who engineered McKinley's election to the governorship of Ohio in 1891 and the presidency in 1896. He served as chairman of the Republican National Committee in 1896-1897 and U.S. Senator from Ohio, 1897-1904.

who come among us to make war upon society, to diminish the dignity and rewards of American workmen, and to degrade our labor to their level."[50]

Economic prosperity and good citizenship were mutually reinforcing, according to McKinley, and immigration restriction aided both. High wages produced a better citizenry as well as a higher standard of living. Better-paid workers could afford to live in more wholesome environments and educate their families, McKinley explained to a Cincinnati audience in 1891. "The first duty of a nation is to enact those laws which will give to its citizens the widest opportunity for labor and the best rewards for work done. You cannot have the best citizenship without these encouragements," he said, and the "citizenship must be protected in every way possible, for upon it rests the permanency and glory of our institutions."[51]

McKinley believed that the education provided by the public schools was the key to assimilation and good citizenship. At the 1887 dedication of a public school building in Canal Fulton, Ohio he noted that schools were "open to the children of the humblest citizen or exiled sojourner within our gates, as freely and ungrudgingly as to the native-born, or the children of the most opulent." He praised the public schools as places where "all distinctions, social, political, and religious, are banished; all differences hushed; all barriers removed."[52] Likewise, in 1892 McKinley told the Baptist Young People's Assembly in Lakeside, Ohio: "Upon education and morality rest the strength and destiny of the Republic. They are the firmament of its power. They constitute the force and majesty of free government."[53]

Despite his support for immigration restriction, McKinley was no bigot. He had a record of opposing the anti-Catholic American Protective Association. During the 1893 gubernatorial campaign, he did not answer when asked if he were an Association member. But when the Association requested him to fire two Catholic guards at the state penitentiary, McKinley refused, and Hanna spread the news among the Catholic clergy of Ohio. Although the American Protective Association's executive committee initially opposed McKinley's nomination for president in 1896, its national convention ultimately put him on an approved list of candidates in May, and

---

[50] William McKinley, *Speeches and Addresses of William McKinley, from His Election to Congress to the Present Time* (New York: D. Appleton & Co., 1893) 237–38.

[51] Ibid., 559–60.

[52] Ibid., 215.

[53] Ibid., 587.

its magazine endorsed him. Hanna countered by recruiting Catholic clergy to campaign for McKinley and issuing a denial that McKinley was a member of either the Association or Roman Catholic organizations.[54]

The Republican platform of 1896 said that in order to protect "the quality of our American citizenship" and "the wages of our workingmen," the immigration laws should be "thoroughly enforced and so extended as to exclude from entrance to the United States those who can neither read nor write." McKinley's letter accepting the nomination agreed that immigration restriction was "of peculiar importance at this time, when our own laboring people are in such great distress" due to the lingering economic depression. The Ohio Governor expressed support for legislation that "will secure the United States from invasion by the debased and criminal classes of the Old World."[55]

McKinley believed that immigration restriction, the gold standard and particularly the protective tariff which he championed, worked together to protect the wages and standard of living of American workers. "We want in the United States neither cheap money nor cheap labor," he said in the 1896 campaign, insisting that "nothing is cheap to the American people which comes from abroad and when it entails idleness upon our own laborers."[56]

McKinley, however, never discussed restriction during the campaign, even when addressing labor groups. To the Hungarian-Americans of Cleveland, he spoke of the egalitarian premise of American citizenship. "The pride and boast of America is that every man, native born or naturalized, no matter what may be his creed or religion, politics or place of birth, is equal before the law and entitled to the enjoyment of equal privileges with every other citizen," he declared. "Those of you who were born in a foreign country come here because you love liberty and because you love our free institutions and want to enjoy equal privileges with those already here," he told them, "and...I know you can be relied upon to stand

---

[54] Morgan, *William McKinley*, 191–92; and Donald L. Kinzer, *An Episode in Anti-Catholicism: The American Protective Association* (Seattle: University of Washington Press, 1964) 119–21, 214–17, 224–25.

[55] Lewis L. Gould, *The Presidency of William McKinley* (Lawrence: University Press of Kansas, 1980) 31; and Hutchinson, *Legislative History*, 629.

[56] William McKinley, "To Delegation of Colored Citizens and Military, of Cleveland, Ohio, at Canton," 17 August 1896, William McKinley Presidential Papers, Library of Congress, Washington DC, Series 4, reel 81.

by the honor of our country and for the preservation of our free institutions."[57]

Despite his support for immigration restriction, McKinley appears to have appealed successfully to foreign-born voters. He defeated Democratic and Populist candidate William Jennings Bryan with a vote of 7,100,000 to 6,500,000 (271 to 176 in the electoral college), the largest margin of victory for any presidential candidate since Ulysses S. Grant defeated Horace Greeley in 1872. One half of the total popular vote was cast in eight immigrant-rich states, and McKinley carried them all: New York, New Jersey, Pennsylvania, Ohio, Indiana, Illinois, Michigan and Wisconsin. The Republican candidate carried all 67 counties in New England and all but 12 counties in the Mid-Atlantic states, all regions with numerous foreign-born voters. He garnered support from most ethnic groups except Irish-American Catholics.[58]

McKinley echoed the language of the platform plank when he spoke on the subject of immigration in his first inaugural address. "Our naturalization and immigration laws should be further improved to the constant promotion of a safer, a better, and a higher citizenship," he declared. While he once again stopped short of endorsing the literacy test, he said, "A grave peril to the Republic would be a citizenship too ignorant to understand or too vicious to appreciate the great value and beneficence of our institutions and laws, and against all who come here to make war upon them our gates must be promptly and tightly closed." He then went on to mention the need to reduce illiteracy among citizens.[59]

President McKinley appointed former Knights of Labor leader Terence V. Powderly as Commissioner-General of Immigration. Powderly had testified before Chandler's Senate committee in 1890 that the quality of recent immigrants was deteriorating, and he criticized the lax enforcement of the contract labor law. He was an opponent of the literacy test, however, and

---

[57] William McKinley, "To Hungarian-Americans of Cleveland, O[hio]," 19 September 1896, William McKinley Presidential Papers, Library of Congress, Washington DC, Series 4, reel 81.

[58] Gould, *Presidency of McKinley*, 12-13. Morgan, *William McKinley*, 246–47; and Edgar Eugene Robinson, *The Presidential Vote, 1896–1932* (Palo Alto: Stanford University Press, 1934) 4–7. The Democratic party platform also condemned "the importation of foreign pauper labor." Hutchinson, Legislative History, 629.

[59] Gould, *Presidency of William McKinley*, 30–31; and Hutchinson, *Legislative History*, 122.

his appointment worried Lodge.[60] Powderly tried to clean up the administration of the Immigration Bureau and secure strict enforcement of the laws. He investigated a scandal concerning the contract labor inspectors at Ellis Island in 1899–1900, but his report was filed away and forgotten at the Treasury Department by friends of Ellis Island Commissioner Thomas Fitchie and his assistant, Edward F. McSweeney.[61]

McKinley largely avoided immigration issues during his time in office. He did not remind Congress of the platform plank or encourage restriction efforts, despite his call for "prompt action" in his inaugural address. In his annual messages of 1899 and 1900, he deplored mob violence against foreigners, specifically condemning the lynching of five Italians in Tallulah, Louisiana. Like his predecessors, McKinley called for legislation to protect aliens in their treaty rights. McKinley also asked that the Contract Labor law be amended to give it greater force.[62] Beyond this, however, McKinley made no use of the bully pulpit to discuss immigration issues.

Congress likewise took no action on immigration during McKinley's term of office. In March 1897 Lodge and Chandler reintroduced in the Senate the literacy test bill which Cleveland had vetoed. The House Immigration Committee also resubmitted the bill. The only substantive change was the omission of the Corliss Amendment barring "birds of passage," which Madison Grant and the Immigration Restriction League believed was the real reason Cleveland had vetoed the bill.[63] When the Senate allowed the bill to go over to the next session, Lodge resigned the chairmanship of the Immigration Committee. He was replaced by Charles Fairbanks of Indiana in June. The Senate passed the literacy test 42 to 28 in January 1898, but it was stymied in the House of Representatives where only 92 out of 207 Republicans voted to take it up. Most of the bipartisan opposition to the bill came from the South and West.[64]

In 1898, however, Congress did move to create the Industrial Commission. It was assigned the task, among other things, of investigating immigration. Legislators decided to wait for its report and leave the issue alone for a while. The Industrial Commission heard from many different

---

[60] Pitkin, 15 Keepers; and Zeidel, "Literacy Test," 170.

[61] Pitkin, Keepers, 27–29.

[62] Hutchinson, Legislative History, 125–26.

[63] Hershfield, "Immigration Restriction League," 60–61; and Zeidel, "Literacy Test," 155–58.

[64] Zeidel, "Literacy Test," 164–69, 174–78.

witnesses on the subject of further restriction of immigration. The Commission recommended increasing the head tax to three dollars to make it restrictive, establishing inspection of immigrants on the land borders, extending inspection to cabin passengers, ensuring the exclusion and deportation of anarchists, continuing and strengthening the Chinese Exclusion and Contract Labor laws, extending the statute of limitations on deportations to five years, and penalizing the steamship companies for the transport of diseased aliens. Only two members of the Commission favored a literacy test, and so it was not part of the recommendations. Prescott F. Hall of the Immigration Restriction League had testified that while an educational test did not necessarily indicate moral worth, statistical evidence showed that illiteracy accompanied pauperism and criminality. But Dr. Edward Senner, the former commissioner of immigration at New York, and Terence V. Powderly, Commissioner-General of Immigration, argued that a literacy test made sense for naturalization rather than for admission to the country.[65]

By the time the Industrial Commission reported back to Congress in 1901, William McKinley had been assassinated by Leon Czolgosz, a second-generation Polish American, and Theodore Roosevelt, a close friend of Henry Cabot Lodge, had become president. Czolgosz, although a native-born citizen, seemed to embody the threat posed by foreign radicals. Congress responded to the heightened fears by excluding anarchists in 1903. Although new categories of excludable and deportable aliens were created and the head tax was increased, Lodge's literacy test never reached Roosevelt. Instead, the president accepted a new immigration commission to study the issue in more detail.

William McKinley shared the conflicting attitudes of many Americans toward immigration at the end of the nineteenth century. He was a moderate restrictionist, but he rejected the racial and religious prejudices of nativists. He supported immigration restriction to protect the wages and living

---

[65] Hutchinson, *Legislative History*, 128; United States Industrial Commission, *Reports of the Industrial Commission*, vol. 15 (Washington: Government Printing Office, 1901) cxiv–cxvi. The Industrial Commission's members were US Senators Boies Penrose, Stephen R. Mallory, John W. Daniel, and Thomas R. Bard, Congressional Representatives John J. Gardner, L. F. Livingston, John C. Bell, and Theobald Otjen, and from the "private sector" William Lorimer, Andrew L. Harris, John M. Farquhar, Eugene D. Conger, Thomas W. Phillips, Charles J. Harris, John L. Kennedy, Charles H. Litchman, and D. A. Tompkins. E. Dana Durand served as secretary. John R. Commons wrote the report on immigration.

standards of American workers, just as he supported the protective tariff to help businesses. Had Lodge's literacy test bill been presented to him, McKinley almost certainly would have signed it into law. He believed firmly in the melting pot, but he did not publicly discuss America's traditional offer of asylum for political and religious refugees. Although he did not alter the historically lenient immigration policy of the United States, McKinley failed to use the bully pulpit to champion the admission and assimilation of immigrants.

CHAPTER 2

THEODORE ROOSEVELT AND "IMMIGRATION OF THE RIGHT KIND"

Theodore Roosevelt became president in September 1901 following the assassination of William McKinley. He was an imperialist who believed in the superiority of the White race, but he believed it was a historical rather than biological superiority. Because he did not believe other races were inherently inferior, he took seriously the "White man's burden" to elevate them to the American standard of civilization.[1] This obligation was best fulfilled in acquiring overseas colonies like the Philippines and Puerto Rico, but it also applied to the immigrants who came to the United States. Although Roosevelt believed in the melting pot concept as characteristic of the American immigration experience, he cautiously pushed for a more rigorous selection of immigrants and exclusion of "undesirable immigration." He thereby imposed a pragmatic limit to America's offer of asylum to the "poor huddled masses, yearning to breathe free."

Like many of his fellow Republicans, Roosevelt generally supported immigration restriction, but he wanted a method that would uphold the old ideals of the melting pot and asylum, safeguard a labor supply for big business without antagonizing labor unions too much, and emphasize Americanization rather than racial intolerance. He was trying to keep the progressive and conservative factions of the Republican party together, while attempting to make inroads on traditional Democratic constituencies in the Southern states and among urban immigrants. With regard to Asian

---

[1] George Mowry described Roosevelt's attitude perfectly when he wrote of the typical progressive of that era, "he might have thought of himself as one of the racial lords of creation, but he was also extremely responsive to the Christian ethic and to the democratic tradition. It was just not in his character to be ruthless toward a helpless minority, especially when the minority was one of his own." George Mowry, *The Era of Theodore Roosevelt, 1900–1912* (New York: Harper & Row, 1958) 94.

immigration, the solution was a class-based restriction that accepted Chinese and Japanese businessmen, professionals, and students as equals in civilization, but excluded the working-class "coolies" as too different to be assimilated and accepted by White society. Roosevelt proposed the same sort of solution for European immigrants. Here it was not politically possible to achieve since, unlike their Asian counterparts, European immigrants were allowed to vote. Roosevelt initially supported his good friend Henry Cabot Lodge's literacy test, but political pressure from both conservatives and liberals led him to abandon it and wait instead for an Immigration Commission recommendation.

While maneuvering politically to achieve class-based restriction, Roosevelt declared his abiding faith in the melting pot concept to his fellow Americans at every opportunity. Long before he became president and long after he left office he was reminding his compatriots to treat immigrants with dignity and justice. A natural preacher, Roosevelt was delighted to have "such a bully pulpit" as the presidency from which to proclaim his moral standards.[2] He urged his audiences to live in accordance with "the great rule of righteousness which bids us treat each man on his worth as a man." Roosevelt's corollary to the golden rule meant that when a member of an inferior race acted "in a way which would entitle him to respect and reward if he was one of our own stock, he is just as entitled to that respect and reward if he comes of [sic] another stock, even though that stock produces a much smaller proportion of men of his type than does our own."[3] It was the duty of civilized people to lead by example. Only by adhering to the highest standard of Christian morality could men of Northern European descent hope to bring the rest of the world up to the same standard. As William Allen White observed, the message that Roosevelt preached from the bully pulpit was, "Be good, be good, be good; live for righteousness, fight for righteousness, and if need be die for it. Nothing else matters but to be militantly decent."[4] Americans had to be militantly decent toward immigrants if they hoped to assimilate them.

---

[2] Roosevelt's phrase is quoted in Lyman Abbott, "A Review of President Roosevelt's Administration , IV: It's Influence on Patriotism and Public Service," The Outlook 91 (27 Feb. 1909), 430.

[3] Theodore Rosevelt, *The Works of Theodore Roosevelt, National Edition,* 20 vols. (New York: Charles Scribner's Sons, 1926), 12:57-58.

[4] Ibid., 13.xi.

Theodore Roosevelt believed in the melting pot because he was a product of it. His ancestor Claes Martenszen van Rosenvelt settled in New Amsterdam by 1648. Roosevelt was proud of his Dutch roots, maintaining membership in the same Dutch Reformed church in New York to which Peter Stuyvesant belonged. He was also quick to point out his Scottish, English, French, German, Irish, and Welsh ancestors, and not just at election time.[5] Born into a wealthy family in 1858, Roosevelt was able to tour the Middle East and Europe as a child. He spent one summer living in Dresden, Germany.[6] As a twelve-year-old boy he recorded in his diary how he and his father had made sport of Italian beggars at Finale and Pompeii, tossing bread and pennies to them for performing degrading tricks and giving three cheers for the United States of America.[7] Thus he was taught early on that he belonged to a privileged, civilized upper-class of society—a belief he never lost. His father, however, also imparted to him a strong sense of *noblesse oblige*. The senior Theodore Roosevelt helped to found the New York Orthopedic Hospital, the Children's Aid Society, and the Newsboys' Lodging House. Similarly, his namesake engaged public service not as perfunctory duty but with passion. Although his first love was natural history, he turned readily to politics in the early 1880s.

Joe Murray, an Irish Catholic and former Democrat, helped Roosevelt to win his first election to the New York state legislature in 1881. Years later Roosevelt credited Murray with showing him a public servant's need for "a genuine fellow-feeling for, understanding of, and sympathy with his fellow Americans, whatever their creed or birthplace, the section in which they live, or the work which they do." Significantly, Roosevelt appointed Murray as Assistant Commissioner of Ellis Island in 1901.[8] Roosevelt's more deeply set aristocratic prejudices, however, only wore off gradually. In his diary for

---

[5] Nathan Miller, *Theodore Roosevelt: A Life* (New York: William Morrow & Co., 1992) 25–26; and Edmund Morris, *The Rise of Theodore Roosevelt* (New York: Ballantine Books, 1979) 36–37.

[6] Miller, *Roosevelt: A Life*, 57–60.

[7] Morris, *Rise of Theodore Roosevelt*, 55. His hostile attitude toward Italians continued well into adulthood. See Roosevelt to Anna Roosevelt, 30 January 1887, and Roosevelt to Corinne Roosevelt Robinson, 8 February 1887, *The Letters of Theodore Roosevelt*, ed. Elting Morison and John Blum, 8 vols. (Cambridge: Harvard University Press, 1951–54) 1:120–21.

[8] Theodore Roosevelt, *An Autobiography* (New York: Macmillan Co., 1913) 70; and Thomas M. Pitkin, *Keepers of the Gate: A History of Ellis Island* (New York: New York University Press, 1975) 35–36, 41.

1882, he described the Irish Democrats in the New York State House of Representatives as "a stupid, sodden, vicious lot." When one of them, J. J. Costello, insulted Roosevelt in an Albany bar, he beat him up. The thrashing ended with Costello being admonished to conduct himself like a gentleman in the presence of one.[9] There is little question that most of his support in New York's twenty-first district came from the "silk stocking" set.

Roosevelt first became aware of the suffering of the city's poor when Samuel Gompers escorted him on a tour of the tenements where immigrant families made cigars under squalid conditions. Years later, as New York City Police Commissioner (1895–1897), the Danish immigrant Jacob Riis showed Roosevelt "how the other half lived" and instilled in him even more sympathy for the foreign-born. Roosevelt also learned much from University Settlement's James Bronson Reynolds, upon whom he later relied as a confidential advisor on immigration matters while Governor of New York and President of the United States. Both Riis and Reynolds taught Roosevelt that the immigrants' environment, rather than any innate racial traits, was largely responsible for their objectionable characteristics.[10]

As US Civil Service Commissioner (1889–1895), Roosevelt stood solidly against racial or religious persecution. He publicly denounced the American Protective Association at every opportunity, surpassing McKinley's quieter opposition to the anti-Catholic group. When the Association opposed one candidate for a local civil service board in Michigan because of his Roman Catholic faith, Roosevelt promptly placed him in the position and fired an Association member from a board for openly displaying bigoted material.[11] In an 1894 article entitled "True Americanism," he branded the American Protective Association as an ugly revival of "Know-nothingism" that was "as utterly un-American, as alien to our school of political thought, as the worst immigrants who land on our shores." He argued that such intolerance only hindered the process of

---

[9] Miller, *Roosevelt: A Life*, 124; Morris, *Rise of Theodore Roosevelt*, 166–67. See also Roosevelt to C. Connolly, 11 April 1894, in *Letters of Theodore Roosevelt*, 1:372–73, where he writes that he supported the good Irish and only "warred against the bad."

[10] Roosevelt, *Autobiography*, 70, 313; Roosevelt to Josephine Shaw Lowell, 20 February 1900, in *Letters of Theodore Roosevelt*, 2:1199; Roosevelt to Winston Churchill, 4 August 1915, in ibid., 8:958; and Roosevelt, "How I Became a Progressive," *The Outlook* (12 October 1912), in *Works*, 17:316–17.

[11] Roosevelt to C. Connolly, 11 April 1894, in *Letters of Theodore Roosevelt*, 1:372; and Roosevelt to T. T. Hudson, 12 October 1894, in ibid., 1:403.

assimilation. He opposed spending public money on parochial schools, and he insisted that English be the only language of instruction in all schools to "Americanize [the immigrants] in every way." But, he proclaimed, "It is a base outrage to oppose a man because of his religion or birthplace, and all good citizens will hold any such effort in abhorrence."[12]

Roosevelt struck more blows against bigotry as police commissioner. When an anti-Semitic preacher named Hermann Ahlwardt came to New York, Roosevelt assigned an all-Jewish contingent of police officers to protect him.[13] He also opened up the police department to Jews for the first time, as part of a deliberate effort to help them become accepted members of society by restoring to them a martial spirit and undoing the stereotype of the "money-hungry Jew." He called his Jewish officers "Maccabees," in honor of the ancient Jewish revolutionaries who overthrew Seleucid rule in Israel. "I was confident that nothing would do more to put a stop to the unreasoning prejudice against them," he explained to George Briggs Aiton, "than to have it understood that not only were they successful and thrifty businessmen and high-minded philanthropists, but also able to do their part in the rough, manly work which is no less necessary."[14] Roosevelt had transformed himself from a sickly, asthmatic boy into a strapping athletic dynamo, and he was certain he could do the same for the Jews. Martial valor was always the hallmark of his Americanism, and so Jewish immigrants needed to do such "rough, manly work" to become true Americans.

In 1896 Roosevelt visited Ellis Island. As police commissioner, he was interested in the appeals process, so he observed the review board at work. He applauded a decision by Robert Watchorn to admit a Swedish stowaway, telling the inspector that "We need lots of good, vigorous, healthy blood to mingle with the national stream." Roosevelt later appointed Watchorn as Commissioner of Ellis Island in 1905.[15]

Roosevelt described his New York City police force as a microcosm of the melting pot. Indeed, he believed that the camaraderie of serving with the police hastened the process of assimilation. Commenting on the variety of

---

[12] "True Americanism," *The Forum*, April 1894, in Roosevelt, *Works*, 13:22, 25. See also his Boston speech on "Religion and the Public Schools," November 1893, in ibid., 13:275 80.

[13] Roosevelt, *Autobiography*, 205–206.

[14] Roosevelt to George Briggs Aiton, 15 May 1901, in Roosevelt, *Letters of Theodore Roosevelt*, 3:78–79; and Miller, *Roosevelt: A Life*, 232.

[15] Robert Watchorn, *The Autobiography of Robert Watchorn*, ed. Herbert Faulkner West (Oklahoma City: The Robert Watchorn Charities Ltd., 1958) 145–46.

ethnic backgrounds of his officers, he wrote, "All soon became welded into one body." He wrote to his good friend, British diplomat Cecil Arthur Spring-Rice, in 1896, "the children and grandchildren of the German and Irish immigrants, whom we appoint on our force, are scarcely distinguishable from one another, and the best of them are not distinguishable from the best of the appointees of old American stock."[16] There was still a slight distinction between those of immigrant stock and those of native stock, Roosevelt believed, but the discipline and teamwork of the police force would soon eliminate it.

Similarly, Roosevelt celebrated the diversity of the Rough Riders, his beloved Spanish-American War unit, as evidence of the effectiveness of the melting pot. Standing in front of the Alamo addressing his troops at their 1905 reunion, the colonel claimed that the regiment was "a typical American body" because it was comprised of "the Northerner and the Southerner, the Easterner and the Westerner,…men who worshiped their Creator some according to one creed, some according to another," and "men who had been born abroad and men who had been born here." Not only did the army, like the police force, bring them all together, Roosevelt asserted, but it rewarded and punished them according to their individual merits, not on the basis of their religion or ancestry. And each man was "glad to get in on his worth as a man only, and content to be judged purely by what he could show himself to be."[17]

Addressing the Brotherhood of Locomotive Firemen in Chattanooga three years before, he had made the same point about the Rough Riders' unity despite their diversity, and applied the lesson to all Americans. "I firmly believe in my countrymen, and therefore I believe that the chief thing necessary in order that they shall work together is that they shall know one another," he declared, "so that we may realize that the things which divide us are superficial, are unimportant, and that we are, and must ever be, knit together into one indissoluble mass by our common American brotherhood."[18] Just as Roosevelt had learned to appreciate his less fortunate

---

[16] Roosevelt, *Autobiography*, 205; and Roosevelt to Cecil Arthur Spring-Rice, 5 August 1896, in *Letters of Theodore Roosevelt*, 1:555.

[17] Roosevelt, *Works*, 11:177. Of course, African Americans were excluded from the Rough Riders, and though Roosevelt praised the African American soldiers who had fought with him in Cuba at first, as time went on he denigrated them. See Gary Gerstle, *American Crucible: Race and Nation in the Twentieth Century* (Princeton: Princeton University Press, 2001) 32–38.

[18] Roosevelt, *Works*, 16:157–58.

fellow Americans when he actually met them, so would all Americans come to respect their fellow citizens as they worked together for the common good.

Although his circle of friends included nativists like Henry Cabot Lodge, Madison Grant, and Owen Wister, Roosevelt was too optimistic to be more than temporarily swayed by their fears of new immigrants undermining "Anglo-Saxon" democracy in the United States. Praising James Bryce's book *American Commonwealth*, he told the British author, "You have...thoroughly understood that instead of the old American stock being 'swamped' by immigration, it has absorbed the immigrants and remained nearly unchanged."[19] Occasionally he complained about the quality of recent immigrants and called for greater restriction. He groused to Lodge in 1892, "I wish the cholera would result in a permanent quarantine against most immigrants!" He confided to his friend Brander Matthews, a Columbia University professor and literary critic, "I am very glad the immigration has come to a standstill for the last year. We are getting some very undesirable elements right now, and I wish that a check could be put to it."[20] Nevertheless, the occasional bouts of pessimism did not damage his faith in the melting pot. After pointing out to historian Francis Parkman the irony that French Canadian immigrants were now taking over parts of New England that their seventeenth and eighteenth-century ancestors had failed to conquer, Roosevelt asserted, "I am a firm believer that the future will somehow bring things right in the end for our land."[21]

Theodore Roosevelt's confidence in assimilation, despite what he viewed as the negative aspects of the new immigration, had much to do with his interest in and understanding of both natural history and human history. He dismissed the facile arguments of the eugenicists and Social Darwinists, well aware that they grossly oversimplified natural selection in order to arrive at their racist conclusions. Commenting on Benjamin Kidd's *Social*

---

[19] Roosevelt to James Bryce, 6 January 1888, in *Letters of Theodore Roosevelt*, 1:135. However, he also realized that assimilation took time, writing to Bryce on 30 November 1897 (ibid., 722) that good government in New York City will take a while because the "mass of foreigners will take at least a couple of generations before they can be educated to the proper point."

[20] Roosevelt to Lodge, 25 September 1892, in ibid., 291; Roosevelt to Brander Matthews, 29 June 1894, in ibid., 389; and *The Letters of Roosevelt and Brander Matthews*, ed. Lawrence J. Oliver (Knoxville: University of Tennessee Press, 1995) 82.

[21] Roosevelt to Francis Parkman, 22 May 1892, in *Letters of Theodore Roosevelt*, 1:282–83.

Evolution in the *North American Review* in 1895, Roosevelt criticized the British Social Darwinist for ignoring the tendency of the "unfit" not only to survive, but also to become more fit.[22] Roosevelt's well-known fears of "race suicide," in fact, were based on the concern that the fittest would *not* survive if they did not breed. He wrote to Spring-Rice in 1897, "The one ugly fact all over the world is the diminution of the birth rate among the highest races." At the same time, however, he cautioned that the history of Ireland and Italy demonstrated a high birth rate and national greatness did not always go together.[23] Roosevelt also understood that the melting pot functioned primarily through interbreeding, so the refusal of White, upper-class Americans to participate in the "warfare of the cradle" meant that they would lose control of assimilation.[24]

Nativists distorted American history just as they oversimplified natural history. The historical battles then raging over what role the various ethnic groups had played in the founding of America seemed pointless to Roosevelt. Discussing the ethnic makeup of the colonists in a 1900 letter to Robert J. Thompson, he dismissed the term "Anglo-Saxon" as "an utterly unscientific word," and likewise called "purely artificial" the idea that "nationality coincides with race and language." Any estimates of English "blood" in the colonists were mere guesses and arguments about percentages missed what Roosevelt considered to be the important point: "the English, and especially the Puritans, made the mold into which the other races were run." In other words, however many English colonists there actually were, they controlled and shaped the culture to which the settlers from different races and ethnic groups were assimilated. That process of assimilation was

---

[22] Richard Hofstadter, *Social Darwinism in American Thought*, rev. ed. (New York: George Braziller, 1959) 101–02. Likewise, in reviewing Houston Stewart Chamberlain's *Foundations of the Nineteenth Century* for *The Outlook* in 1911, Roosevelt blasted Chamberlain's "foolish hatred" of Jews, Catholics, and Southern Europeans, and derided his use of the fictitious labels "Aryan" and "Teutonic" for any historical figure of whom he approved. Roosevelt, *Works*, 12:106–112.

[23] Roosevelt to Cecil Arthur Spring-Rice, 13 August 1897, in *Letters of Theodore Roosevelt*, 1:647. See also Roosevelt to Spring-Rice, 16 March 1901, in ibid., 3:15–16.

[24] In a 1911 article ("Race Decadence," *The Outlook* (8 April 1911), in Roosevelt, *Works*, 12:187), Roosevelt lamented that the American-born children of immigrants were exhibiting the "same wilful sterility" as the "old-stock Americans," thus preventing the melting pot from working. In another article ("Twisted Eugenics," *The Outlook*, 3 January 1914, in ibid., 12:201), he argued that since there was no way to prevent all undesirable people from breeding, he was instead encouraging desirable people to procreate.

still at work, Roosevelt declared, and "the astonishing thing is how the nationalities have fused" so that "the sons of the German, Scandinavian and other immigrants of the present day in the vast majority of cases become absolutely indistinguishable in feeling and interest, and above all, in patriotic devotion, from their fellow countrymen" whose ancestors came in the 1600s and 1700s.[25]

Roosevelt believed that it took longer for the melting pot to assimilate some peoples than others, but he firmly believed that the melting pot was creating a new American race, just as Crèvecoeur had said. He conceded that there were "curious differences between the different races in point of rapidity and thoroughness of mixture" in a letter to Ernest Bruncken, author of a pamphlet on *How Germans Become Americans*. But fast or slow, all races were "melted down," usually by "the second generation born on American soil." Roosevelt followed historian Frederick Jackson Turner in attributing great significance to the role of the frontier in the process of assimilation. "The frontier has always had a tremendous effect in Americanizing people," the former Badlands rancher wrote and added, "A single generation of life upon it has invariably beaten all the frontiersmen of Europe into one mould [sic], and this a mould different from any in Europe."[26]

Immigrants and native-born Americans alike bore the responsibility of Americanization, according to Roosevelt. It was the duty of the native-born to treat as equals immigrants who had to assimilate and become just like old-stock Americans in speech, behavior and political thought. In Roosevelt's mind, America stood for all that was good, just and decent; therefore, immigrants who failed to embrace America wholeheartedly were *ipso facto* immoral. In his 1894 *Forum* article "True Americanism," he declared that "where immigrants, or the sons of immigrants, do not heartily and in good faith throw in their lot with us, but cling to the speech, the customs, the ways of life, and the habits of thought of the Old World which they have left, they thereby harm both themselves and us." In fact, he continued, they harmed themselves more because they rejected "the most honorable [of] titles"—that of being a true American. It was, however, an honor that should be given only to the worthy. Although he preached that "Americanism is a question of spirit, conviction, and purpose, not of creed or birthplace," he called for

---

[25] Roosevelt to Robert J. Thompson, 30 April 1900, in *Letters of Theodore Roosevelt*, 2:1273–275.

[26] Roosevelt to Ernest Bruncken, 1 March 1898, in ibid., 1:786–87.

restriction to "keep out races which do not assimilate readily with our own," as well as "laborers who tend to depress the labor market" and "unworthy individuals of all races."[27] In essence, he would limit immigration to the European middle and upper classes.

Within these limits the melting pot could work and Roosevelt wanted all Americans, not just the foreign-born, to be molded together. His concern about "hyphenated Americans" came long before World War I, also extending to Anglophiles and others who prided themselves on their colonial pedigrees. "We have a right to demand that every man, native-born or foreign-born, shall in American public life act merely as an American," he told a Boston audience in November 1893. "To quote a phrase I have used more than once before, we don't wish any hyphenated Americans," he elaborated, "we do not want you to act as Irish-Americans or British-Americans or native-Americans, but as Americans pure and simple."[28]

Roosevelt's definition of an "American pure and simple" was based mostly on his moral creed. In his Independence Day oration at Oyster Bay in 1906, Roosevelt proclaimed, "None of you are worth anything as American citizens, none of you can be worth anything as citizens, if you have not the fund of moral qualities which find expression in love of country, love of neighbors, love of home, which make you honest, decent, clean-living, right-thinking." In addition, he said, they needed "the courage, physical and moral, without which no American citizen can do his full duty as a citizen."[29] Courage and decency were the heart of Roosevelt's "muscular Christianity," and they also formed the core of his conception of citizenship.

Pride in one's ancestry was understandable and acceptable, according to Roosevelt, but pride in the United States and its unique place in the world must take precedence in one's estimation. Continuing to fight old world battles on new world soil was forbidden, because it distracted America from its manifest destiny. Coming into its own as a world power, America still had to be the "city set on a hill" for which the Puritans had called and it needed every citizen to be patriotic and courageous in order to fulfill that mission. "Let us keep our pride in the stocks from which we have sprung," he told the Friendly Sons of St. Patrick in 1905, "but let us show that pride, not by holding aloof from one another, least of all by preserving the Old World jealousies and bitternesses [sic], but by joining in a spirit of generous

---

[27] "True Americanism," *The Forum* (April 1894), in Roosevelt, *Works*, 13:21-23, 25.
[28] Ibid., 13:275–76.
[29] Ibid., 16:6.

rivalry to see which can do most for our great common country." It was crucial to maintain loyalty and devotion to the United States, he explained, because "the fate of the twentieth century" would "in no small degree depend upon the type of citizenship developed on this continent." Since the United States was destined for greatness, Roosevelt believed, its citizens must be great to do their duty. He insisted, "Surely such a thought must thrill us with the resolute purpose so to bear ourselves that the name American shall stand as the symbol of just, generous, and fearless treatment of all men and all nations."[30] America's destiny, as he imagined it, thrilled Roosevelt and made him more resolute in calling his countrymen to account.

Roosevelt did not, of course, always practice what he preached. He was a master politician who both appealed to ethnic voters and loudly denied so doing. As Police Commissioner he offended German-Americans by enforcing the Sunday closing laws that prohibited the sale of alcoholic beverages, but then reviewed their protest march and spoke to them in German.[31] He also cultivated the support of prominent German-Americans such as Arthur von Briesen, who was president of the German Legal Aid Society and the Citizens' Union. President Roosevelt later appointed him to the Ellis Island Commission in 1903. Defending his record in the 1900 campaign for the vice-presidency, he listed all the German-Americans he had appointed to office or worked with while cleverly denying that he had merely filled ethnic quotas. "I did not appoint them because they were Germans," he explained, "but because I thought they were men best fitted to do duty."[32] By insisting that his appointments were the best men for the job, he flattered the ethnic groups while maintaining the façade of his declared standard of impartial treatment.

As president, Roosevelt took a much more active role in managing immigration policy than had William McKinley. He inherited the ongoing dispute between Terence V. Powderly, the former Knights of Labor leader who had been McKinley's Commissioner-General of Immigration, Ellis Island Commissioner Thomas Fitchie and Assistant Commissioner Edward McSweeney. Powderly had investigated a scandal involving the contract labor inspectors, but friends of Fitchie and McSweeney in the Treasury Department had buried the report. In the summer of 1901 a new scandal

---

[30] Ibid.,16:43–44.

[31] Miller, *Roosevelt: A Life*, 238.

[32] Roosevelt to George L. Viereck, 1 September 1900, in *Letters of Theodore Roosevelt*, 2:1396–397.

broke involving the sale of as many as 10,000 fraudulent citizenship certificates at five dollars each. Angry and embarrassed, Roosevelt fired all three men, replacing Powderly with Frank L. Sargent of the Brotherhood of Locomotive Firemen and appointing Wall Street attorney William Williams to the post at Ellis Island, along with his old political mentor, Joe Murray.[33]

Williams got rid of the corrupt Immigration officials and the contractors who owed their positions to political patronage. He insisted on treating all immigrants equally, and Jacob Riis wrote approvingly in a March 1903 *Century Magazine* article, "The law of kindness rules on Ellis Island." But Williams repeatedly urged the restriction of the "new" immigration, telling a New York *Times* reporter that the recent arrivals were "inferior" to the "old" immigrants and were often "undesirable and unintelligent people." Williams tried to accomplish such restriction by promulgating a rule which required all immigrants to be in possession of ten dollars, in addition to the money to purchase tickets to their final destination. If they did not have the correct amount, they would be excluded as likely to become a public charge. Commissioner-General Sargent approved the new policy, as long as it did not apply to "sturdy Scotchmen, Irishmen or Germans," but only to "other nationalities who are not of that type."[34]

Not content with cleaning up the Immigration Bureau, Roosevelt pushed for a comprehensive immigration policy that would restrict the ever-increasing flow of immigrants while avoiding overt discrimination. In his first annual message to Congress in December 1901, he used McKinley's assassination as a vehicle to call for the exclusion of anarchists and other unwelcome immigrants. He declared that the United States needed "every honest and efficient immigrant fitted to become an American citizen," meaning a person "who comes here to stay, who brings a strong body, a stout heart, a good head, and a resolute purpose to do his duty well in every way and to bring up his children as law-abiding and God-fearing members of the community."At the same time, however, Roosevelt called for three essential reforms in the immigration laws that would have a restricting effect on the flow of new-comers to America.

The first was the exclusion of anarchists and "all persons who are of a low moral tendency or of unsavory reputation" through inspection abroad as

---

[33] Pitkin, *Keepers of the Gate*, 27–29, 33–36; and Terence V. Powderly, *The Path I Trod: The Autobiography of Terence V. Powderly*, ed. Harry J. Carman, Henry David and Paul N. Guthrie (New York: Columbia University Press, 1940) 298-302.

[34] Ibid., 36–40, 43–44, 56.

well as at the ports of entry. Inspection in the ports of embarkation had been recommended by Powderly as well as the Industrial Commission. Such a process, however, would require negotiating treaties with the countries in which the proposed inspections were to take place. The second reform was a "careful and not merely perfunctory educational test" to gauge the immigrants' "capacity to appreciate American institutions and act sanely as American citizens," a reference to the literacy test which Cleveland had vetoed and the Industrial Commission had failed to recommend. The third reform required immigrants to provide "proper proof of personal capacity to earn an American living and enough money to insure a decent start under American conditions," a financial restriction meant to stop "the influx of cheap labor."[35]

Roosevelt's second reform avoided an outright endorsement of his friend Henry Cabot Lodge's literacy test. This was not merely a matter of politics; the president had genuine misgivings about the test because it was "perfunctory" and unscientific. He was willing to accept it, however, as long as the political cost was not too high. To House Speaker Joseph Cannon he explained in May 1906 that while he would personally prefer "a most rigid inspection…in the foreign countries from which the immigrants come" and severe limitations on the number of passengers allowed on steamships so as to eliminate steerage, such solutions did not seem "at present practicable." A literacy test was, in the end, "very much better than nothing."[36]

Some of Roosevelt's recommendations, along with those of the Industrial Commission, were included in a bill drafted by William Williams and Commissioner-General Frank Sargent in conjunction with House Immigration and Naturalization Committee Chair William B. Shattuc of Ohio. The bill raised the head tax to three dollars, established inspection on the land borders, provided for the exclusion and deportation of anarchists, as well as prostitutes and persons transporting them, and raised the statute of limitations on deportation to five years. It was introduced in the House of Representatives in March 1902, where Democrat Oscar Underwood of

---

[35] Roosevelt, *Works*, 15:95–97.

[36] Roosevelt to Joseph Cannon, 27 May 1906, in *Letters of Theodore Roosevelt*, 5:285–86. In 1915, addressing the Knights of Columbus at Carnegie Hall, he said, "I entirely agree with those who feel that many very excellent possible citizens would be barred improperly by an illiteracy test." He proposed instead that aliens be admitted under bond, with a time limit for them to learn English. Those who failed to learn it would then be deported. Roosevelt, *Works*, 18:398–99.

Alabama amended it by adding a literacy test. The bill passed the House in May, but the Senate delayed action until the following session. Roosevelt endorsed the House bill in his second annual message, and the Senate took it up promptly that winter. The Senators lowered the head tax from three to two dollars and dropped the literacy test. The House agreed to these amendments and Roosevelt signed the bill into law on 3 March 1903.[37]

The 1903 Immigration Act reorganized the existing jumble of related legislation and added several new features. The head tax was raised to two dollars to cover the increased cost of administration because of more rigorous inspection at the points of entry, which now included land border crossings. Time limits on, and reasons for, deportation were increased. The familiar categories prevailed; idiots, insane persons, epileptics, persons with a "loathsome or contagious disease," paupers, persons likely to become a public charge, anarchists, polygamists, prostitutes and those who recruited them, and contract laborers (except for professional classes such as teachers, ministers, actors and artists) were all excluded from admission to the United States. When skilled labor could not be found in sufficient numbers, businesses were allowed to import it. Aliens who entered illegally or became public charges could be deported up to three years, rather than one, after arrival. Steamship companies were fined for bringing any alien who was diseased or became a public charge due to preexisting health conditions, and were required to pay for transporting them back home.[38]

Congress passed only the first of Roosevelt's three proposed reforms, and he was not satisfied with the result. He decided that he would resort to the investigatory commission, a device he had used several times as governor of New York to impress legislators and the public with the need for reform. The pretext was a campaign against Williams' harsh enforcement of the exclusion and deportation laws begun by a German-American newspaper, the New York *Staats-Zeitung*, in 1903. The president warned

---

[37] John R. Jenswold, "Leaving the Door Ajar: Politics and Prejudices in the Making of the 1907 Immigration Law," *Mid-America* 67/1 (Jan. 1985): 5; Edward P. Hutchinson, *Legislative History of American Immigration Policy, 1798–1965* (Philadelphia: University of Pennsylvania Press, 1981) 128–33; and Roosevelt, *Works,* 15:147.

[38] United States Immigration Commission, *Reports of the Immigration Commission*, 42 vols., Vol. 39, *Immigration Legislation*, 61st Cong., 2nd sess., S. Doc. 758, serial 5879 (Washington: Government Printing Office, 1911), 51–55; and Hutchinson, *Legislative History*, 131–35. The law was amended on 28 April 1904 to reflect the transfer of the Immigration Bureau to the new Department of Commerce and Labor created in 1903.

Williams that "the so-called Star Chamber business in reference to the deported aliens" had to stop. He reminded the commissioner that deportation, while necessary in some cases, was often a punishment "only less severe than death itself," and therefore government officials had to be sure "not merely that we are acting aright but that we are able to show others that we are acting aright."[39] As always, he was acutely sensitive to public opinion.

In September 1903 Roosevelt appointed Arthur von Briesen, Eugene A. Philbin (the Irish Catholic District Attorney for New York City), Lee Frankel, Thomas W. Hynes, and Ralph Trautmann to a commission charged with investigating the alleged abuses at Ellis Island. Roosevelt pointed out to Trautmann that one newspaper denounced him for appointing "'two Germans, two Irishmen and a Jew—not a single native American!'" He further commented, "Evidently *that* writer did not regard me as a 'nativist'!"[40] That, of course, was the reason that he had appointed representatives of New York's most politically active ethnic groups: so that he could not be accused of nativism.

Briesen sent the committee's report to the president on 1 December 1903, but it was not made public until the following February. The Ellis Island Commission exonerated Williams, but contrary to his opinion it recommended that steamship companies be represented at review board meetings and their liability be limited. The commission also suggested that a second commission be sent abroad to determine conditions in the European ports of embarkation and what methods could be used to select or exclude emigrants "with regard to the ascertainment of the *character* of each individual." The Commission's concern for determining the character of would-be immigrants led them to reject the literacy test, arguing that "a law which would draw an educational rather than a character line" would be "an almost fatal error."[41]

These were not the results Roosevelt had hoped for, but he tried to twist them into support for his position. The day after receiving Briesen's

---

[39] Roosevelt to William Williams, 23 January 1903, *Letters of Theodore Roosevelt*, 3:411–12; and Pitkin, *Keepers of the Gate*, 49–50, 53–54.

[40] Roosevelt to Ralph Trautmann, 28 November 1903, in *Letters of Theodore Roosevelt*, 3:659–60 (emphasis in the original).

[41] Arthur von Briesen to Roosevelt, 1 December 1903, Theodore Roosevelt Presidential Papers, Library of Congress, Washington DC, Series 1, Reel 38 (emphasis in the original); and Pitkin, *Keepers of the Gate*, 49–50.

communiqué he replied: "I have considered the educational qualification simply as a possible makeshift—that is, one to be taken into account if, on investigation, it was found that it did roughly coincide with a proper test of character in the immigrant. It is, of course, character, not education, that counts."[42] Despite the Commission's findings, Roosevelt remained convinced that a literacy test did roughly coincide with a proper test of character. He denied to Trautmann any responsibility for or involvement with Lodge's bill reintroducing the literacy test in the autumn of 1903. By the same token, he also insisted that, according to Lodge, the literacy test would be a legitimate test of character. Appealing to Trautmann's ethnic pride, he wrote, "[Lodge] informs me, for instance, that his bill would not keep out any German immigrants at all, but would restrict immigration of some undesirable elements."[43]

He agreed that a commission should be sent to Europe, but not until after the 1904 presidential election, so that it would not become an emotional issue exploited by "extreme partisans."[44] Roosevelt again clearly sought to avoid any accusations of anti-immigrant bias in the upcoming campaign. In his third annual message to Congress on 7 December 1903, Roosevelt emphasized the Commission's findings of fraud with regard to naturalization and malpractice on Ellis Island rather than its recommendations in favor of a second commission and against a literacy test. He called for better selection and distribution of immigrants, writing what became his mantra on immigration, "We cannot have too much immigration of the right kind, and we should have none at all of the wrong kind." He stated his goal clearly: "The need is to devise some system by which undesirable immigrants shall be kept out entirely, while desirable immigrants are properly distributed throughout the country."[45] Such a system, however, proved difficult to design.

Due to concerns over the presidential campaign, Roosevelt did not push immigration reform at all in 1904. He warned Lodge of this in a 23 May 1904 letter, writing in an unusually passive, third-person style. "There seems to be a good deal of uneasiness as to saying anything about immigration this year," he explained. "It is not believed it would help us to getting [sic]

---

[42] Roosevelt to Arthur von Briesen, 2 December 1903, in *Letters of Theodore Roosevelt*, 3:664.

[43] Roosevelt to Ralph Trautmann, 28 November 1903, in ibid., 659–60.

[44] Roosevelt to Arthur von Briesen, 2 December 1903, in ibid., 664.

[45] Roosevelt, *Works*, 15:175–77.

legislation. There is no question but that there will be a sharp lookout kept to see if they cannot catch us tripping on it," he added. Roosevelt suggested that the party platform simply repeat his right immigrant/wrong immigrant dialectic.[46] In fact, the resultant platform was even more cautious. Whereas the 1896 platform had endorsed the literacy test and the 1900 platform had called for "a more effective restriction of the immigration of cheap labor from foreign lands," the 1904 platform simply promised to continue Chinese exclusion.[47]

Roosevelt easily defeated Democrat Alton B. Parker in the 1904 presidential election. The Rough Rider carried every state outside the South, losing only the immigrant-rich cities of Boston in New England and New York in his home state. He ran well among German, Swedish, Polish, Italian and Jewish Americans.[48] Following his victory, he wrote to humorist Finley Peter Dunne, taking issue with Mr. Dooley's assertion that Roosevelt "regards his iliction as a great triumph f'r th' Anglo-Saxon race." He protested, "I have always insisted that we are not Anglo-Saxons at all—even admitting for the sake of argument, which I do not, that there are any Anglo-Saxons—but a new and mixed race—a race drawing its blood from many different sources."[49] Roosevelt fiercely resented any attempt to portray him as an Anglo-Saxon nativist, and he continued to promote the melting pot concept from his bully pulpit.

With victory secured in November 1904, Roosevelt turned again to the subject of immigration restriction in his fourth annual message. This time, however, he began with a lengthy and impassioned defense of the melting pot. He warned legislators that they should always "remember that the question of being a good American has nothing whatever to do with a man's birthplace any more than it has to do with his creed." He pointed out that "in every generation from the time this government was founded men of foreign birth have stood in the very foremost rank of good citizenship," citing in particular several Congressional Medal of Honor recipients. "Good Americanism is a matter of heart, of conscience, of lofty aspiration, of sound

---

[46] Roosevelt to Lodge, 23 May 1904, in *Letters of Theodore Roosevelt*, 4:803.

[47] Hutchinson, *Legislative History*, 629–30. Roosevelt wrote candidly to Lodge on 28 June 1904, "I don't know what the Chinese exclusion plank amounts to." *Letters of Theodore Roosevelt*, 4:849.

[48] Miller, *Roosevelt: A Life*, 441; and Edgar Eugene Robinson, *The Presidential Vote, 1896–1932* (Palo Alto: Stanford University Press, 1934) 9–13.

[49] Roosevelt to Finley Peter Dunne, 23 Nov. 1904, in *Letters of Theodore Roosevelt*, 4:1040–041.

common sense, but not of birthplace or creed," he explained, while insisting that "each must stand on his worth as a man and each is entitled to be judged solely thereby." Roosevelt nevertheless warned that "the citizenship of this country should not be debased;" therefore, the wages and standard of living of American workers must be protected, "and above all we should not admit any man of an unworthy type, any man concerning whom we can say that he himself will be a bad citizen, or that his children and grandchildren will detract from instead of adding to the sum of good citizenship of the country."[50]

In his second term, Roosevelt appointed more lenient officials to key posts in the Bureau of Immigration. William Williams resigned his post as Ellis Island Commissioner in January 1905. On the advice of then-Secretary of Commerce and Labor George B. Cortelyou, Roosevelt replaced Williams with Robert Watchorn, who had been working in Montreal to seal the Canadian border against illegal Chinese immigrants. Watchorn overturned Williams' monetary requirement and in general looked more favorably on all immigrants. A Welsh immigrant himself, he wrote in a December 1907 *Outlook* article that he was confident that the United States could absorb all immigrants, "old" or "new." The same issue commended Watchorn for combining "rigid administration" with "a broad human sympathy," and Secretary of Commerce and Labor Oscar Straus praised Watchorn for "tempering justice with mercy."[51]

Such appointments were part of an attempt to appeal to foreign-born voters. In the autumn of 1906, when Republican Charles Evans Hughes was facing stiff opposition from immigrant-friendly publisher William Randolph Hearst in the New York gubernatorial race, Roosevelt shrewdly appointed Oscar Straus as the first Jewish cabinet member and suggested to Hughes that the New York Republicans needed to nominate more Jews and Catholics.[52] Straus was a prominent member of the American Jewish Committee, an organization founded to fight the restriction of immigration, and as Secretary of Commerce and Labor he would have control over the

---

[50] Roosevelt, *Works*, 15:245–46.

[51] Pitkin, *Keepers of the Gate*, 41–42, 56; and Watchorn, *Autobiography*, 36–46, 104–108.

[52] Roosevelt to Charles Evans Hughes, 4 October 1906, in *Letters of Theodore Roosevelt*, 5:442; Roosevelt to Hughes, 5 October 1906, in ibid., 443; John Higham, *Strangers in the Land: Patterns of American Nativism, 1860–1925*, 2nd ed. (New Brunswick: Rutgers University Press, 1988), 127–28; and Jenswold, "Leaving the Door Ajar," 12–13.

Immigration Bureau. The apocryphal story was told that at the dinner celebrating Straus' appointment, the president turned to Jacob Schiff for affirmation that Straus had been selected simply because he was the best man for the job. Schiff, who was very hard of hearing, responded, "Dot's right, Mr. President. You came to me and said, 'Chake, who is der best Jew I can appoint Segretary of Commerce?'"[53] Even if the story was not true, its circulation revealed that Roosevelt's penchant for playing ethnic politics was well-known.

Despite appointing more lenient men like Straus and Watchorn, Roosevelt continued to call for greater restriction of immigration. In his December 1905 annual message, the president pointed out that 1,026,000 immigrants had come to the United States in the year ending 30 June 1905, "a greater number of people than came here during the 169 years of our colonial life." He brought to the attention of Congress the Commissioner-General's warning that "a considerable proportion is undesirable," and that many were lured here, "often against their best interest," by the steamship companies. Following up his previous call for better distribution of the immigrant population, Roosevelt specifically recommended limiting the number of immigrants allowed to enter through Northern cities while allowing unlimited immigration to the South, to "distribute the immigrants upon the land and keep them away from the congested tenement-house districts of the great cities." But he cautioned that "distribution is a palliative, not a cure" and asserted once again that "the prime need is to keep out all immigrants who will not make good citizens."[54]

To restrict immigration further, the president recommended that only native Canadians and Mexicans be allowed to cross the land borders, that harsher penalties be imposed on steamship and other companies that violated the ban on contract labor, and that the immigrants-to-ship-tonnage ratio be greatly reduced in order to virtually eliminate steerage and "insure the coming hither of as good a class of aliens as possible." He also called for an international conference to discuss the possibility of allowing US officials to examine potential immigrants before they embarked in Europe. He concluded with the caveat that "in dealing with this question it is unwise to depart from the old American tradition and to discriminate for or against any man who desires to come here and become a citizen." Nevertheless, he

---

[53] John Morton Blum, *The Republican Roosevelt* (New York: Atheneum, 1972) 37.
[54] Roosevelt, Works, 15:317-19.

insisted, the United States had a "right and duty" to consider immigrants' "moral and social quality."[55]

It was the social quality of the immigrant with which Roosevelt was most concerned, since he believed that social standing and moral rectitude generally went together. By eliminating steerage Roosevelt hoped to prevent the lower classes who, he believed, contributed most of the "people of bad character, the incompetent, the lazy, the vicious, the physically unfit, defective or degenerate" from coming to the United States. He wished by these means to avoid any overt racial or religious discrimination. "If the man who seeks to come here is from the moral and social standpoint of such a character as to bid fair to add value to the community he should be heartily welcomed," he told Congress. "We cannot afford to consider whether he is Catholic or Protestant, Jew or Gentile; whether he is [sic] Englishman or Irishman, Frenchman or German, Japanese, Italian, Scandinavian, Slav, or Magyar," he argued.[56] It is significant that Roosevelt included the Japanese among the European nations, because it was in the context of Asian restriction that Roosevelt developed his proposal of class-based restriction.

Of course, class-based restriction of Asian immigration preceded Roosevelt's presidency. The Chinese Exclusion Act, originally passed in 1882 and renewed indefinitely in 1902, banned all working-class Chinese immigrants (the so-called "coolies") but permitted the merchants, professionals and students of the upper classes to immigrate freely. The 1892 Geary Act required all Chinese aliens to register with the Immigration Bureau, and both exclusion and registration were extended to Hawaii in 1900 and the Philippines in 1902.[57] Immigration inspectors subjected Chinese immigrants to harsh treatment, assuming that they all lied to gain admittance fraudulently as merchants, students, or "paper sons." They cross-examined aliens and their witnesses on minutiae, such as how many steps there were out the back door of their house in China, or how many houses there were in their village. Inconsistencies were taken to prove that the immigrants were lying, while corroboration suggested coaching. The

---

[55] Roosevelt, *Works*, 15:318–19.

[56] Ibid., 319–20. Of course, class-based restriction went against Roosevelt's insistence on judging immigrants on the basis of individual merit. Roosevelt's patrician bias prevented him from seeing that, however.

[57] Lucy E. Salyer, *Laws Harsh as Tigers: Chinese Immigrants and the Shaping of Modern Immigration Law* (Chapel Hill: University of North Carolina Press, 1996) 46–55, 103–106.

Supreme Court ruled in 1905 that the Bureau had the final power to determine if claims of citizenship were legitimate, thus denying Chinese and other immigrants the constitutional rights to a trial by jury and due process of law.[58]

Roosevelt put pressure on the Immigration Bureau to treat Chinese merchants, professionals and students with dignity and respect. He wrote to Commerce and Labor Secretary George B. Cortelyou on 25 January 1904 to ask that a certain Chinese merchant with whom he was personally acquainted be admitted, as Roosevelt could personally testify that the gentleman was a *bona fide* merchant returning to the United States. The president further suggested that this case serve as precedent for treating the Chinese fairly: "I have been for a long time uneasy about the way in which Chinese merchants and Chinese students have all kinds of obstacles thrown in their way when they come to this country." Roosevelt noted that such official harassment hurt US attempts to increase economic and political ties to the Middle Kingdom.[59]

Cortelyou was replaced later that year by Victor H. Metcalf, a former Republican Congressman from California, the state that received the most Asian immigrants. Roosevelt wrote two letters to Metcalf in June 1905, asking him to inform Immigration Bureau officials that there was "not the slightest excuse for severity in the administration of this law" and insisting that they together draw up "a circular of instructions sufficiently drastic to prevent the continuance of the very oppressive conduct of many of our officials toward Chinese gentlemen, merchants, travelers, students, and so forth."[60] His concern was prompted by a Chinese boycott of American goods begun by the Shanghai Chamber of Commerce. James B. Reynolds wrote to him from East Asia in May 1905, suggesting that fair treatment of Chinese gentlemen would "immeasurably" improve relations with China. In his 1905 annual message, Roosevelt demanded that legitimate Chinese immigrants be

---

[58] *United States v. Ju Toy*, 198 US 263 (1905); and Salyer, *Laws Harsh as Tigers*, 53–55, 59, 111–14. The Court had previously ruled in *Fong Yue Ting v. United States*, 149 US 698 (1893), that constitutional standards of due process did not apply in deportation hearings because they were not criminal proceedings.

[59] Roosevelt to George B. Cortelyou, 25 January 1904, in *Letters of Theodore Roosevelt*, 3:709–10.

[60] Roosevelt to Victor H. Metcalf, 16 June 1905, in ibid., 4:1235–236; and Roosevelt to Victor H. Metcalf, 19 June 1905, in ibid., 1240. Roosevelt wrote to Acting Secretary of State Herbert Henry Davis Pierce on 24 June 1905 a similarly stern letter warning the diplomatic and consular staff to treat Chinese with respect and courtesy. Ibid., 1251–252.

welcomed and treated fairly, noting that the Chinese boycott was a protest against discriminatory treatment.[61]

Frustrated with the seeming intransigence of the Immigration Bureau with respect to Chinese immigrants, Roosevelt once again created investigatory commissions. In February 1906, he appointed Reynolds, along with Ralph M. Easley of the National Civic Federation and Columbia economics professor Jeremiah W. Jenks to investigate the Bureau's role in precipitating the boycott. The following November he again appointed Reynolds and Jenks to investigate the smuggling of Chinese "coolies," a move prompted by the complaints of American Federation of Labor president Samuel Gompers.[62]

Roosevelt was even more uneasy about the growing anti-Japanese movement on the West Coast. Japanese immigrants began to arrive in the United States after 1891, renewing West Coast fears of a "yellow peril." By 1900, 27,000 Japanese were living in America; 100,000 more arrived by 1908.[63] Japan's success in its war with Russia and his personal contacts with Japanese leaders taught him a healthy respect for the island empire, and he was well aware that the United States was not in a position to defend the Philippines from a determined attack. He wrote to Lodge in May 1905, "I am utterly disgusted at the manifestations which have begun to appear on the Pacific slope in favor of excluding the Japanese exactly as the Chinese are excluded." The California state legislature and various other bodies, he complained, had "acted in the worst possible taste and in the most offensive manner to Japan." It was ironic, Roosevelt contended, that the West Coast congressional delegation had been reluctant to support increased naval expenditures, thus "refusing to take steps to defend themselves against the formidable foe whom they are ready with such careless insolence to antagonize."[64]

---

[61] James B. Reynolds to Roosevelt, 16 May 1905, Roosevelt Papers, Series 1, reel 54; Roosevelt, *Works*, 15:320–22; and Salyer, *Laws Harsh as Tigers*, 162–68.

[62] Roosevelt to Ralph M. Easley, Jeremiah W. Jenks and James B. Reynolds, 24 February 1906, in *Letters of Theodore Roosevelt*, 5:165; Roosevelt to Jeremiah W. Jenks and James B. Reynolds, 6 November 1906, Roosevelt Papers, Series II, Vol. 68, 265; and Samuel Gompers, *Seventy Years of Life and Labor: An Autobiography*, 2 vols. (New York: E. Dutton & Co., 1925) 2:162–65.

[63] Salyer, *Laws Harsh as Tigers*, 124.

[64] Roosevelt to Lodge, 15 May 1905, in *Letters of Theodore Roosevelt*, 4:1180–181. See also Roosevelt to Lodge, 5 June 1905, in ibid., 1205–1206; and Roosevelt to George Kennan, 6 May 1905, in ibid., 1168–169.

Roosevelt's regard for the Japanese was not merely political and diplomatic posturing. He wrote to Spring-Rice in June 1904 that the Japanese people "interest me and I like them." The president rejected the argument that Americans should support the Russians in their war with Japan because they were members of the same race. Experience had taught him that even widely different races or cultures had roughly the same proportions of bad and good people. "A good man is a good man and a bad man is a bad man wherever they are found," he concluded.[65]

In December 1904 he wrote again to Spring-Rice, expressing concern that the rudeness and racism of Americans caused the Japanese to view them as "white devils inferior to themselves." In addition to his military concerns, this mutual racial antipathy bothered him personally. "There are many individual Japanese for whom I have a sincere liking," he said, "and there is much in their civilization from which we can with advantage learn."[66] Roosevelt learned judo from and wrestled with Japanese instructors in Washington, and their physical and military prowess impressed him. Perhaps for this reason he wrote to his son Kermit in May 1907, "I want to try to keep on the best possible terms with Japan and never do her any wrong."[67]

Roosevelt tried to forestall a diplomatic crisis in July 1905 by instructing the US Minister to Japan, Lloyd Carpenter Grissom, to let the Japanese government and people know that "the American government and the American people at large have not the slightest sympathy with the outrageous agitation against the Japanese in certain small sections along the Pacific slope." As long as he was president, Roosevelt declared, "the Japanese will be treated just exactly like the English, Germans, French, or other civilized peoples."[68] But the crisis came anyway in October 1906, when the San Francisco school board ordered that Japanese and Korean schoolchildren be segregated as were the Chinese already. The people of Japan were naturally outraged. Roosevelt was, too.

He sent Victor Metcalf out to California to confer with the authorities and labor leaders. Metcalf reported that the lone "Oriental school" was in a

---

[65] Roosevelt to Cecil Arthur Spring-Rice, 13 June 1904, in ibid., 831–32.

[66] Roosevelt to Cecil Arthur Spring-Rice, 27 December 1904, in ibid., 1085–087.

[67] Roosevelt to Kermit Roosevelt, 5 March 1904, in *Works*, 19:463; Roosevelt to William Sturgis, Bigelow, 14 January 1905, in ibid., 479; and Roosevelt to Kermit Roosevelt, 12 May 1907, in ibid., 525.

[68] Roosevelt to Lloyd Carpenter Grissom, 15 July 1905, in *Letters of Theodore Roosevelt*, 4:1274–275.

burned-out section of the city, too far away to allow many students to attend. He was unable to make any headway in two weeks of negotiations with his fellow Californians. Robert Devlin, the US District Attorney for San Francisco, told Metcalf that the most favored nation clause in the 1895 treaty with Japan did not apply to education. Secretary of State Elihu Root believed that it did, however, so he supported a lawsuit filed by several Japanese-American parents. Root was on shaky legal ground, especially considering the Supreme Court's 1896 "separate but equal" ruling allowing segregation in *Plessey v. Ferguson*. Nevertheless, Root and Roosevelt were determined to prevent any diplomatic breach with Japan. Roosevelt wrote Root on 5 December 1906 that the suit "should be prest [sic] as rapidly as possible."[69]

Roosevelt decided that the only solution to the problem which would placate West Coast voters and avoid war was to apply the same class-based restriction to the Japanese that was already in effect for the Chinese, but to do it through an informal "Gentlemen's Agreement." The name given to this deal is apt, since it restricted Japanese immigration to those members of the upper classes who were the social equals of American and European gentlemen. Roosevelt appealed to Japanese leaders as fellow gentlemen, excusing American racism as a product of working-class ignorance which could be prevented by keeping the American and Japanese working classes apart. In a letter to Baron Kentaro Kaneko in May 1907, he explained that just as it had taken centuries for the working classes of the various European nations to lose their racial antipathies and adopt the enlightened, cosmopolitan outlook of the aristocrats, so time must be given for American and Japanese laborers to overcome their animosities. "Now gentlemen, all educated people, members of the professions, and the like, get on so well together that they not only travel in each other's country, but associate on the most intimate terms," he wrote, noting that several Japanese gentlemen were his valued friends. Unfortunately, such enlightened attitudes did not prevail among laborers from the two countries.[70]

---

[69] Roosevelt to Eugene Hale, 27 October 1906, in ibid., 5:473–75; Roosevelt to Victor Metcalf, 27 Nov. 1906, in ibid., 510-11; Roosevelt to Elihu Root, 5 December 1906, in ibid., 521; and Frank Chuman, *The Bamboo People: The Law and Japanese-Americans* (Del Mar CA: Publisher's Inc., 1976) 24–26. Korea had been annexed by Japan in 1905; hence their inclusion in the segregation order.

[70] Roosevelt to Kentaro Kaneko, 23 May 1907, in *Letters of Theodore Roosevelt*, 5:671–72. See also Roosevelt to Kogora Takahira, 28 April 1907, in ibid., 5:656–67; Roosevelt to Kentaro Kaneko, 8 May 1913, in ibid., 7:727–29; and Roosevelt to Sir Edward Grey, 18 December 1906, in ibid., 5:527–29.

Roosevelt's sixth annual message to Congress on 3 December 1906 laid out his solution. He had prepared his remarks carefully, allowing the Japanese Ambassador to read and approve them before sending them to Congress. The message condemned the anti-Japanese agitation because "it is most discreditable to us as a people, and it may be fraught with the gravest consequences to the nation." He pointed out to those who prided themselves on being "Anglo-Saxon" that Japan had a "glorious and ancient past" as a civilization far older than Northern Europe's. He also praised Japan's recent industrialization and militarization, declaring that "the Japanese have won in a single generation the right to stand abreast of the foremost and most enlightened peoples of Europe and America," and therefore "the right to treatment on a basis of full and frank equality."[71]

The president explicitly linked the treatment of Japanese and European immigrants, saying, "Not only must we treat all nations fairly, but we must treat with justice and goodwill all immigrants who come here under the law. Whether they are Catholic or Protestant, Jew or gentile, whether they come from England or Germany, Russia, Japan or Italy, means nothing." He referred to the Mosaic law's command to do justice to "the stranger within our gates" and noted, "It is the sure sign of a low civilization, a low morality, to abuse or discriminate against or in any way humiliate such a stranger who has come here lawfully and who is conducting himself properly." Then he proposed two pieces of legislation whose aim was in fact to make Japanese and European immigrants equal before the law: naturalization of the Japanese, and a ban on *all* working-class immigrants.[72]

Roosevelt's message was hailed with gratitude in Japan, but roundly condemned by nativists in the United States. He defended himself in a letter to Lyman Abott in January 1907. While the president believed that Japanese laborers should be excluded, he maintained that "it does no possible good to deprive those who are here of the franchise. On the contrary, I think that we should studiously give the franchise and school facilities to, and in other ways treat as well as possible, all the Japanese that come." Roosevelt understood that prejudice only hindered assimilation. While Japanese immigrants were barred from naturalization, their American-born children were citizens who should learn to love their country. "We cannot afford to

---

[71] Roosevelt, Works, 15:385-86.

[72] Roosevelt, *Works,* 15:387–88. He also asked, as Harrison, Cleveland and McKinley had, for greater power to protect aliens in their treaty rights., On the biblical command, see e.g.; Exodus 20:10, Leviticus 19:33-34 and Deuteronomy 5:14.

regard any immigrant as a laborer; we must regard him as a citizen," he insisted.[73]

Theodore Roosevelt retained his faith in the eventual assimilation of even those whom he considered to be extremely different on a racial basis. But assimilation had to be encouraged by treating the immigrants with dignity and respect so that they would want to join American society. To conservative Los Angeles publisher Harrison Gray Otis the president wrote, "I entirely agree with you as to the great undesirability of the large influx of Japanese to the United States. As you probably know, I should like greatly to restrict the immigration hither of the classes of the lowest standard of living, even from Europe." Nevertheless, the Japanese who were already in the country, should be treated "just as well as anybody else." Their children should attend the common public schools, just like the children of European immigrants. "The cry against them is simply nonsense," Roosevelt declared, since "they cannot possibly contaminate the other scholars."[74]

Roosevelt summoned to Washington the mayor and school board members of San Francisco to work out an acceptable compromise with the Japanese Ambassador and himself. Meanwhile Oscar Straus, the new Secretary of Commerce and Labor, investigated Japanese immigration at Root's behest and found that two-thirds of the previous year's total had come from Hawaii. Straus and Root drafted an amendment to the immigration bill (then in conference committee) allowing the president to exclude aliens trying to enter from Canada, Mexico, or a US territory if he had reason to believe that they had entered the territory for the sole reason of gaining access to the US mainland and that their entry would be detrimental to labor conditions. The Californians and Japanese agreed to it. The bill, with the amendment, was passed and signed into law on 20 February 1907. On 13 March the San Francisco school board rescinded its segregation order and the following day Roosevelt invoked the amendment to bar Japanese and Korean aliens.[75]

---

[73] Roosevelt to Lyman Abbott, 3 January 1907, in *Letters of Theodore Roosevelt*, 5:537; and Chuman, *Bamboo People*, 28.

[74] Roosevelt to Harrison Gray Otis, 8 Jan. 1907, in *Letters of Theodore Roosevelt*, 5:541.

[75] Hutchinson, *Legistlative History,* 142; Chuman, *Bamboo People*, 28–32; and Oscar Straus, *Under Four Administrations: From Cleveland to Taft* (Boston: Houghton Mifflin, 1922) 217–19.

Unrest, however, continued in California because politicians knew that racist scapegoating made for good politics. Roosevelt railed against the "hideous cowardice and stupidity" of the people and the "hideous sensationalism and offensiveness" of the press in a July 1907 letter to Root. The situation concerned him more than any other crisis, especially since Japanese diplomats were insisting that exclusion of Japanese immigrants be on the same terms as European immigrants rather than those applying to Chinese immigrants.[76] Concerned about the threat of war with Japan, he quietly contacted British Foreign Secretary Arthur Balfour and Canadian Premier Mackenzie King to secure a common front against Japanese immigration by the United States, Canada and Australia.[77]

Roosevelt determined that the only way to reduce the racial tensions that threatened to turn into a Pacific war was to persuade Japan to allow only students and members of the business and professional classes to emigrate. This was the purpose of the "Gentlemen's Agreement," worked out in correspondence between US Ambassador Thomas J. O'Brien and Japanese Foreign Minister Hayashi between January and March 1908. The exact terms—if, indeed, there were any recorded in writing—are unknown, but the 1908 report of the Commissioner-General of Immigration stated that the Japanese government would only issue passports to students, merchants, professionals, and laborers returning to property acquired before 1906 or to their spouses. The result was an immediate and drastic cut in Japanese immigration: whereas 12,999 Japanese had come in 1907, only 8,340 came in 1908, and 1,596 in 1909.[78]

Despite the success of the Gentlemen's Agreement, Roosevelt had to quash yet another attempt by California to insult Japan in the last months of his term. He wrote to Governor James N. Gillett on 16 January 1909 expressing deep concern over proposed legislation that would have both banned Japanese ownership of land and also segregated Japanese schoolchildren. He pointed out that over the past six months departures of Japanese persons from the US had exceeded arrivals, proving that the agreement was working. Ten days later he passed along Root's observation

---

[76] Roosevelt to Elihu Root, 13 July 1907, in *Letters of Theodore Roosevelt*, 5:717–19.

[77] Roosevelt to Arthur James Balfour, 5 March 1908, in ibid., 6:959–63; and Roosevelt to Whitelaw Reid, 30 March 1908, in ibid., 985.

[78] Chuman, *Bamboo People*, 33–37; and memo enclosed with Philander C. Knox to William Howard Taft, 12 January 1911, William Howard Taft Presidential Papers, Library of Congress, Washington DC, Series 6, Case File 749 (reel 405).

that reinstating segregation in the schools would only cause Japan to abrogate the Gentlemen's Agreement, and thus lead to more Japanese immigration. He also noted that by treaty Japanese aliens could own residential and commercial property. Since it was the case that treaties took precedence over state laws, the most the California legislature could do was to bar Japanese-Americans from owning farm land.[79] Ultimately, Gillett convinced the legislature to reconsider its actions.

Roosevelt explained his policy to Taft's incoming Secretary of State, Philander C. Knox, in February 1909. He said that despite the odiousness of anti-Japanese prejudice on the West Coast, he had reluctantly come to believe that Japanese immigrants must be excluded because their continued admission would "cause a race problem and invite and insure a race contest." He also insisted that it was necessary to show "all possible courtesy and consideration" in carrying out this policy, and he added in a handwritten note that the Japanese should be shown "that our keeping them out means not that they are inferior to us—in some ways they are superior—but that they are *different*; so different that, whatever the future may hold, at present the two races ought not to come together in masses." Roosevelt knew, however, that such logic would not be convincing to the Japanese. The United States government was clearly catering to the racism of some of its citizens who did consider the Japanese to be inferior. Knowing that Japanese resentment could not readily be mollified, the president also urged Knox to make sure the nation was "thoroly [sic] armed," and to begin replacing Japanese workers in Hawaii with Europeans.[80]

The 1907 Immigration Act had many important provisions beyond those dealing with the Japanese. Representative Augustus Gardner of Massachusetts, Henry Cabot Lodge's son-in-law, introduced a bill from the House Committee on Immigration and Naturalization on 9 April 1906. It raised the head tax from two to five dollars, with part of the increased revenue going to fund a new division of information that would help to facilitate Roosevelt's desire for better distribution of immigrants to rural

---

[79] Roosevelt to James N. Gillett, 16 January 1909, in *Letters of Theodore Roosevelt*, 6:1477–478; and Roosevelt to Gillett, 26 January 1909, in ibid., 1483–486. See also Roosevelt to Speaker of the California House of Representatives Philip A. Stanton, 8 February 1909, in ibid., 1509–510.

[80] Roosevelt to Philander C. Knox, 8 February 1909, in ibid., 6:1510–514 (emphasis in original). See also Roosevelt, "The Japanese Question," The Outlook, 8 may 1909, in Works, 16:288-91; and Roosevelt, *Autobiography*, 411–15.

areas. To meet his recommendation of an economic qualification, the bill required adult males to be in possession of twenty-five dollars, while females and children had to have fifteen dollars, unless the head of a family entering together had fifty dollars. Reflecting eugenic fears, the bill added imbeciles, the feeble-minded, consumptives, those who had been insane at any time, and persons of poor physique to the list of excluded immigrants. The time limit for deportation was extended from one to three years in certain cases to weed out more criminals and paupers. Finally, it prescribed a literacy test whose form would be determined by the Secretary of Commerce and Labor.[81]

The biggest obstacle to the passage of the bill was the Speaker of the House, Republican Joseph Cannon of Illinois. Roosevelt wrote Cannon to seek his support on 27 May 1906. He denied that Wall Street was behind the bill, blaming opposition to it on steamship companies and businesses that wanted "cheap labor." He also downplayed Cannon's fears of German and Scandinavian opposition. While he declared that personally he would prefer inspection abroad and the elimination of steerage to the literacy test, the test was "very much better than nothing." He concluded that he wanted a law that would "prevent the admission of immigrants who by their competition tend to lower the standard of living, and therefore the standard of wages, of our own laboring men," while at the same time bringing in "elements which would be of advantage to our community." He expressly denied any prejudice: "I do not care what the man's creed or nationality may be, so long as his character is all right and so long as he has the amount of physical and mental fitness that we should be able to demand." He did not want to be "afraid of their grandchildren intermingling with ours as their political, social and industrial equals."[82]

Cannon, however, was not persuaded. He was a believer in the economic doctrine of *laissez-faire*, and he opposed the labor unions which were clamoring for restrictions. The fact that millions of workers wanted to come to the United States for higher wages and more personal liberty proved to Cannon that "America was a hell of a success." He also viewed the president's growing power as a threat to his own. Cannon's Rules Committee strictly limited debate on the bill. Cannon himself led the floor fight against it, temporarily turning the duties of the speaker over to his ally,

---

[81] Hutchinson, *Legislative History*, 138–29.

[82] Roosevelt to Joseph Cannon, 27 May 1906, in *Letters of Theodore Roosevelt*, 5:285–86.

James Watson of Indiana. Another ally, Charles Grosvenor, successfully amended the bill by eliminating the literacy test and substituting a commission to study the immigration question. When the time came to form a conference committee to reconcile the House and Senate versions, Cannon appointed Republican William S. Bennet and Democrat Jacob Ruppert, Jr., the New York City representatives who had filed the minority report for the Immigration Committee opposing the literacy test, along with Committee chair Benjamin Howell of New Jersey, who was bound to support Cannon despite his personal preference for the literacy test.[83]

The proposed legislation became a central issue in the 1906 national elections. Cannon and Bennet were also members of the National Liberal Immigration League, a group founded in 1906 by Jewish, German, and Irish leaders to oppose immigration restriction. Another group, the American Jewish Committee, lobbied against the legislation more discreetly.[84] Under such circumstances, Roosevelt did not publicly support the bill. He wrote to Cannon in August that although Lodge was putting pressure on him to speak in its favor, he was "afraid that any allusion to it would do harm rather than good." He also reassured Gardner that although he had received much information regarding the political damage caused by the bill, he remained confident that it was the right thing to do from the "national standpoint."[85] Restrictionists were dismayed, however, when Roosevelt announced in September that Oscar Straus would become the next Secretary of Commerce and Labor, with control over the Bureau of Immigration. Their fears proved correct: the first Jewish cabinet member in American history proceeded to work diligently against passage of the literacy test.[86]

As the House and Senate conference committee met in February 1907, Roosevelt sent Secretary of State Root to plead with Cannon to adopt the amendment worked out by the president, the San Francisco officials, and the

---

[83] Blair Bolles, *Tyrant from Illinois: Uncle Joe Cannon's Experiment with Personal Power* (New York: W. W. Norton & Co., 1951) 72–74; Hutchinson, *Legislative History*, 141; and Jenswold, "Leaving the Door Ajar," 14–16. Ruppert later became the owner of the New York Yankees baseball club.

[84] Rivka Shpak Lissak, "The National Liberal Immigration League and Immigration Restriction, 1906–1917," *American Jewish Archives* 46/2 (1994): 197–246; Henry B. Leonard, "Louis Marshall and Immigration Restriction, 1906–1924," *American Jewish Archives* 24/1 (1972): 6–26; and Higham, *Strangers in the Land*, 123–28.

[85] Roosevelt to Joseph Cannon, 15 August 1906, in *Letters of Theodore Roosevelt*, 5:360; and Roosevelt to Augustus Gardner, 4 September 1906, in ibid., 5:393.

[86] Higham, *Strangers in the Land*, 127–29.

Japanese ambassador. Cannon agreed, on the condition that the Senate drop its insistence on the literacy test. Root and Roosevelt then convinced Lodge and his fellow Senate conferees, William Dillingham of Vermont and Anselm McLaurin of Mississippi, to agree to Cannon's demands. The conference committee also set the head tax at four dollars, raised the amount of deck space per passenger and created an Immigration Commission composed of three senators, three representatives and three presidential appointees.[87] Restrictionists like Gardner and Alabama Democrat John L. Burnett felt betrayed by Roosevelt. "When it came to a showdown," Burnett complained, "the President was not to be seen, and his hand was not to be felt."[88] From the beginning, Roosevelt's support for the literacy test had only been lukewarm. He had no qualms about abandoning it to secure what he thought was the greater good of peace with Japan. Besides, Cannon's opposition had already doomed the literacy test: stubbornness on the part of Lodge, Dillingham and McLaurin would only have resulted in the failure of any bill to pass at all.

After securing most of what he wanted in the 1907 act, Roosevelt gave no further attention to the subject of immigration for the remainder of his term in office. Secretary of Commerce and Labor Straus continued his campaign against restriction and pressed for naturalization of Japanese Americans in the cabinet. Well aware that the decisions of review boards depended almost entirely on whether the board members were restrictionists—especially in cases involving the highly subjective "likely to become a public charge" clause—he reviewed all appeals that came to him. He also issued a circular to secure greater cooperation between the police and immigration officials in deporting alien criminals and anarchists, and tried to curtail fraudulent naturalization.[89] Immigration Restriction League secretary Prescott F. Hall accused Straus of failure to enforce the existing

[87] Bolles, *Tyrant from Illinois*, 75–77; Roger Daniels, *The Politics of Prejudice: The Anti-Japanese Movement in California and the Struggle for Japanese Exclusion* (Berkeley: University of California Press, 1962) 41–42; Hutchinson, *Legislative History*, 142 n. 111; Jenswold, "Leaving the Door Ajar," 14–16; and Rachel Leah Hershfield, "The Immigration Restriction League: A Study of the League's Impact on American Immigration Policy, 1894–1924," (M.A. thesis, University of Calgary, April 1993) 65–66.

[88] Jenswold, "Leaving the Door Ajar," 17.

[89] Straus, *Under Four Administrations*, 216–17, 220–21, 226–27, 231–34. While serving as US Minister to Turkey, Straus had complained to McKinley about immigrants who used naturalization as a way of avoiding obligations in their homelands.

laws, but when asked by Roosevelt to investigate the charge, Lodge replied that surprise inspections at Baltimore, Philadelphia, New York City and Boston turned up no evidence against him: Straus was enforcing the law, however reluctantly.[90] Roosevelt grew very fond of Straus, and requested of incoming President Taft that he be kept on as Commerce and Labor Secretary. Taft, however, did not continue Straus's appointment.

Roosevelt did try to influence the nature of the Immigration Commission. To remove it from politics, he wrote to Cannon in June 1906 to request that Immigration Commissioner Frank Sargent and Labor Commissioner Charles Neill be allowed to investigate immigration, rather than a congressional committee. In fact, he secretly ordered Sargent and Neill to begin such an investigation, and in the fall of 1906 he had James Reynolds investigate Ellis Island once again.[91] On 12 January 1907, the president wrote Cannon that he wanted the conference committee's report on the immigration bill to propose a commission that would thoroughly investigate the subject and allow Roosevelt, after his successor's election, to lay before Congress a plan offering "a definite solution of this immigration business." Such a plan would exclude "the unfit, physically, morally or mentally," and distribute immigrants for their "more rapid assimilation with our people."[92] Like the Immigration Commission itself, Roosevelt knew the conclusions they would reach before they began their investigations.

After he left the White House, Theodore Roosevelt continued to champion the melting pot and oppose the pseudo-science of eugenics. In his Romanes Lecture at Oxford in 1910, Roosevelt undercut the very basis for Social Darwinism when he declared that there was "no exact parallelism between the birth, growth and death of species in the animal world, and the

---

[90] Roosevelt to Prescott F. Hall, 24 June 1908, in *Letters of Theodore Roosevelt*, 6:1096–097; Henry Cabot Lodge, *Selections from the Correspondence of Theodore Roosevelt and Henry Cabot Lodge, 1884–1918*, 2 vols. (New York: Charles Scribner's Sons, 1925) 2:306; Roosevelt to Lodge, 8 Aug. 1908, in *Letters of Theodore Roosevelt*, 6:1160; and Barbara Miller Solomon, *Ancestors and Immigrants: A Changing New England Tradition* (Cambridge: Harvard University Press, 1963; reprint, New York: J. Wiley & Sons, 1965) 196–97.

[91] Roosevelt to Joseph Cannon, 27 June 1906, in *Letters of Theodore Roosevelt*, 5:322–23; Roosevelt to Charles Neill, 28 June 1906, in ibid., 323–24; and Roosevelt to James B. Reynolds, 12 October 1906, Roosevelt Papers, Series II, Vol. 67, 328.

[92] Roosevelt to Joseph Cannon, 12 Jan. 1907, in *Letters of Theodore Roosevelt*, 5:550.

birth, growth and death of societies in the world of man."[93] He understood, as eugenicists Madison Grant, Charles Davenport and Harry H. Laughlin did not, that not only were there no pure races, but that they were not desirable because the great cultures and civilizations of history grew out of the intermingling of races. "A great nation rarely belongs to any one race, though its citizens generally have one essentially national speech," he observed.[94]

He also had little patience for historians who gloried in an "Anglo-Saxon" past and worried about a multiethnic future. "The anthropologist and the historian of today realize much more clearly than their predecessors of a couple of generations back how artificial most great nationalities are, and how loose is the terminology usually employed to describe them," he explained to his Oxford audience. He noted a "pathetic humor" in the reverential way that some historians spoke of "the Aryan and the Teuton," and compared such history to the old pagan beliefs that certain humans were descended from the gods. "Nowadays, of course, all students recognize that there may not be, and often is not, the slightest connection between kinship in blood and kinship in tongue," he said, and nowhere was that more true than in America.[95] Roosevelt offered himself as an example of the melting pot's work, noting that he had "the blood of men who came from many different European races." He was a microcosm of American society, which was producing a race "more and more akin to that of those Americans like myself who are of the old stock but not mainly of English stock."[96]

Roosevelt set limits on which immigrants could be assimilated, basing them more on his view of the history of the United States than on racism. He was willing to give the benefit of the doubt to the most recent immigrants. He wrote to *Outlook* editor Lyman Abbott in 1908, "I grow extremely indignant at the attitude of coarse hostility to the immigrant taken by so many natives." He admitted that he "never had much chance to deal with the Slav, Magyar, or Italian," but he asserted that when he had dealt with them, he "tried to do with them as with the German and the Irishman, the Catholic and the Jew, and that is, treat them so as to appeal to their self-respect and make it easy for them to become enthusiastically loyal Americans as well as good citizens." That was why he had appointed two Catholics (Charles J.

---

[93] Roosevelt, *Works*, 12:29. He did concede that there were "strange analogies."
[94] Ibid., 12:41.
[95] Ibid., 12:40.
[96] Ibid., 12:25.

Bonaparte and Robert J. Wynne) and one Jew (Oscar Straus) to his cabinet: he wanted "to implant in the minds of our fellow-Americans of Catholic or of Jewish faith, or of foreign ancestry or birth, the knowledge that they have in this country just the same rights and opportunities as everyone else…and therefore just the same ideals as a standard toward which to strive."[97] All men may not have been created equal, Roosevelt believed, but it was necessary to treat them as if they were, and thereby encourage them to the highest standard of conduct.

In the end, Roosevelt was a politician dealing with the unfortunate racist realities of his day, a racism that he himself only partially overcame. He wrote in December 1906 to English journalist and friend, John St. Loe Strachey, that he had hoped to get a general immigration bill to "keep out all people who have difficulty in assimilating with our own" without offending any nation, but it had been impossible. "I have to recognize facts," he said, "one fact being governmental conditions as they actually exist in a democracy, and the other being, what so many sentimentalists tend to forget, the great fact of difference of race."[98] Roosevelt believed that racial differences were real, but based on history rather than biology. Although he deplored the racist animosities based on those differences as immoral and unworthy of a great Christian civilization, he thought it best to avoid situations that would inflame such prejudice. He used the bully pulpit to extol the melting pot, even though he did not desire the United States to be a universal asylum for the downtrodden any longer. A supporter of restricted immigration, he tried to find a method that would differentiate between the "right kind" and "wrong kind" of immigrants without overt racial discrimination. The literacy test failed in Congress, however, and his class-based solution held no popular appeal. In this, as in many other policy areas, Roosevelt left an uncertain legacy for Taft to follow.

---

[97] Roosevelt to Lyman Abbott, 29 May 1908, in *Letters of Theodore Roosevelt*, 6:1042–043. Abbott had succeeded Henry Ward Beecher as the pastor of Plymouth Congregational Church in Brooklyn.

[98] Roosevelt to John St. Loe Strachey, 21 December 1906, in ibid., 5:532–33.

CHAPTER 3

WILLIAM HOWARD TAFT AND
THE DILLINGHAM COMMISSION

William Howard Taft inherited a stable immigration policy from Theodore Roosevelt. The Gentlemen's Agreement barred Japanese laborers from immigrating to the United States while minimizing tension with Japan. Further congressional attempts at restriction awaited the report of the Immigration Commission. Taft, unlike his predecessor, had little personal interest in immigration matters; he was content to maintain the status quo. In terms of their attitude toward racial and ethnic groups, Taft and Roosevelt were similar. Taft was a benevolent imperialist who believed in the possibility of "uplifting" peoples whom he considered inferior. He had the opportunity to put his ideas into practice as Governor of the Philippines. He had an abiding faith in both the economic benefits of immigration and the assimilation of immigrants. Furthermore, he particularly valued America's role as an asylum from religious persecution. Influenced by his German-American Secretary of Commerce and Labor, Charles Nagel, Taft vetoed the literacy test bill recommended by the Immigration Commission.

The Immigration Commission was created by the Immigration Act of 1907. Senate Immigration Committee chairman, William P. Dillingham of Vermont, chaired the commission. He was joined by fellow Senate committee members Henry Cabot Lodge of Massachusetts and Anselm McLaurin of Mississippi, along with House Immigration Committee members William S. Bennet of New York, John L. Burnett of Alabama and Benjamin Howell of New Jersey.[1] Roosevelt appointed the other three commissioners: Labor Commissioner Charles P. Neill, who had previously

---

[1] McLaurin initially declined, and was replaced by South Carolina Senator Asbury C. Latimer. However, Latimer died on 20 Feb. 1908, and McLaurin took his place. McLaurin died on 22 Dec. 1909, and was replaced in the Senate and on the Commission by LeRoy Percy.

been a professor of political economy at Catholic University; Columbia economics professor Jeremiah W. Jenks, who had served on the 1903 Ellis Island Commission and investigated Chinese immigration with James B. Reynolds; and Oakland, California, transportation executive William R. Wheeler, active in the Republican party and presumably representing both California and the transportation companies. Morton E. Crane, whom Lodge described as "safe and loyal" on immigration, served as secretary, along with the Senate and House Committee clerks, William Walter Husband and C. S. Atkinson. With the sole exception of Bennet, all were committed to increased immigration restrictions in general and the literacy test in particular.

The Dillingham Commission was a substitute for the literacy test that restrictionists had been demanding, and it was widely viewed as a delaying tactic. Immigration Restriction League lobbyist James Patten privately referred to the Vermont senator as "Dilly-Dally," accusing him of dragging out the commission's work.[2] William S. Bennet explained in a letter to President Taft's secretary, Charles D. Hilles, in 1911 that Congress had been trying hard to avoid dealing decisively with the immigration issue: "During my six years in Congress it was my aim to so handle immigration legislation as not to blow us up. The whole question is filled with dynamite." Speaking of the 1907 Immigration Act and the 1910 Mann White Slave Traffic Act, he wrote, "Our congressmen from restrictive districts could point with pride to these while those from liberal districts could stand on the fact that the educational test remained unadopted. Thus this dangerous question was kept out of politics and from doing us harm." He went on to recommend that similar inconsequential pieces of legislation be passed by every Congress, to maintain the illusion that the federal government was addressing the issue.[3]

Despite Bennet's cynical analysis, one cannot simply dismiss the Immigration Commission as an attempt to whitewash the problem. The forty-two volumes of its reports represent an exhaustive study of immigration, and indeed the chief complaint made by Bennet in his brief minority report was that the Commission's recommendation of a literacy test was not warranted by the evidence assembled, which showed that "in the

---

[2] Robert Fredric Zeidel, "The Literacy Test for Immigrants: A Question of Progress" (Ph.D. diss., Marquette University, 1986) 253–54, 263.

[3] William S. Bennet to Charles D. Hilles, n.d. [1911], enclosure with Philander C. Knox to Taft, 21 April 1911, William Howard Taft Presidential Papers, Library of Congress, Washington DC, Series 6, Case File 77 (Immigration), reel 364.

main the present immigrants are not criminal, pauper, insane, or seekers of charity in so great a degree as their predecessors."[4] Bennet, however, was the lone liberal on the Commission. The rest of the members were committed to a literacy test even before the investigations began, and thus their recommendation was a foregone conclusion.[5]

The final report declared: "The chief basis of the Commission's work was the changed character of the immigration movement to the United States during the past twenty-five years." In other words, the commissioners accepted as fact the distinction between old and new immigrants assumed by restrictionists and eugenicists. According to the report, the "old immigrants"—the British, Irish, German and Scandinavian immigrants who came in the first eight decades of the nineteenth century—had been "settlers" and "pioneers" who came during a "period of agricultural development" and became landowners. Furthermore, they "mingled freely with the native Americans and were quickly assimilated" so that "the racial identity of their children and was almost entirely lost and forgotten." By contrast, the "new immigrants"—the Italians, Poles, Slavs, and Jews who came in the late 1800s and early 1900s—were described as "unskilled laboring men who have come, in large part temporarily, from the less progressive and advanced countries of Europe." They worked in factories rather than on farms, and they kept to themselves in crowded city tenements. They were "far less intelligent" than their predecessors, did not readily assimilate, and were motivated by sordid pecuniary interests rather than the ideals of pioneers. "Consequently the Commission paid but little attention to the foreign-born element of the old immigrant class and directed its efforts almost entirely to an inquiry relative to the general status of the newer immigrants."[6]

The perceived change in the recent immigrants' motivation to come to the United States was particularly important because it indicated to the commissioners that the nation was no longer needed as an asylum for the

---

[4] United States Immigration Commission, *Reports of the Immigration Commission*, 42 vols., 61st Cong., 3d sess., S. Doc. 747, serial 5865 (Washington: Government Printing Office, 1911) 1:49. For a scathing attack on the Commission's conclusions, see Oscar Handlin, *Race and Nationality in American Life* (Boston: Little, Brown & Co, 1957) 98–131.

[5] Zeidel, "Literacy Test ," 255–56, 266. Patten and the Immigration Restriction League worked to discredit Bennet by making him appear to be secretly antisemitic and hostile to immigrants.

[6] US Immigration Commission, *Reports*, 1:13–14.

oppressed. The "birds of passage," who came to work only to earn enough money to move back to their homeland and support a family there, demonstrated that they did not come to America as refugees from tyranny. The report observed that "emigration from Europe is not now an absolute economic necessity, and as a rule, those who emigrate to the United States are impelled by a desire for betterment rather than by the necessity of escaping intolerable conditions." The commissioners added tartly, "This fact should largely modify the natural incentive to treat the immigration movement from the standpoint of sentiment and permit its consideration primarily as an economic problem."[7] Like the eugenicists, the commissioners urged Americans to give up their old sentimental notions of the melting pot and asylum, and instead face the stern realities of scientific facts.

The facts discovered by their investigations, however, did not always support the suggested dichotomy between good "old" immigrants and bad "new" ones. Despite the fears raised by such language, it appeared that existing immigration laws were functioning well. The commission found that while prior to 1882 "the diseased, defective, delinquent, and dependent entered the country practically at will," the immigration laws passed since then did "effectively debar paupers and the physically unsound and generally the mentally unsound," although difficulty in getting proof made the laws "largely ineffectual in preventing the coming of criminals and other moral delinquents." The report also admitted that the steamship companies' inspections abroad were very effective in keeping out the medically unfit, and an experiment with American medical examiners in Italian ports showed no improvement in the overall quality of those who arrived as immigrants on US shores.[8]

Even in the one area where the laws did not seem effective, it was unclear whether it had much impact on American society. While the officials of the Immigration Bureau seemed unable to check effectively the admission of criminals, the Dillingham Commission concluded that "it does not appear from available statistics that criminality among the foreign-born increases the volume of crime in proportion to the total population." The statistics did seem to show that the number of convictions for crimes was proportionally greater among the foreign-born than among the native-born, but the report cautioned: "The proportion of persons of what may be termed the criminal

---

[7] Ibid., 24-25.
[8] Ibid., 26–27.

age is greater among the foreign-born than among natives, and when due allowance is made for this fact it appears that criminality, judged by convictions, is about equally prevalent in each class." The report added another caveat that recognized how the statistics were skewed unfavorably against the newer immigrants: Many of the convictions were for violations that only applied to unnaturalized aliens. Nevertheless, the commissioners asserted that despite this ambiguous evidence, the immigration of criminals "constitutes one of the serious social effects of the immigration movement" and that the present laws were insufficient to either exclude or deport alien criminals.[9]

One reason that the crime rate was not as high among the foreign-born as expected was that the poverty rate was also less than expected. The commission found that contract labor was not a problem and that the "padrone" system, in which labor brokers arranged transportation and employment for immigrants belonging to the same ethnic group in exchange for hefty fees, died out as immigrant groups became established enough to rely on family and friends to help them get jobs.[10] It also discovered that "pauperism among the newly admitted immigrants is relatively at a minimum," and that "the number of those admitted who receive assistance from organized charity is relatively small." In fact, the commission found that at New York's Bellevue and Allied Hospitals, a higher percentage of native-born than foreign-born were treated for alcoholism, and that almost all the foreign-born were "old immigrants."[11] This ran counter to the claims of restrictionists and eugenicists that the foreign-born, particularly the most recent immigrants, were overburdening eleemosynary institutions.

Although most of the new immigrants lived in poor urban neighborhoods, the commissioners found that even there conditions were not as bad as they had assumed. Investigating immigrant ghettoes in New York, Philadelphia, Chicago, Boston, Cleveland, Buffalo and Milwaukee, they were surprised to learn that "the average conditions were found materially

---

[9] Ibid., 27, 33–34. Even Bennet agreed with this conclusion, and he had submitted bills in 1908 and 1909 to allow for the deportation of alien convicts after they had served their sentences. Edward P. Hutchinson, *Legislative History of American Immigration Policy, 1798–1965* (Philadelphia: University of Pennsylvania Press, 1981) 144, 146.

[10] US Immigration Commission, *Reports*, 1:29–30. It did find, however, that the importation of prostitutes (the "white slave traffic") was a problem. The report expressed confidence that the new 1910 Mann Act, "if vigorously enforced," would solve it. Ibid., 30.

[11] Ibid., 35–37.

better than had been anticipated," and in fact better than in many smaller industrial towns. Furthermore, the commissioners realized that the new immigrants were not always responsible for the squalor in which some of them lived. The report noted that deplorable conditions were often "due in part, at any rate, to circumstances over which the inhabitants have little direct control ... matters that should be attended to by city authorities." Investigators found that the turnover in such districts was high, with the successful moving out and newcomers taking their place. While they still believed that "racial standards" played a role in living conditions, their investigations revealed that the single biggest determining factor was whether the immigrants lived in groups of single men or in families. Families were not only much neater, but they were much more likely to assimilate quickly, largely due to the influence of children who learned English in the public schools and got better-paying jobs that enabled their families to move to nicer neighborhoods.[12]

The economic impact of immigration, according to the report, was mixed. There was no evidence that the new immigrants had any effect on the skilled trades whose unions demanded restriction. The commission, however, did find evidence that immigration "kept conditions in the semiskilled and unskilled occupations from advancing." The culprits were once again single men, "whose standard of living is so far below that of the native American or older immigrant worker that it is impossible for the latter to successfully compete with them." Living crowded together, with no families to support, they could accept lower wages and still save money. Because many of them were "birds of passage" who returned to their native land after a few years, they were unconcerned about their long-term standard of living in America. Families were better, the commission argued, but even the most stable families generally took "a long time before they even approach the ordinary standard of the American or the older immigrant families in the same grade of occupation."[13] The report did not note that it took time for anyone, native or foreign-born, to accumulate financial resources, and thus the most recent arrivals would always be lagging behind those who had been there for a while.

The Dillingham Commission endorsed Roosevelt's immigration policy in several areas. It called for distributing immigrants around the country to break up the congested urban areas, and criticized the Immigration Bureau's

---

[12] Ibid., 36–37, 42.
[13] Ibid., 38–39.

Division of Information for acting as an employment agency rather than encouraging distribution as it was intended to do.[14] It also avoided dealing directly with the subject of Asian immigration, simply commenting: "Though sentiment is divided in the matter of Asiatic immigration, the people of the coast [sic] states as a whole are opposed to such immigration, and the force and validity of their objections are recognized."[15]

Most surprisingly, given the commissioners' explicit bias, they even saw grounds for optimism concerning assimilation in Columbia anthropologist Franz Boas' study of "Changes in Bodily Form of Descendants of Immigrants." Boas contradicted eugenicists' claims that racial traits were immutable by demonstrating that immigrants changed in bodily form after residing in America, and their children did so to an even greater extent.[16] Boas' study suggested that environment (diet, living conditions, etc.) was more important than heredity, consequently meaning that the melting pot might work after all. If he was correct, the commissioners marveled, it meant that "even racial physical characteristics do not survive under the new social and climatic environment of America."[17] The majority's call, however, for a literacy test to exclude Southern and Eastern European immigrants, as well as a continuation of Asian restriction, indicated that they were not completely reassured by Boas' research.

The Dillingham Commission's report was more optimistic in tone than one would have expected, given the restrictionist bias of all but one of the commission's members. The evidence showed that the immigration laws were effective, and the report did not call for an overhaul of the system. This was, however, proof to the majority on the commission that a literacy test was needed. If laws excluding paupers, criminals, and the physically and mentally disabled were not effectively stemming the tide of immigration from Southern and Eastern Europe, then a more direct measure was needed. The commission members were still unwilling to write overt racial prejudice into the immigration code. The literacy test consequently provided a reasonable, if transparent, disguise. Americans believed that an educated

---

[14] Ibid., 40.

[15] Ibid., 41.

[16] United States Immigration Commission, *Reports of the Immigration Commission*, 42 vols., Vol. 38, 61st Cong., 2d sess., S. Doc. 208, serial 5663.

[17] US Immigration Commission, *Reports*, 1:44. By contrast, Madison Grant ridiculed Boas' theory in a 22 November 1910 letter to Taft. Taft Papers, Series 6, Case File 77 (reel 364).

citizenry was necessary to insure the continuation of effective popular government. Uneducated immigrants, whose political traditions were non-democratic, seemed to pose a threat to the continuance of the Republic.

The literacy test was explicitly designed to discriminate against the new immigrants from Southern and Eastern Europe. Middle-class progressive reformers, used to battling the urban political machines, were quick to blame the immigrant voters who kept those machines in power. Union leaders lashed out at immigrant strikebreakers because they were easier targets to hit than the factory owners who hired them. Such frustration easily merged with scorn and revulsion at the immigrants' physical appearance, strange languages and customs. But the literacy test was seemingly objective and unprejudiced: it allowed those Jews, Italians, Poles, and Slavs who could read and write to enter the United States.

The Dillingham Commission began its recommendations by declaring that the United States should remain an asylum, but only for a limited number of those whom Roosevelt had called the "right kind" of immigrants. "While the American people, as in the past, welcome the oppressed of other lands," they wrote, "care should be taken that immigration be such both in quality and quantity as not to make too difficult the process of assimilation." They argued further that economic growth had to be secondary to maintaining the American culture and standard of living: "A slow expansion of industry which would permit the adaptation and assimilation of the incoming labor supply is preferable to a very rapid industrial expansion which results in the immigration of laborers…who imperil the American standard of wages and conditions of employment."[18] These sentiments served as the guiding principles for the commission's recommendations.

The commission proposed several administrative reforms. They advised that the time limit for deportation of alien criminals be increased to five years after entry, and the period for aliens who became public charges raised to three years after arrival. They suggested the negotiation of agreements with foreign countries to obtain the criminal records of would-be immigrants. They urged the continuation of the commission's practice of placing disguised investigators in the steerage quarters of transatlantic steamers to make sure that the passenger laws were being followed. They recommended that states regulate immigrant banks and employment agencies to discourage the sending of money abroad and protect immigrants

---

[18] US Immigration Commission, *Reports*, 1:45.

against fraud. They also called on the Division of Information to work with those states desiring immigrants to ensure better distribution.[19]

With regard to restriction, the majority report endorsed the continued exclusion of Asian laborers. The commission recommended that the Chinese Exclusion Act and the Gentlemen's Agreement with Japan remain in effect, and called for an additional agreement with Great Britain to prevent the immigration of East Indians. As for European workers, the report called for further general restriction of immigration to relieve the oversupply of unskilled labor, with the purpose of excluding "birds of passage" (usually single men) and "those who, by reason of their personal qualities or habits, would least readily be assimilated or would make the least desirable citizens." The commission considered several different methods for accomplishing the restrictions: a literacy test; a yearly quota based on the percentage of each nationality already living in America; the exclusion of unskilled laborers unaccompanied by wives or families; a yearly limit on the number of arrivals at each port; a requirement that immigrants be in possession of a certain amount of money on arrival; and an increase in the head tax, with a preferential rate for families and a prohibitive one for the unmarried. While the majority said that "all these methods would be effective in one way or another," they preferred the literacy test as "the most feasible single method of restricting undesirable immigration."[20] They did not explain why it was the most feasible, or why a single method was preferable to a combination of measures.

William S. Bennet, the sole dissenting commission member, wrote a brief minority report. He agreed that "a slowing down of the present rate of immigration of unskilled labor is justified by the report," but the evidence indicated that "restriction should be limited to unmarried male aliens or married aliens unaccompanied by their wives and families." The volumes of data collected by the commission showed that the key factor determining better living conditions and more rapid assimilation and naturalization was whether the immigrant lived in a family. There was no evidence to suggest that the ability to read and write correlated in any way with desirable immigration. "The educational test proposed is a selective test for which no logical argument can be based on the report," Bennet charged.[21]

---

[19] Ibid., 45–47.
[20] Ibid., 47–48.
[21] Ibid., 49.

Roosevelt had thought that the Immigration Commission would complete its work in a little over a year; it took three. William Howard Taft was completing his second year in the presidency when the commission reported to Congress in December 1910. Taft was thus thrust into the middle of the renewed debate over immigration restriction, and specifically the literacy test. Unlike his predecessor, Taft had never given much thought to immigration and he was unprepared to lead Congress and the voting public on this issue.

William Howard Taft was descended from seventeenth-century English settlers in Massachusetts Bay on both sides of his family, and thus his "Anglo-Saxon" credentials were as established as those of Henry Cabot Lodge or any other proponent of restrictionism. But he was not one to dwell on his ancestry, or to exploit it for votes, as Roosevelt had done.[22] He was born in Cincinnati in 1857 into an upper-middle-class family with political connections, and graduated as salutatorian from Yale in 1878. After studying at the Cincinnati Law School he was admitted to the Ohio bar, and began to build a legal career. He served as assistant prosecuting attorney and collector of internal revenue in Cincinnati, and then as assistant county solicitor, before becoming a state superior court judge. Benjamin Harrison appointed him Solicitor General of the United States, and then a US circuit court judge. While Taft's wife was known to have ambitions for the White House, his ultimate goal was to be appointed to a seat on the Supreme Court. In 1900 William McKinley appointed him president of the Second Philippine Commission, and a year later Taft became the first civil governor of that American colony. In 1904, after Taft—at his wife's insistence—reluctantly turned down Theodore Roosevelt's offer of a seat on the Supreme Court, Roosevelt named him Secretary of War.[23]

Taft genuinely liked the Filipinos and showed them far more respect than did his fellow commissioners or the US Army. He believed that they would not be ready for self-government for decades, and he denigrated several of the native peoples, in particular the Muslim Moros and the darker-skinned Negritos. He saw hope, however, for those Filipinos who had embraced the civilizing influence of Spanish culture and Roman Catholic

---

[22] Henry F. Pringle, *The Life and Times of William Howard Taft*, 2 vols. (New York: Farrar & Rinehart, 1939) 1:16–18.

[23] Paolo E. Coletta, *The Presidency of William Howard Taft* (Lawrence: University Press of Kansas, 1973) 1–8.

Christianity.[24] "They are a Christian people, and they have been educated in Christianity for three hundred years," he explained to the Yale Alumni Association at a banquet in Washington D.C. in 1904. "Sometimes the Christianity which was taught them seems a little different from our Christianity," Taft conceded to his mostly Protestant audience. Nevertheless, "their ideals are all European or American."[25] Taft recognized that most Filipinos and Americans shared at least one basis of civilization: a common religious faith.

The chief obstacle to civilizing the Philippines completely, according to Taft, was the wide variety of languages spoken there. The governor therefore pursued a policy of teaching English to the Filipinos as "a means not only of intercommunication between the different tribes, but also as a medium through which to grasp the principles of popular government and the traditions of Anglo-Saxon individual liberty." Moreover, the Filipinos themselves evinced a desire to learn the language, which proved to Taft that they had a "future capacity for self-government."[26] Like Roosevelt, Taft shared the romantic notion that national culture could only be expressed through a national language: "Anglo-Saxon ideals" could only be understood in the English tongue. To fully embrace democracy, Filipinos had to adopt America's language. It did not occur to Taft that concepts like political liberty could be translated into Spanish or Tagalog.

A benevolent imperialist like his predecessor, Taft accepted unquestioningly the racist views of the men of his class and era. He believed, however, that it was possible to civilize the Filipinos; the "White man's burden" otherwise would be a waste of time. He did not see the Filipinos as permanently, biologically inferior and therefore incapable of meeting "Anglo-Saxon" standards. Taft recognized as well that the Spanish government and Roman Catholic church had begun the civilizing process, and he appreciated their efforts, however incomplete he thought they were. This attitude of acceptance and patience toward peoples he considered

[24] Pringle, *William Howard Taft*, 1:205; William H. Taft, "The People of the Philippine Islands," *The Independent* (1 May 1902): 1018a–020; and ibid. (8 May 1902): 1099–1104; Taft Papers, Series 9A, vol.1, 11–20 (reel 563).

[25] Taft, Speech at Yale Alumni Association Dinner, Washington DC, 1 February 1904, ibid., 84.

[26] Taft, "The People of the Philippine Islands," ibid., 14, 18. See also Taft, "Civil Government in the Philippines" *The Outlook* (31 May 1902): 305–21, in ibid., 21–37, where he also endorses Roman Catholic schools as an acceptable means of teaching the English language and American ideas.

inferior to White Americans, patronizing as it was, carried over into his willingness to accept the new immigrants from Southern and Eastern Europe whom the Dillingham Commission had castigated.

Taft showed a similar patronizing respect for the Chinese and Japanese, although he supported the Roosevelt Administration's exclusionist policy. He initially called for the admission of Chinese laborers to speed up the economic development of the Philippines, but later changed his stance in the face of disapproval in both the islands and the mainland.[27] Taft also supported Roosevelt's order to treat Chinese merchants, professionals and students with courtesy and respect. Presenting the commencement address at Miami University in Ohio on 15 June 1905, the Secretary of War supported the exclusion of Chinese laborers because they did not "become a part of the real population of the country," but instead refused "to amalgamate and to stake their all as citizens of this Republic." Furthermore, their "habits and views of life are so much at variance with those of our civilization as to make it impossible for them to ever become a useful and intelligent part in this self-governing community." He did not mention that the Chinese were barred by law from becoming citizens and generally were not welcomed in American communities.

Despite his disparaging remarks about Chinese immigrants, Taft did not think it just or wise—in the effort to exclude "coolies"—to harass legally admissible Chinese merchants and students, especially since they came to the United States to foster commercial ties between the two nations. He suggested that in addition to gaining wealth or education, such Chinese immigrants might also gain "familiarity with the best of our institutions to aid the older but retarded civilization of the Chinese Empire." He dwelt in particular on the negative economic impact of the Chinese boycott and declared that Congress and the executive had a duty to "disregard the unreasonable demands of a portion of the community deeply prejudiced upon this subject in the far West, and insist on extending justice and courtesy to a people from whom we are deriving and are likely to derive such immense benefit in the way of international trade."[28]

In similar fashion, Taft supported the Gentlemen's Agreement with Japan. He wrote to Martin Egan on 25 March 1905: "The truth is that the governing classes of the Japanese have elevated the people, and it is the aim

---

[27] Taft, "The People of the Philippines," ibid., 18; and Taft, Address to Union Reading College, 17 December 1903, ibid., 76.

[28] Taft Papers, Series 9A, vol. 2, 234–36 (reel 563).

of the governing classes that is important. I have no fear of a yellow peril through them."[29] Roosevelt sent Taft to Japan in the autumn of 1907 to mollify Japan's wounded pride in the wake of the San Francisco school board crisis. In an after-dinner speech at the Imperial Hotel in Tokyo on 30 September, Roosevelt's envoy congratulated the Japanese on their recent military successes and compared their rule over Korea to American rule in the Philippines. He did not specifically address the subject of immigration, but he alluded to it when he called the talk of war between the United States and Japan "absurd," dismissing it as "a little cloud [that] has come over the sunshine of a fast friendship of fifty years."[30]

Taft continued to support the Gentlemen's Agreement in the 1908 presidential campaign. Addressing the Trenton, New Jersey, Chamber of Commerce on 23 March 1908 with Japanese Ambassador Takahira in attendance, Taft dismissed rumors of war as inventions of the press. "The question of immigration," he said, "seems quite within the power of the two governments without legislation on either side, to bring to a satisfactory adjustment."[31] This was in keeping with Roosevelt's efforts to calm public opinion on both sides of the Pacific, while quietly preparing for a possible war. In his speech accepting the Republican nomination in 1908, Taft once again affirmed the Gentlemen's Agreement and promised to continue by its terms.[32]

While he wished to continue restricting Japanese immigration, Taft welcomed European immigrants of all classes into the melting pot, confident that they would assimilate. Addressing the Ohio Society of Philadelphia on 14 January 1908, he explained that his native state had become great due to its "open door of welcome to the immigrants" and its "liberality of dealing with everybody that came there." Ohio's population was thus a microcosm of the American population: "an amalgamation, not English, not German, not French, not Italian, not New England, but simply American," in which everyone had the "facility of becoming somebody out of nobody and settling down and taking part in the community in which one lives."[33] Taft accepted

---

[29] Pringle, *William Howard Taft*, 1:296–97.

[30] Taft Papers, Series 9A, vol. 8, 2 (reel 564); also in William Howard Taft, *Present Day Problems: a collection of Addresses Delivered on Various Occasions* (New York: Dodd, Mead & Co. 1908), 55.

[31] Taft Papers, Series 9A, vol. 9, 166 (reel 565).

[32] Taft, Acceptance Speech, Cincinnati, 28 July 1908, ibid., vol. 11, 8 (reel 565).

[33] Ibid., vol. 8, 157 (reel 564).

immigrants in large part because he appreciated the role they played in building up the material prosperity of America.

At a St. Patrick's Day dinner at Delmonico's in New York City in 1908, he praised the Irish-Americans for their contributions from colonial times onward and argued that the nativist societies did not have a monopoly on revolutionary war heroes and patriotism: "The truth is, the meeting of the Friendly Sons of St. Patrick is not unlike the meeting of the Society of the Cincinnati in its memories of the American Revolution and its preservation of the highest ideals of American patriotism." He also celebrated the success of the American melting pot: "Never in the history of the world has there been for the making of a new citizenship such a commingling and mixture of races as we have had in this country to make a typical American...The atmosphere of civil liberty, the guaranty of life, liberty and property under due process of law, complete freedom of religious worship, have given to every race coming under the stars and stripes an opportunity to flower and manifest its best and most enduring traits."

These traits, in turn, were blended into Crèvecouer's new American race. Taft explained "that the races transplanted to America, mixing with each other on a basis of complete equality, are gradually forming a race distinct from all of those who entered originally into the combination, but which will unite the high and admirable qualities of all." He did not believe that assimilation required that the immigrants abandon the culture of their old homelands. Instead, he argued that because America brought out the best in them and was made up of the best in them, the immigrants were affirming their American identity even as they celebrated their ethnic heritage. "Recollection and pride in our origin do not lessen our Americanism," he said, "but only strengthen us in our understanding of how it was made and why it is what it is."[34]

Since the melting pot was working successfully, Taft believed that America should continue to offer asylum to the political and religious refugees. "We have in this country offered a refuge to the oppressed of all nations, and they have come here and they have been received on an equality," he told the Order of Railway Conductors in Chicago in April 1908. Like the Filipinos, these refugees "have been given the opportunity at common schools to receive an education which should give them an opportunity to go on climbing the ladder of success." The recent surge in

---

[34] Taft, "Address to Friendly Sons of St. Patrick Banquet," New York, 17 March 1908, ibid., vol. 9, 153–54, 161 (reel 565).

immigration had been "a test of our people," he conceded, but he was proud to announce that America had passed the test. He had visited the lower east side of New York City and seen the immigrants "learning American patriotism and striving to become good citizens," and he said, "I thanked God that we belong to a nation that offered to the world such an opportunity for improvement as this nation has proved to be."[35]

The Republican presidential candidate gave the same report to the notoriously nativist Sons and Daughters of the American Revolution, offering it as proof of the success of their Americanization efforts. "I came into contact with the young Hungarian Jews who had been educated in the schools of the East Side, and never in all this country have I seen the love of country so deeply implanted and a desire to express it so emphatically as in those young Jews," he told them.[36] No doubt it was a compliment that his listeners were not sure how to take.

Taft believed that religious freedom was the most important aspect of America's role as an asylum, as his reference to Jewish immigrants as exemplars of American patriotism suggests. The concept of America as a haven of religious toleration appealed especially to Taft, a Unitarian, because he was subject to religious bigotry. He had declined to pursue the presidency of his alma mater, Yale University, in 1899 because he knew that anyone who denied the divinity of Christ and other orthodox doctrines would not be accepted. Evangelical Protestants attacked Taft in the 1908 campaign as a heretic, especially in contrast to his evangelical opponent, William Jennings Bryan. Taft wrote to John W. Hill on 12 August 1908 that he refused "to go into a dogmatic discussion of creed," and that "if the American public is so narrow as to not elect a Unitarian, well and good. I can stand it."[37] In both the 1908 and 1912 campaigns, the support he had given to the Roman Catholic church in the Philippines also became an issue, spawning rumors that his wife was secretly Catholic and that military aide Archie Butt, who died in the wreck of the *Titanic* in 1912, had been on a

---

[35] Taft, Address to Order of Railway Conductors of America, Div. No. 1, Chicago, 5 April 1908, ibid., 260 (reel 565).

[36] Taft, Address to Sons and Daughters of the American Revolution, Chicago, 4 April 1908, ibid., 266–67 (reel 565).

secret mission to the Vatican. Taft was forced to issue public denials of these absurdities and reassure voters that his wife was Episcopalian.[38]

Despite his liberal views on immigration, Taft was nowhere near as adept at appealing to ethnic voters as was Roosevelt. Not only was he a poor public speaker, he was also ignorant of the needs and desires of most immigrants. Despite having grown up in Cincinnati, a city famous for its German-American population, Taft had to confess to the city's German Club in the 1908 campaign that he had never followed his father's advice to learn German and so he could not address them in that language.[39] By contrast, Roosevelt had taken pride in hailing German-born New Yorkers in their native tongue. In St. Paul, Minnesota, Taft touted his proposed postal savings banks as a way for immigrants to save money in the United States instead of sending their earnings abroad. He did not know that immigrants sent their money home to help their families, not because they did not trust American banks.[40] After a speech on labor and capital at Cooper Union in New York City in January, Taft was asked a question about immigration since he had failed to mention the subject during his address. Taft declined to answer the question, deferring to the judgment of Congressman William Bennet, who was present.[41] Taft's response indicated little interest in or knowledge of the subject, but revealed a generally liberal leaning by referring the question to an opponent of the literacy test.

Taft's inability to appeal to immigrant voters mattered little, however, in the 1908 campaign. Immigration was not a major issue, as both parties downplayed it while awaiting the results of the Immigration Commission's investigations. The Democratic party platform opposed Asian immigration, while the Republican platform omitted any discussion of the issue.[42] Taft's only proposal with regard to immigration policy was to ask Congress to give the executive branch the power to protect aliens in their treaty rights, a request that both McKinley and Roosevelt had made without success. In a

---

[38] Pringle, *William Howard Taft*, 1:45, 373–74, 2: 833–34; and Taft Papers, Series 6, Case File 2139 (Catholic Matters–Politics), reels 426–27.

[39] Taft, Remarks to Taft German Club of Cincinnati, 17 September 1908, Taft Papers, Series 9A, vol. 11, 254–55 (reel 565).

[40] Taft, "Postal Savings Banks and Guarantee of Bank Deposits," St. Paul, 28 September 1908, ibid., vol. 12, 68 (reel 565).

[41] Taft, "Questions and Answers Following Cooper Union Speech," 10 Jan. 1908, ibid., vol. 8, 151 (reel 564). Bennet was, of course, the lone liberal on the Dillingham Commission.

[42] Hutchinson, *Legislative History*, 631.

speech to the Brooklyn Bar Association, Taft used the examples of the 1891 lynching of Italians in New Orleans and the recent anti-Japanese riots in San Francisco to argue that "Congress ought to take some steps directly authorizing the Executive to use the forces at his command to protect the treaty rights of such aliens and ought to vest the courts of the United States with power to punish the person who would violate such alien rights."[43]

William Howard Taft easily defeated Democrat William Jennings Bryan, running for the third time in 1908. The Republican candidate enjoyed mixed success among foreign-born voters. He carried every county in New England and did better than Roosevelt had in New York and New Jersey, but he did not do as well as his predecessor in Pennsylvania and the Midwestern states. Two-thirds of Bryan's total popular vote came from the mid-Atlantic and Midwestern states, although he carried only his home state of Nebraska outside of the South.[44]

In his inaugural address Taft repeated his pledge of support for the Gentlemen's Agreement and added: "We must take every precaution to prevent, or failing that, to punish, outbursts of race feeling among our own people against foreigners of whatever nationality who have by our grant a treaty right to pursue lawful business here and to be protected against lawless assault or injury." He requested federal legislation to protect aliens in their treaty rights. "We can not permit the possible failure of justice, due to local prejudice, in any State or municipal government to expose us to the risk of a war," he warned, obviously referring to the recent strained relations with Japan.[45] The former federal judge (and future Supreme Court justice) believed that federal courts would avoid the passions and prejudices of state courts. Congress, however, again failed to act on the matter.

Taft followed Roosevelt's lead in personally negotiating with both Japanese and Californian officials to avoid embarrassing incidents. Even though the 1895 commercial treaty did not expire until July 1912, the Japanese government sought to negotiate a new pact in the winter of 1910–1911, hoping that Taft's Asian experience would lead him to be more moderate on immigration issues. Secretary of State Philander C. Knox asked

---

[43] Taft, Address to Brooklyn Bar Association, 29 February 1908, Taft Papers, Series 9A, vol. 9, 77 (reel 565).

[44] Edgar Eugene Robinson, *The Presidential Vote, 1896–1932* (Palo Alto: Stanford University Press, 1934) 13–14.

[45] Taft, Inaugural Address, 4 March 1909, Taft Papers, Series 9A, vol. 14, 4 (reel 566).

the Japanese government to send him their proposals, which he secretly submitted to the Senate Foreign Relations committee for advance approval. The Japanese asked Knox to drop the clause from the 1895 treaty which stated the United States' right to exclude Japanese laborers. Knox agreed, reasoning that the Gentlemen's Agreement had proven effective and that the right to regulate immigration was an inherent aspect of sovereignty, whether stated in a treaty or not.[46] Taft became involved in the negotiations, and summoned California Governor Hiram Johnson to Washington to discuss the likely response on the West Coast. Taft flatly warned Johnson that San Francisco would not host the Panama Pacific International Exhibition planned for 1915 if there was a recrudescence of anti-Japanese hysteria and violence. Johnson promised to keep his state quiet until the new treaty was ratified. Knox and Japanese Ambassador Yasuya Uchida signed the treaty on 1 February 1911 and the Senate ratified it three days later.[47]

The new treaty of 1911 did not alter the Gentlemen's Agreement. On 5 April Taft issued an official proclamation, noting that the treaty "shall not be deemed to repeal or affect any of the provisions" of the 1907 Immigration Act. The Japanese government attached a declaration to the treaty which stated that they were "fully prepared to maintain with equal effectiveness the limitation and control which they have for the past three years exercised in regulation of the emigration of laborers to the United States." Nevertheless, the California state senate passed a resolution on 22 February (introduced by Anthony Caminetti, who would later serve as Commissioner-General of Immigration in the Wilson Administration) decrying the omission of an exclusion clause, and demanding either the president withdraw the treaty from consideration or that the Senate refuse to ratify it. Both US senators from California, Republicans Frank P. Flint and George C. Perkins, publicly supported the treaty, however, and Hiram Johnson maintained silence.[48] When California Congressman John E. Raker got the House of Representatives to pass his resolution requesting that the executive branch

---

[46] Philander C. Knox to Taft, 12 January 1911, with enclosure Knox to Senator Shelby M. Cullom, 10 January 1911, Taft Papers, Series 6, Case File 749 (reel 405); and Pringle, William Howard Taft, 2:713-15.

[47] Pringle, William Howard Taft, 2:712-13; and Frank Chuman, The Bamboo People: The Law and Japanese-Americans (Del Mar CA: Publisher's Inc., 1976) 43–44.

[48] Hiram W. Johnson, telegram to Taft, 22–23 February 1911, Taft Papers, Series 6, Case File 749 (reel 405); Chuman, Bamboo People, 44–45; and Coletta, William Howard Taft, 199–200.

turn over all correspondence with Japanese and California officials, Taft and Knox firmly refused to do so.[49]

Unlike Roosevelt, Taft did not focus on immigration issues, nor did he offer extensive recommendations to Congress on the subject. His only immigration policy initiative that met with success was his call for better legislation to prohibit the admission of prostitutes in his 1909 annual message. Congress responded by passing the Mann White Slave Traffic Act, which prohibited the transportation of prostitutes across national or state borders, and the Act of 26 March 1910, which amended the 1907 Immigration Act by adding to the list of excludable and deportable persons those "who are supported by or receive in whole or in part the proceeds of prostitution." Former Ellis Island Commissioner Robert Watchorn's attempts to enforce the tougher anti-prostitution provisions in the 1907 Immigration Act had led to the sale of fraudulent documents establishing a three-year residence, so the 1910 law eliminated the time limit on deportation for such persons and prostitutes themselves.[50]

In his annual message of 1910, Taft echoed Roosevelt's call for better distribution of immigrants which he saw as a way to alleviate overcrowding at Ellis Island, while avoiding the costly expansion of facilities recommended by the immigration commissioner there. He was unsuccessful, however, in his attempts to convince Southerners that competition from Southern and Eastern European workers would stimulate African Americans to more productive labor.[51] The Immigration Restriction League also opposed distribution, warning Taft that it "will act as a force pump to create a vacuum which will serve to draw in still more immigration and nullify the

---

[49] US Congress, House of Representatives, 62d Cong., 1st sess., H. R. 92, 14 April 1911, copy in Taft Papers, Series 6, Case File 749 (reel 405); John E. Raker to Taft, 5 June 1911; Taft to Raker, 16 June 1911; Raker to Taft, 20 June 1911; and Philander C. Knox to Charles D. Hilles, 23 June 1911; in ibid.

[50] Taft, Annual Message to Congress, 7 Dec. 1909, Taft Papers, Series 9A, vol. 17, 38 (reel 567); Hutchinson, *Legislative History*, 146–48; US Immigration Commission, *Reports*, 39:65–66; and Thomas M. Pitkin, *Keepers of the Gate: A History of Ellis Island* (New York: New York University Press, 1975) 102–104.

[51] Editorial, *New York Times*, 20 October 1910, Taft Papers, Series 5, Case File 3 (Dept. of Commerce & Labor), reel 323; Taft, "The South and the National Government," Address to North Carolina Society of New York, 7 December 1908, Taft Papers, Series 9A, vol. 13, 20 (reel 566); Taft, "Speech to Armstrong Association at Carnegie Hall to Benefit Hampton Institute," 23 February 1909, ibid., 190–91; and Hutchinson, *Legislative History*, 148.

very good aimed at."[52] Taft appears to have made no efforts to influence the Immigration Commission and he paid little attention to the publication of its reports in 1911. He had enough to worry about, however, with the Ballinger-Pinchot affair, the fight over the tariff and his deteriorating relationship with Roosevelt and the insurgent Republicans.

Taft's approach to racial and ethnic diversity in America was to focus instead on unity through assimilation. On his cross-country speaking tour in the summer and fall of 1909, President Taft commented repeatedly about the homogeneity of the American people, despite the diversity of their backgrounds. In Salem, Oregon, after singling out the city's German Americans for praise, he declared: "We are not English, we are not Irish, we are not German or French, but we are all of that mixed up." Rather than leading to confusion, the mix produced "a homogenous population of ninety millions," according to Taft. He described the patriotic pride he had felt as he traveled across the country and seen "people with the same aspirations, with the same clothing, with the same method of speech, with the same hearty manner, and with the same determination to go on whether you find him [sic] on the streets of Boston or in your own beautiful city."[53]

In Merced, California, Taft used the analogy of a mixing bowl: "We have Englishmen, Germans, Frenchmen, Scotchmen, Irishmen, Bohemians, Hungarians, Italians and Greeks, and we have shaken them all up in a bowl and we have got a new type," he explained, and "that type is a unit [sic] of the virtues of all those who are its constituents, leaving out their vices; so that we have bred a character of person or citizen whom it is a pride to meet."[54] Noticeably absent from Taft's mix were Asian and African Americans. Their inclusion would have ruined Taft's claims of homogeneity.

Secretary of Commerce and Labor Charles Nagel, a second-generation German American from St. Louis, shared Taft's confidence in the melting pot. Nagel had been German-American brewer Adolphus Busch's attorney. For both personal and professional reasons he was sympathetic to immigrants and opposed to overly strict enforcement of existing legislation, let alone further restrictive measures. In response to a letter from John Noyes

---

[52] Prescott F. Hall to Taft, 8 November 1910, Taft Papers, Series 6, Case File 77 (reel 364).

[53] Taft, Remarks at Salem OR, 3 October 1909, Taft Papers, Series 9A, vol. 15, 305 (reel 566).

[54] Taft, Address at Merced CA, 5 October 1909, ibid., vol. 16, 46 (reel 566).

of the nativist Junior Order United American Mechanics to Taft criticizing different remarks by Nagel opposing the literacy test and suggesting that the spirit rather than the letter of the law was being enforced, Nagel agreed that the charges were true. He had expressed opposition to a literacy test many times, and as for enforcing the existing laws, "without disregarding the purpose and command of the law I have endeavored to relieve against its extreme hardships in individual cases whenever I could find a way to do so." He argued that it was easier to make rules than enforce them, and pointed out that even some members of the Immigration Commission had asked him "not to inflict the hardships of the law upon particular sufferers."[55] He might well have added that he was continuing the practice of his predecessor, Oscar Straus.

Commissioner-General Daniel Keefe and Ellis Island Commissioner William Williams, on the other hand, were just as forthright in their demands for greater restriction. Williams had been Ellis Island Commissioner in Roosevelt's first term. In his first annual report to Keefe in August 1909, Williams declared that the current list of excluded categories of people "keep out only what may be termed 'scum,' or the very worst elements that seek to come here." He implied strongly that more restrictive legislation was needed. He criticized the lax administration of his predecessor, Robert Watchorn, and gave notice to the steamship companies on 4 June 1909 that the immigration statutes would now be strictly enforced. He also reinstated his earlier monetary requirement, which Watchorn had waived, despite the fact that a monetary requirement had been dropped from the final version of the 1907 Immigration Act. On 28 June Williams issued a circular stating that "in most cases it will be unsafe for immigrants to arrive with less than twenty-five ($25) besides railroad ticket to destination, while in many instances they should have more." Only in exceptional circumstances would charitable gifts to immigrants after arrival be taken into consideration when determining if they were likely to become a public charge.[56]

---

[55] Charles Nagel to Charles D. Hilles, 17 January 1912, Taft Papers, Series 6, Case File 3 (reel 354).

[56] William A. Williams to Daniel J. Keefe, 16 August 1909, Taft Papers, Series 6, Case File 1579 (Ellis Island–William Williams), reel 419; and Pitkin, *Keepers of the Gate*, 56–59. Keefe was rarely consulted by Taft or Nagel, and had to ask Hilles' help in securing an invitation to Taft's hearings on the immigration bill in 1913. Daniel J. Keefe to Charles D. Hilles, 3 February 1913, Taft Papers, Series 6, Case File 3D (Dept. of Commerce & Labor, Bureau of Immigration), reel 355.

Williams was greatly influenced by the eugenicists, and in his 1910 and 1911 reports he called for more doctors to inspect immigrants (especially "new immigrants") for feeble-mindedness. He recommended that Congress amend the law to permit investigations of immigrants' heredity. He was harshly critical of the "new immigration," which he claimed came from the "backward races" of Southern and Eastern Europe, who had "very low standards of living, possess filthy habits and are of an ignorance which passes belief." He also asked for separate detention facilities for cabin passengers, so that they could be spared mingling with the steerage passengers and "accommodated in a manner appropriate to their condition in life."[57] Prescott F. Hall of the Immigration Restriction League wrote to Williams in 1909, "Nothing has made me so happy for a long time as feeling you are there and seeing ... how you are clearing things up." Eugenicist Madison Grant likewise praised Williams for "proper enforcement of the laws and regulations of immigration."[58]

Immigrant aid societies, on the other hand, were outraged by Williams' blatant hostility to the immigrants and his strict enforcement of the rules. New York Congressman William Sulzer introduced a resolution in 1911 calling for an investigation into the "atrocities, cruelties, and inhumanities practiced at Ellis Island," while the National German-American Alliance called for his resignation. The New York *Staats-Zeitung* renewed its earlier campaign against Williams, and the Hearst newspapers joined in the attack. Nisam Behar of the National Liberal Immigration League and Henry J. Dannenbaum of B'nai B'rith, however, defended him as a fair and impartial administrator.[59]

The Taft administration thus pleased no one. The restrictionists praised Williams but excoriated Nagel; the immigrants and their allies were grateful for Nagel's restraining influence on Williams. Nagel summarized the political position of the administration to Taft in April 1912: "Those who are in favor of a liberal interpretation or even disregard for the law center their attacks upon Commissioner Williams, while those who are in favor of a

---

[57] William A. Williams to Daniel J. Keefe, 10 September 1910; and Williams to Keefe, 10 October 1911; Taft Papers, Series 6, Case File 1579 (reel 419).

[58] Pitkin, *Keepers of the Gate*, 62.

[59] US Congress, House of Representatives, Committee on Rules, *Hearings on House Resolution 166, July 10–11, 1911,* H. R. 166, copy in Taft Papers, Series 6, Case File 1579 (reel 419); Charles Nagel to Charles D. Hilles, 18 October 1911, in ibid.; and Pitkin, *Keepers of the Gate*, 50–53, 60, 63–64.

strict and technical interpretation regard me as a more fit subject for attack."
He acknowledged that "Commissioner Williams is disposed to be more strict
and even severe than I am." He argued, however, that this was as it should
be because "the strict officials should be in charge of the detention stations"
while "the general supervision, with the right to hear appeals, should be in
the hands of men more liberally inclined."[60]

Despite lurid newspaper accounts and immigrants' traumatic
recollections, Williams and the Immigration Bureau generally treated new
arrivals as well as possible in cramped facilities. The average immigrant
spent only a few hours at Ellis Island. Over eighty percent passed through
inspections, and the majority of detentions were only temporary. The
maximum percentage of exclusions was two percent in 1911, when 13,000
aliens were rejected and 637,000 admitted. The review boards excluded only
fifteen to twenty percent of the cases they heard on appeal.[61]

The president found out for himself how difficult it was to pass
judgment on the aliens who crowded Ellis Island. When Taft and Nagel
visited the immigration station in the fall of 1910, they attended meetings of
the review board. Taft overrode the board's decision to deny admission to a
Welsh miner named George Thornton due to a hernia. Thornton later proved
unable to work due to his injury and his relatives refused to support him.
After Secretary Nagel personally found employment for him, Thornton
refused to work. He was deported for becoming a public charge, and the
administration consequently embarrassed. In explaining the case to the
American Association of Foreign Language Newspapers, Taft used it to
prove both that Williams was "a very just and kindly man" whose judgment
was usually correct, and that Nagel and Taft were committed to carry out the
laws "not sternly but mercifully."[62]

Taft believed wholeheartedly that criminals and the mentally and
physically defective should not be allowed to immigrate to the United States,
and looked for ways to tighten the restrictions on such aliens. He endorsed a
suggestion from Professor Bernardo Attolico, the Italian Commissioner of

---

[60] Charles Nagel to Taft, 16 April 1912, Taft Papers, Series 6, Case File 3D (reel 355).

[61] Pitkin, *Keepers of the Gate*, 67, 73.

[62] Charles Nagel to Charles D. Norton, 10 and 13 December 1910; Nagel to Taft, 7 January 1911; and Taft, "Remarks of President Taft to the Board of Directors of the American Association of Foreign Newspapers [sic]," 4 January 1911; Taft Papers, Series 6, Case File 77 (reel 364).

Immigration in New York City, that Italian immigrants be required to present a "certificate of character" from their local police when they applied to a US consul for a passport. Nagel and Williams agreed that certificates showing a clean police record would be helpful, but at present they could not require such documents because not all European countries issued them, and immigrants did not necessarily embark from their native lands. Secretary of State Knox agreed to sound out other countries about such a plan. In the end the plan died because Great Britain, Russia, and Romania refused to negotiate the necessary agreements, and Germany and Turkey failed to respond to the secretary's inquiries.[63]

Even before the Dillingham Commission's recommendations were published in early December 1910, restrictionists in Congress had begun to push again for the imposition of a literacy test on new immigrants to the United States. Taft told a delegation from the American Association of Foreign Language Newspapers when a literacy test bill was introduced in Congress in 1910 that he was "not familiar" with it, but noted that Congress had rejected such a test in the past because "it did not shut out those whom we most desired to shut out," as anarchists "could easily pass a mental examination." He did not commit himself to any course of action, but promised to hold public hearings if the bill was passed by Congress.[64] The association's good will was important because it controlled national advertising contracts for four hundred thirty-nine immigrant newspapers published in twenty-seven different languages with a combined circulation of 6,500,000, and thus its director, Louis Hammerling, could influence editorial policy through blackmail. Hammerling was on the advisory board of the National Liberal Immigration League and he used his association's clout to lobby against immigration restriction.[65]

---

[63] E. G. Fabbri to John D. Rockefeller, 24 August 1910 [hand delivered to Taft by Senator Nelson Aldrich]; Charles Nagel to Charles D. Norton, 28 November 1910; Norton to Nagel, 29 November 1910; Nagel to Norton, 10 December 1910; Philander C. Knox to Taft, 22 and 29 December 1910; Knox to Taft, 21 April 1911; and Huntington Wilson to Charles D. Hilles, 14 May 1912; ibid.

[64] Taft, "Remarks of President Taft to a delegation from the American Association of Foreign Language Newspapers, at the Executive Office," 28 February 1910, ibid.

[65] Louis Hammerling to Taft, 31 December 1910, ibid.; John Higham, *Strangers in the Land: Patterns in American Nativism, 1860–1925,* 2nd ed. (New Brunswick: Rutgers University Press, 1988) 126; and Rivka Shpak Lissak, "The National Liberal Immigration League and Immigration Restriction, 1906–1917," *American Jewish Archives* 46/2 (1994): 221.

Taft relied heavily on Nagel for advice on handling immigration issues; as a result, his stance became more liberal than either McKinley's or Roosevelt's. When Taft asked him to comment on a letter from Harvard President A. Lawrence Lowell advocating a literacy test, Nagel replied that restrictionists placed too much emphasis on the ability to read and write, noting that most of the appeals from rejected immigrants were from those who could read and write. He also pointed out that the Immigration Bureau already took literacy into consideration as a factor in determining whether the immigrant was likely to become a public charge. "For the present, a sound body, a square look out of the eye, a willingness to work, without the ability to read or write, is preferable to a broken system, a hangdog appearance, with proof of the ability to read and write," he asserted. Nagel also challenged Lowell's conclusion that without the power to read assimilation was very difficult: literacy in the immigrants' native languages "furnishes the means to perpetuate a distinct social life" in the ethnic enclaves, particularly through the foreign-language press. Illiterate immigrants, however, would be immune from such influences, and most likely to learn English, while illiterate parents would be more likely to encourage their children to learn English than literate parents who would probably insist that their children learn their native tongue.[66] Taft forwarded Nagel's response to Lowell as representing his own views.

The real fight over the literacy test came in 1912. The Senate passed Dillingham's bill, which embodied all of the Immigration Commission's recommendations, including a literacy test of twenty to twenty-five words from the US Constitution. While the Vermont senator insisted that the new immigrants were not racially inferior, he maintained the United States simply did not need as many immigrants as before, particularly unskilled, unmarried ones. He argued that "while the test as a practical means of improving the quality of immigration may be considered of doubtful value by some, as a practical means of reducing immigration of the class referred to it undoubtedly would be a success."[67] Immigration Restriction League lobbyist Joseph Lee told his fellow members that they were "going easy" on the racist arguments and instead emphasizing the protection of workers'

---

[66] A. Lawrence Lowell to Taft, 4 November 1910; Charles Nagel to Taft, 8 November 1910; and Nagel to Taft, 7 December 1910, Taft Papers, Case File 77 (reel 364). Nagel acknowledged the value of the foreign language press for those who could not read English, but worried that it retarded assimilation.

[67] *Congressional Record*, 62d Cong., 2d sess., 1912, 48:4916; and Zeidel, 289–91.

wages.[68] But few were fooled by the new strategy. New Jersey Democrat James E. Martine pointed out that many old immigrants would have been unable to pass the literacy test, and he declared his faith in assimilation: "Let our test be clear morals, sound and clean bodies, and, with a public-school system, we can safely trust the rest to God."[69]

The chairman of the House Immigration Committee, Alabama Democrat John L. Burnett, substituted his own bill for Dillingham's, consisting solely of a literacy test based on thirty to forty words in common usage and exempting those fleeing religious persecution. While Burnett's version of the test was a little easier, both had the same explicit goal: to bar Southern and Eastern Europeans from entering the United States.[70] Nagel doggedly fought the literacy test, writing to presidential secretary Charles D. Hilles: "I still regard the provision as too sweeping, too well calculated to accomplish wholesale exclusions, and perhaps too difficult to apply where different members of the same family would not be similarly affected by such a law." Burnett's bill in the House was an improvement on Dillingham's Senate bill, he conceded, but only as the lesser of two evils.[71]

This proposed change in immigration policy became a key issue in the 1912 presidential campaign, as the Senate and House delayed the meeting of a conference committee to reconcile the two different immigration bills until after the election. Roosevelt's Progressive party staked out a liberal position on immigration, largely due to the influence of former Commerce and Labor Secretary Oscar Straus and social worker Frances Kellor, who was the director of the New York State Bureau of Industries and Immigration and headed the New York branch of the North American Civic League for Immigrants. The Progressive platform did not mention restriction, but denounced "the fatal policy of indifference and neglect which has left our enormous immigrant population to become the prey of chance and cupidity." Further, it called for "governmental action to encourage the distribution of immigrants away from the congested cities, to rigidly supervise all private

---

[68] Zeidel, "Literacy Test," 271.

[69] *Congressional Record*, 62d Cong., 2d sess., 1912, 48:4969; and Zeidel, "Literacy Test," 292.

[70] Hutchinson, *Legislative History*, 150–53; and Zeidel, "Literacy Test," 295–97. Patten and other Immigration Restriction League members feared that Burnett would insist on his stand-alone literacy test in order to embarrass Taft and Senate Republicans.

[71] Charles Nagel to Charles D. Hilles, 10 March, 6 April 1912, Taft Papers, Case File 77 (reel 364).

agencies dealing with them and to promote their assimilation, education and advancement."[72]

The Democratic platform did not mention immigration issues at all, but New Jersey governor Woodrow Wilson, the Democratic nominee, faced heavy criticism for his earlier derogatory statements about immigrants in his *History of the American People*. The Hearst newspapers reprinted passages which described the "new immigrants" as men "of the lowest class" who had "neither skill nor energy nor any initiative of quick intelligence," and claimed that European governments "were disburdening themselves of the more sordid and hapless elements of their population."[73] Wilson tried mightily to overcome his nativist image. He had been on the advisory committee of the National Liberal Immigration League, and League president Edward Lauterbach defended him. Newer immigrant groups such as the Italians and Poles were not mollified, however, deserting the Democratic Party for the upstart Progressives.[74]

The Republican platform pledged the party "to the enactment of appropriate laws to give relief from the constantly growing evil of induced or undesirable immigration, which is inimical to the progress and welfare of the people of the United States." Nevertheless, Taft rejected this restrictionist stance and made an effort to win the immigrant vote—amounting to almost the only campaigning he engaged in following the convention. Hammerling distributed pro-Taft editorials to the newspapers in his association and disbursed over $100,000 of campaign funds to support Taft's bid for re-election. The National Liberal Immigration League published a pamphlet containing the anti-restriction views of several leading professors and statesmen, including Nagel. Charles D. Hilles, now chairman of the Republican National Committee, released an interview with Taft on 31 October in which the president endorsed the opinions of Nagel and opposed the literacy test as a revival of the Know-Nothing spirit. Robert

---

[72] Higham, *Strangers in the Land*, 190, 239–42; and Hutchinson, *Legislative History*, 631–32. Kellor went on to found the Committee for Immigrants in America in 1914, which subsidized the Americanization work of the Division of Immigrant Education in the federal Bureau of Education.

[73] Woodrow Wilson, *A History of the American People*, 5 vols. (New York: Harper & Brothers, 1902) 5:212–13.

[74] Higham, *Strangers in the Land*, 190; and Arthur S. Link, *Wilson: The Road to the White House* (Princeton: Princeton University Press, 1947) 382–87, 493–99.

DeCourcy Ward, president of the Immigration Restriction League, hotly denied being a Know-Nothing and vowed to vote for Wilson.[75]

Taft also directly attacked Wilson on immigration. The Republican National Committee issued a statement in July to the foreign language press which said, "President Taft has shown himself to be a friend of the immigrant, while Woodrow Wilson has publicly condemned all immigrants except Chinese." The statement quoted Wilson's infamous passage from his *History* to illustrate his anti-immigrant bias. "President Taft has not only discouraged the enactment of laws for the unreasonable and unfair restriction of immigration," the statement continued, "but on more than one occasion has conferred with representatives of the Foreign-Language Press, and with various committees representing the foreign-born element of this country, in regard to immigration problems."[76]

When the Hungarian newspaper *Amerikai Magyar Nepszava* published an interview favorable to Wilson, Hammerling urged Taft to respond. He did so, sending the newspaper a statement drafted by Nagel. The statement said that he had appointed Nagel with "immigration in mind," trusting in "his respect for the law and his sympathy with immigrants." The statement specifically endorsed Nagel's opposition to the literacy test: "Character, ability and willingness to work in some capacity must constitute the true test." It concluded that immigrants were still needed to build up the nation and called for maintaining "a policy that will extend the blessings of our free institutions to all those who come with a will to aid and with the dream of liberty as their guide."[77]

Taft made very few campaign speeches after Congress recessed in August. Two of them, however, were addresses to immigrant groups in which he implied that his two opponents were nativists. He also continued to follow the lead of his Secretary of Commerce and Labor in opposing the literacy test. Nagel was the only cabinet member other than Secretary of

---

[75] Higham, *Strangers in the Land*, 189–90; Hutchinson, *Legislative History*, 632; Lissak, "National Liberal Immigration League," 226; Zeidel, "Literacy Test," 300–301; Robert DeC. Ward to Taft, 31 October 1912; and William A. Pike to Taft, 1 November 1912; Taft Papers, Series 6, Case File 77 (reel 364).

[76] Charles D. Hilles to Taft, 24 July 1912, Taft Papers, Series 6, Case File 423 (American Association of Foreign Language Newspapers), reel 384.

[77] Louis Hammerling to Taft, 3 September 1912; and Charles Nagel to Rudolph Forster, 19 September 1912; Taft Papers, Series 6, Case File 77 (reel 364). Memoranda indicate that copies of this statement were later sent to the Italian American Alliance and the National German American Alliance.

Agriculture James Wilson to campaign for him, and this demonstration of loyalty undoubtedly influenced Taft to reject immigration restriction.[78]

Addressing Italian Americans who came to his "summer White House" in Beverly, Massachusetts, Taft offered a higher opinion of them than Wilson had in his *History*, calling them "as prudent, as law-abiding, as successful in business, as home-making and as good citizens as you can find anywhere." He supported the exclusion of those "who are a burden in the old country, the criminals, the undesirable people," but he did not consider uneducated immigrants to be unfit, so long as they were "healthy, useful, law-abiding citizens, capable of amalgamating with those who are here." Contrasting his views to Roosevelt's hostility to "hyphenated Americans," Taft declared that he did not begrudge immigrants' pride in their ethnic heritage: "This pride instead of making you a less worthy American leads you to become a more worthy American citizen."[79]

On 26 October 1912 Taft took part in the dedication of Alliance College in Pennsylvania, founded by the Polish National Alliance of America. Once again he denied that ethnic pride was incompatible with assimilation. Taft told his audience that he was not worried that the college would isolate Polish Americans, keeping them from learning English or participating socially and politically in American life, because "the free air of America creates a natural tendency, on the part of those who come to live with us, and enjoy our institutions, to learn the language, to amalgamate with other peoples, and to take an active interest in the politics of the country." Taft insisted that immigrants could respect "their national traditions, their national language, [and] their national literature," while achieving simultaneously "the assimilation of their aims, political, social and economic, to those of the people of their adopted country."

Discussing the pending immigration legislation, Taft also rejected the invidious distinctions restrictionists made between old and new immigrants. Although he recognized that the founders of America were mostly British, he did not believe that any current immigrants threatened the quality of American citizenship simply because they had different ethnic and cultural backgrounds. Taft supported the exclusion of criminals and those who were mentally or physically disabled, but he rejected a literacy test as unnecessary

---

[78] Donald Anderson, *William Howard Taft: A Conservative's Conception of the Presidency* (Ithaca: Cornell University Press, 1968) 197–98.

[79] Taft, "Address to Italians of Beverly, Mass.," 30 September 1912, Taft Papers, Series 9A, vol. 30, 75–77 (reel 570).

because most immigrants promptly availed themselves of the public educational system. Moreover, while test supporters denied that the "new" immigrants assimilated, Taft asserted "an abiding faith in the influence of our institutions upon all who come here, no matter how lacking in education they may be, if they have the sturdy enterprise to leave home and to come out to this new country to seek their fortunes." He concluded with a rousing defense of America as the asylum for the world. "I am," he declared, "proud of our country that we have had its doors swinging easily open for the industrious peoples of other countries that have sought ours for greater happiness and quicker development."[80]

It is not clear why Taft chose to publicly engage the immigration issue, unless he hoped to detract immigrant voters from Roosevelt and prevent a Progressive victory. He had no illusions of victory for himself, and such efforts would not have made a difference anyway. Taft suffered the worst defeat of any major party presidential candidate in American history. He carried only Vermont and Utah and received just twenty-three percent of the popular vote, which he described as "the irreducible minimum of the Republican Party."[81] But whatever his reasons, the result was that he stood pledged to veto the literacy test that Congress was preparing to send to him in the "lame duck" session.

The conference committee met after the election to reconcile the conflicting House and Senate immigration bills. Its report accepted the more lenient House version of the literacy test. The bill also raised the immigrant head tax to five dollars and excluded all aliens ineligible for citizenship (i.e., Asians) unless otherwise provided for by treaty or executive agreement. It exempted businessmen, professionals, teachers, students, and travelers. Passed by both houses, Taft received it on 1 February 1913. True to his promise, he held hearings, allowing both sides to express their views. On 4 February, thirty-four speakers made their case to the president, with twice as many opposing the bill as favoring it. Two days later two hundred delegates from organizations interested in immigration descended on the White House, many of them connected to the National Liberal Immigration League. Several days after that, Ellis Island Commissioner Williams and American

---

[80] Taft, "Address at Dedication of Polish College, Cambridge Springs, Penn." 26 October 1912, ibid., 178–79, 186–87.

[81] Coletta, *William Howard Taft*, 245–47 (quotation, 246). Alfred Landon also received only eight electoral college votes in 1936, but he captured over thirty-six percent of the popular vote.

Federation of Labor president Samuel Gompers argued with anti-restrictionist Congressmen William S. Bennet of New York and Richard Bartholdt of Missouri for nearly three hours in Taft's presence. Still Taft agonized over the decision.[82]

Finally, on 14 February, Taft vetoed the bill. His message to Congress stated, "The bill contains many valuable amendments to the present immigration law which will insure greater certainty in excluding undesirable immigrants." Nevertheless, he said, "I cannot make up my mind to sign a bill which in its chief provision violates a principle that ought, in my opinion, to be upheld in dealing with our immigration. I refer to the literacy test. For the reasons stated in Secretary Nagel's letter to me, I cannot approve that test."[83] As he had throughout his term in office, Taft relied on his Secretary of Commerce and Labor to guide him on immigration issues.

Nagel's letter, dated 12 February, accompanied Taft's veto message. Nagel began by pointing out technical defects in the law. He objected to the unequal enforcement of the literacy test, as literate men could bring in illiterate wives and children, while the literate wives and children of illiterate husbands and fathers would be barred. Furthermore, illiterate resident aliens who went abroad would be unable to return, as no exception was made for them. He also warned of "very considerable embarrassment" in attempting to enforce the law, as delays would result and many more interpreters and other staff would be needed to administer the test properly.

But Nagel's central argument was that the test could not be defended on its merits. First of all, it was not selective as its proponents claimed. "No doubt the law would exclude a considerable percentage of immigration from Southern Italy, among [sic] the Poles, the Mexicans, and the Greeks. This exclusion would embrace probably in large part undesirable but also a great many desirable people," he said. Secondly, the test would judge European nations' educational systems rather than the abilities of individual immigrants. "The people who come from the countries named are frequently illiterate because opportunities have been denied them," Nagel pointed out, so "they are really striving to free themselves from the conditions under

---

[82] Pencilled notes of 4 February 1913 hearings; Taft to Theodore Burton, 10 February 1913; Taft Papers, Series 6, Case File 77 (reel 364); Lissak, "National Liberal Immigration League," 229; Samuel Gompers, *Seventy Years of Life and Labor: An Autobiography*, 2 vols. (New York: E. P. Dutton & Co., 1925) 1:541; and Higham, *Strangers in the Land*, 191.

[83] *Congressional Record*, 62d Cong., 3d sess., 1913, 49:3269.

which they have been compelled to live." In other words, the opportunity for education was one of the attractions offered by asylum in America.

Finally, Nagel pointed out that the objections to the new immigrants' habits and manners were specious, as indeed the Dillingham Commission's reports, if not its recommendations, had recognized. Taft's Secretary of Commerce and Labor denied that immigrants created an oversupply of labor that drove down wages: "We need labor in this country, and the natives are unwilling to do the work which the aliens come over to do." He noted, "It is perfectly true that in a few cities and localities there are congested conditions. It is equally true that in very much larger areas we are practically without help." Nagel consequently called for "an intelligent distribution of new immigration to meet the needs of our vast country." He insisted that while immigrants in certain areas lived in "deplorable conditions," the same was true of native-born Americans, and in both cases they were the exception not the rule. Likewise, "birds of passage" were a minority, and in fact the census showed that new immigrants were increasingly becoming landowners and farmers. "A careful examination of the character of the people who come to stay and of the employment in which a large part of the new immigration is engaged," he asserted, "will, in my judgment, dispel the apprehension which many of our people entertain." In conclusion, Nagel called the literacy test "a test which is not calculated to reach the truth," conceived in an effort "to find relief from a danger which really does not exist."[84]

The Senate quickly voted to override Taft's veto, 72 to 18, but the effort in the House fell five votes short of the necessary two-thirds majority, 213 to 114.[85] Illinois Republican William W. Wilson sent Taft the results of the House vote sustaining his veto and wrote, "It was deemed by everybody to be one of the most courageous and creditable things you ever did." He said that a Democratic colleague who worked with him to defeat the bill made the remark, "It makes the President bigger than both parties."[86] At the request of Massachusetts Congressman James Curley, the pen with which

---

[84] *Congressional Record,* 62d Cong., 3d sess., 1913, 49:3269–270.

[85] Hutchinson, *Legislative History,* 154; and Zeidel, "Literacy Test," 304. Surprisingly, Massachusetts Republican Augustus Gardner, Lodge's son-in-law and an ardent restrictionist, voted to uphold the veto.

[86] William W. Wilson to Taft, 27 February 1913, Taft Papers, Series 6, Case File 77 (reel 364). It is not clear if the anonymous Democratic congressman was making a joke about Taft's weight.

Taft signed the veto was given to Nisam Behar, the managing director of the National Liberal Immigration League who had organized most of the opposition to the bill.[87] No one was more relieved or pleased at the outcome than Charles Nagel, who wrote to Hilles, "I want to say how deeply I appreciate the recognition which the President has shown me in a matter in which I was so profoundly interested."[88]

The Dillingham Commission had disregarded its own findings to recommend further restriction through a literacy test. Taft's veto of that test was a critical blow to the restriction movement. With the president-elect, Woodrow Wilson, bound by his word and political necessity to oppose such a test, Lodge, Dillingham, and Burnett were counting on Taft to sign the bill into law. But Taft's humiliating defeat in the 1912 election freed him from all political obligations. Following his conscience and the advice of Charles Nagel, he defended his long-standing belief that immigration was an economic boon to the country and that Southern and Eastern Europeans could assimilate as readily as Northern and Western Europeans. While President Taft did not believe that America should also be an asylum for Asians, he did continue the Gentlemen's Agreement and avoided the outright ban on Japanese and other Asian immigrants. Taft left the gates of America open for many immigrants as he left the White House.

---

[87] Nisam Behar to Taft, 24 February 1913, ibid.; and Lissak, "National Liberal Immigration League," 229–230.

[88] Charles Nagel to Charles D. Hilles, 17 February 1913, Taft Papers, Series 6, Case File 77 (reel 364).

CHAPTER 4

WOODROW WILSON AND HYPHENATED AMERICANS

Woodrow Wilson, like Theodore Roosevelt, was a moderate progressive who reacted negatively to the new, upper-class industrialists, but who maintained a strong belief in the triumph of American ideals. In general, Wilson believed that ethnic and class conflict resulted from valuing private interests over the public interest. Immigrants living in the major cities undermined democratic standards by accepting jobs from the political machines in exchange for their votes. Wilson, like most progressives, abhorred the anarchist and socialist beliefs of some of the foreign-born and failed completely to understand their conception of politics as an exchange of favors. Wilson's heroes were great statesmen who selflessly served the common good while rallying the people to patriotic endeavors. He wanted to create an efficient, honest government that citizens could support unashamedly.[1] The solution, according to Wilson, was to unify all classes and ethnic groups into a homogenous middle class, socializing them through education to accept American political, social and economic ideals. Only with a common basis of belief could the body politic agree upon the national interest.[2]

---

[1] Wilson held to the ideal of the selfless, erudite leader throughout his life. See, e.g., "A Christian Statesman," *North Carolina Presbyterian* (6 September 1876) in Woodrow Wilson, *The Papers of Woodrow Wilson*, ed. Arthur S. Link et al., 69 vols. (Princeton: Princeton University Press, 1966–1994) 1:188; and "The Ideal Statesman," ibid., 1:241–43.

[2] In many ways, Wilson resembled the "mugwumps," described by Richard Hofstadter in *The Age of Reform* (New York: Vintage Books, 1955) 131–73, who reacted to the "status revolution" by trying to reestablish themselves as a responsible, elite class guiding democracy. Nevertheless, Robert H. Wiebe's description of progressives in *The Search for Order* (New York: Hill & Wang, 1967) 164-95 is more accurate. Cf. Robert M. Crunden, *Ministers of Reform* (New York: Basic Books, 1982); John H. Ehrenreich,

Born in Staunton, Virginia on 28 December 1856, reared in Augusta, Georgia and Columbia, South Carolina and serving as the first Southern president since Zachary Taylor, Woodrow Wilson often displayed his racial prejudice.[3] He scorned the new immigrants from Southern and Eastern Europe and compared Asian immigrants to African Americans as an unwelcome race. He did, however, also celebrate the melting pot and America's role as an asylum for political and religious refugees, particularly the "old immigrants" from Northern and Western Europe. Wilson's mother, Jesse Woodrow Wilson, was one such old immigrant, having come to the United States as a child with her family from Carlisle, England. Wilson's father, Dr. Joseph Ruggles Wilson, was the son of a Scots-Irish immigrant.[4]

Although Woodrow Wilson did not directly follow in his father's footsteps as a Presbyterian minister, he preached a similar message of Christian morality as a professor of history and government, president of Princeton University, Governor of New Jersey and President of the United States. Wilson's political ideals were the product of both Enlightenment rationalism and his Presbyterian faith. He believed that society was a collection of rational, autonomous men who, given the right education, would always agree how to serve the common good. Furthermore, he believed in the inevitability of progress because he believed in a God who was active in history. His own deep, personal faith in Jesus Christ led him to temper his belief in autonomous Reason with the realization that some truths could only be revealed by the Holy Spirit. But this mattered little, for in Wilson's mind God's will was the same as American national interests.[5]

In addition to these familial and religious influences, Wilson's attitude toward immigration also reflected his belief in the need for national unity and ideological homogeneity in America. He was upset by the fierce class and ethnic conflicts raging in the United States in the latter half of the nineteenth century and the first two decades of the twentieth, a struggle

The Altruistic Imagination (Ithaca: Cornell University Press, 1985); and David Danbom, *The World of Hope* (Philadelphia: Temple University Press, 1987).

[3] Arthur S. Link, *Wilson: The Road to the White House* (Princeton: Princeton University Press, 1947) 1–4; August Heckscher, *Woodrow Wilson: A Biography* (New York: Charles Scribner's Sons, 1991) 10–24.

[4] Link, *Road to the White House*, 1; Heckscher, *Biography*, 4–9.

[5] For an excellent discussion of the strong influence of Wilson's Presbyterian faith on his political thought, see Arthur S. Link, "Woodrow Wilson and his Presbyterian Inheritance," in *The Higher Realism of Woodrow Wilson and Other Essays* (Nashville: Vanderbilt University Press, 1971) 3–20.

which he regarded as a second Civil War. Wilson portrayed himself as imitating his hero, President Grover Cleveland, the Democrat who, in Wilson's view, reunited the rival regional sections and brought peace and prosperity to the United States.[6]

"Hyphenated" immigrants who tried to retain dual national identities were unacceptable to Wilson because they put selfish group interests blindly above the national interest, which he regarded as the interest of all humanity. Along with other moderate progressives, he sought reforms to improve the lives of immigrants, the urban poor and the working class, but he advocated measures designed scientifically to meet objectively the needs of society as a whole.[7] Wilson thus grouped "hyphenates," suffragists, trade unionists and social welfare advocates as selfish special interests. Later on, he would become more sympathetic to some of these groups, but only when he began to see their special interests as embodying the national interest. Immigrant groups never fell into this category. Their disloyalty was bad enough in peacetime; it was intolerable during World War I.[8]

While Wilson opposed hyphenated immigrants, he did not despise the foreign-born in general. Although he was indeed racist towards African and Asian Americans, he was only mildly paternalistic towards the former residents of Southern and Eastern Europe. Wilson thought that literacy tests served a valid purpose in preventing African Americans from voting in the Southern states. But he did not support using such a test to deny admittance to White immigrants. In Wilson's mind, illiteracy did not equate with unassimilability, despite the great stock he placed in education. He did not assume Southern and Eastern Europeans had received a decent education in

---

[6] Wilson, "Mr. Cleveland as President," in Wilson, *Papers*, 10:102–119; Woodrow Wilson, *A History of the American People*, 5 vols. (New York: Harper & Brothers, 1902) 4:145–312, 5:1–114, 171–252.

[7] See Crunden, *Ministers of Reform*, chaps. 1–3; and Danbom, *World of Hope*, chaps. 3–4. Cf. Gabriel Kolko, *The Triumph of Conservatism* (Chicago: Quadrangle, 1967); and James Weinstein, *The Corporate Ideal in the Liberal State* (Boston: Beacon Press, 1968).

[8] Link argued in *Road to the White House* (29–35) that Wilson began as a conservative "mugwump," solely concerned with academic problems. During his presidency at Princeton, however, he became knowledgeable concerning existing economic and social problems, and between 1908 and 1912 he was transformed into a progressive. Link, however, later emphasized the continuity of Wilson's thought as a type of "higher realism" that transformed his Christian ideals into political reality, as far as he deemed practicable, through moderate reform. See Link, "The Higher Realism of Woodrow Wilson," in Link, *Higher Realism*, 127–39.

their homelands. The point was that all Europeans were capable of being educated and assimilated into American culture because they shared a similar moral and cultural background, as well as a similar skin color. More importantly, the United States had to admit the "poor, huddled masses, yearning to breathe free" to fulfill God's purpose in creating the "land of the free and the home of the brave."

In Wilson's historical books, *Division and Reunion* and *A History of the American People*, he deplored the sectionalist loyalties which split the country asunder in the mid-nineteenth century. He criticized both the Confederate leaders and the radical Republicans, whose Reconstruction policies he believed only prolonged the division. Reunion came not with the Compromise of 1877, but with the administration of Grover Cleveland, who as a good, *laissez-faire* Democrat was able to reunite South and North, at least to the extent that Republican Congresses went along with his policies.[9] Wilson feared that the fierce class and ethnic struggles of the 1890s and 1900s constituted a new Civil War, with blood actually being spilt on the picket lines. He longed to intervene and reunify his divided country, and soon transformed this yearning into action.

Stressing the contributions all ethnic groups had made to the United States was one way he tried to reunify the nation. Speaking in a New Jersey synagogue, Wilson asserted: "The reason America grows more and more vigorous and more and more various in its vigor is because it has more and more elements of power, because of the new infusion that is constantly taking place in its blood and thinking," an infusion to which "[e]ach race contributes its own quota."[10] This was more than mere savvy political

---

[9] Wilson, "Mr. Cleveland's Cabinet," in Wilson, *Papers*, 8:160–78; "Mr. Cleveland as President," in ibid., 10:102–119; Woodrow Wilson, *Division and Reunion, 1829–1889* (New York: Longmans, Green, 1893); and Wilson, *History*, 4:145–312, 5:1–114, 171–252. Wilson did not mourn the defeat of the Confederacy largely because it freed the Southern economy to become industrialized. In fact, one of his initial reasons for supporting immigration was that the "New South" needed skilled immigrant laborers to operate its industries, as Blacks were supposedly incapable of doing due to the ascription of inherent laziness. Wilson, "New Southern Industries," *New York Evening Post* (26 April 1882) in Wilson, *Papers*, 2:123–25. For a discussion of Wilson's Whig roots, see David Steigerwald, "The Synthetic Politics of Woodrow Wilson," *Journal of the History of Ideas* 50 (July–September 1989): 465–84; and Nils A. Thorsen, *The Political Thought of Woodrow Wilson, 1875–1910* (Princeton: Princeton University Press, 1988).

[10] Wilson, Address to Temple B'nai Jeshurun, Newark, 8 January 1911, in Wilson, *Papers*, 22:320.

rhetoric. Wilson, like most of the people of his time, believed that each "race" or ethnic group had national characteristics which all of its members possessed. Thus he told the New England Society of New York City "that it is necessary that races of different characters should exchange their ideas as well as their compliments, and that we should understand just what our relative parts are to be in the great game that we are to play upon this continent."[11]

Such immigrant gifts, however, should not impede assimilation. Wilson believed that the melting pot should blend the different national characteristics into a solid blankness, the same way that all colors, when mixed together, produce white. Thus he told countless audiences that Americans had no special human nature and the traits which he attributed to them, such as "alertness, inquisitiveness, unconventionality, readiness for change, eagerness for the newest things and the most convenient," were universal characteristics not limited to any particular "blood strain." He did acknowledge that Americans still held their principles with bigotry, but he confidently stated that they were "learning ever" and that education would foster ideals and "drive out ignorance, provincialism, [and] noxious error."[12] Wilson essentially shared, though with important differences, the view of John Dewey and other progressives that liberal education was the best means of political socialization.

The emergence of the United States as a major world power toward the end of the nineteenth century and as the new century dawned made assimilation and national unity especially important. Woodrow Wilson, like William McKinley, Theodore Roosevelt and William Howard Taft, believed that the new empire and international prestige acquired by the United States through the Spanish-American War offered every promise of a century of American glory if the nation could unite behind moral principle.[13] Hyphenated Americans' insistence upon retaining their old national loyalty, however, stood directly in the way of the triumphal American epoch. Wilson was proud of his own Scots-Irish background, but he firmly believed that

---

[11] Wilson, After-Dinner Speech to the New England Society of New York, 22 December 1900, in ibid., 12:53.

[12] Wilson, Notes for Americanism (a standard speech), delivered to the New Century Club of Wilmington, Delaware, 7 December 1900, in ibid., 12:41–42.

[13] Wilson, Notes for speech to American Philosophical Society, Philadelphia, 14 April 1905, in ibid., 16:53. This bears a striking resemblance to Henry Luce's later proclamation of the "American Century."

ethnic pride must not interfere with loyalty to the United States, the last, best hope of mankind and thus more deserving of loyalty than any lesser land. In a 1902 speech, Wilson defined Americanism as not merely a sentiment, but a principle of action: the Biblical command to "love thy neighbor as thyself." He asked his listeners to view every fellow human being as their neighbor, just as Jesus did when he told the parable of the Good Samaritan. He defined patriotism as "fellowship with many sides, which expends itself in service to all mankind joined in the same citizenship, and who are bound up in the same principles of civilization."[14]

By consistently thinking of America as more of a spiritual concept than a physical entity, Wilson was able to reconcile American ideals with the far-from-perfect reality which he could plainly see. He recognized that it was vital to keep his vision of America, symbolized by the Statue of Liberty, not too far out of line with the reality of Ellis Island. This spiritual conception of America was in reality the old Puritan dream of the New World as the new Jerusalem, the "city set on a hill" about which Jesus spoke; and of the American people as the new Israelites, a people set apart by God to be an example and inspiration to all the world. The biblical texts and the writings of Calvinist preachers were all familiar to the son of a Presbyterian minister and a devout Christian in his own right, and his allusions clearly drew on them.

In a Thanksgiving Day address to the Har Sinai Temple of Trenton (New Jersey) in 1910, he quoted the old New England divine William Stoughton on the subject of God sifting the nations of the world to plant the choicest seed in America. He described the American people as a "conglomerate," with each ethnic group contributing necessary characteristics to the melting pot, "for these stocks are bound by adoption, by mixture and by union."[15] One can hear St. Paul saying, "Theirs is the adoption as sons; theirs the divine glory, the covenants, the receiving of the law, the temple worship and the promises."[16] Wilson concluded that the different "national elements" were not foreigners because "they have come in and been identified with her. They are all instantly recognizable as Americans and

---

[14] Wilson, Speech to Worcester Women's Club, 29 January 1902, in ibid., 12:259.

[15] Wilson, Thanksgiving Address at Har Sinai Temple, Trenton, New Jersey, 24 November 1910, in ibid., 22:89–91. One cannot help but note the appropriateness of such an allusion on Thanksgiving—an appropriateness which was without doubt fully intentional.

[16] Romans 9:4.

America is enriched with the variety of their gifts and the variety of their national characterization."[17]

The adopted citizens received in return the blessings of a free society under a democratic government. As a political scientist, Wilson analyzed that government, hoping someday to be a leader in it. In *Constitutional Government*, published in 1908, Wilson revealed his faith in the leadership of a strong, active president. Inspired by the current example of Theodore Roosevelt, as well as his old heroes, Lincoln and Cleveland, Wilson wrote that the presidency was "the unifying force in our complex system." As such, the president should use his office as a bully pulpit to preach to the masses and convert them, and thus keep Congress honest. Wilson explained that the president "must stand always at the front of our affairs, and the office will be as big and as influential as the man who occupies it."[18] This confidence in presidential leadership also indicated his belief that educated popular opinion would recognize and embrace the common good. A professional educator would thus make the best President. Wilson would have the opportunity to be such a president just four years later.

Wilson's writings came back to haunt him, however, when he ran for political office—especially when they advocated views he no longer held. His *History of the American People,* published in 1902, showed a strong conservative viewpoint, favoring *laissez-faire* economic policies, and opposing labor unions and farmers' alliances as special interest groups that did not foster the common good. The book also portrayed immigrants from Asia and Southern and Eastern Europe unfavorably despite condemning nativist movements such as the Know-Nothing party. Wilson typified the somewhat paradoxical viewpoint of many progressives at that time. By the time he ran successfully in the 1910 New Jersey gubernatorial race, he had come to express much more sympathy for the working class and immigrants. His earlier unkind words, however, were broadcast as part of a hypocritical smear campaign conducted by the Republicans.[19] The Republicans knew

---

[17] Wilson, *Papers*, 22:90–91.

[18] Woodrow Wilson, *Constitutional Government*, in ibid., 18:109, 121; David Burton, *The Learned Presidency: Theodore Roosevelt, William Howard Taft, Woodrow Wilson* (Rutherford: Fairleigh Dickinson University Press, 1988) 174; and Thorsen, *Political Thought*, 64.

[19] The Republican party in New Jersey circulated pamphlets proclaiming Wilson as the enemy of unions, Jews, Catholics, and Southern and Eastern European immigrants, and quoting passages from his earlier writings to prove their point. Wilson fought back by telling these groups that the Republicans were "false friends," and that his earlier

they had him "between a rock and a hard place." Since organized labor, especially the American Federation of Labor, favored severe immigration restrictions to protect their jobs and wages, Wilson could not please both blocs of voters. The Republicans showed anti-labor, pro-immigrant excerpts to the unions and anti-immigrant, pro-labor quotations to the immigrants, a very effective tactic which the national party, as well as opposing Democrats, used as well in the 1912 presidential race.[20]

The passage most often circulated among Polish Americans, Hungarian Americans, Italian Americans, Jewish Americans, and others used the nativist distinction between the old and new immigrants. Wilson wrote that through most of the nineteenth century, "men of the sturdy stocks of the north of Europe had made up the main strain of foreign blood which was every year added to the vital working force of the country, or else men of the Latin-Gallic stocks of France and Northern Italy." By the end of the century, however, there was a frightening influx of "men of the lowest class from the south of Italy and men of the meaner sort out of Hungary and Poland, men out of the ranks where there was neither skill nor energy nor any initiative of quick intelligence." Wilson also repeated the restrictionists' charge that European governments "were disburdening themselves of the more sordid and hapless elements of their population, the men whose standards of life and of work were such as American workmen had never dreamed of hitherto."[21]

The Hearst newspapers broadcast a different excerpt from *A History of the American People* to arouse anti-Wilson sentiment on the Pacific coast in 1912. Wilson wrote that although the Chinese coolies had been excluded from the West Coast, and were seen as "hardly fellow men at all, but evil spirits, rather," they were more desirable than the new European immigrants because they were skilled, intelligent and hardworking. Wilson seemed to argue that the Chinese were driven out because they were good enough to compete with White Americans for jobs, while Southern and Eastern

---

criticisms of them resulted from his fear that group interests would ruin popular government for the common interest. Henry W. Bragdon, *Woodrow Wilson: The Academic Years* (Cambridge: Belknap Press, Harvard University Press, 1967) 399; and Link, *Road to the White House*, 186–87.

[20] For a full description of the smear campaign, see Link, *Road to the White House*, 380–88.

[21] Wilson, *History*, 5:212–13.

Europeans were tolerated because they were only fit for the lowest, unwanted jobs.[22]

James Duval Phelan, the leader of the Wilson forces in California, begged the New Jersey governor to issue a statement upholding the Chinese Exclusion Act to mollify irate White voters. Wilson replied in a published telegram that he stood firmly for the exclusion of Asian immigrants: "The whole question is one of assimilation of diverse races. We cannot make a homogenous population out of people who do not blend with the Caucasian race." He compared Asians on the West Coast with African Americans in his native South. "Oriental coolieism will give us another race problem to solve and surely we have had our lesson," he wrote.[23] Wilson thus blatantly labeled both Blacks and Asians as unassimilable, making his racism all too evident. Nevertheless, he believed that those already living in the United States should be treated as fairly as possible.

The Democratic candidate also wrote letters to European immigrant groups practically every day during the 1912 campaign in order to explain his position to irate voters. Nicholas Piotrowski, the city attorney of Chicago and a leading Democrat, warned Wilson that many of the three million Polish Americans were upset about the passage quoted from Wilson's *History*. Piotrowski said that he could not believe that Wilson meant it, however, and he offered the New Jersey governor the chance to explain himself. In case the governor had been ill-informed about Polish immigrants, Piotrowski supplied him with a brief history of their successes in the United States. He concluded, "In honesty, integrity, thriftiness and respect for the laws, the Poles in this country rank as high as any other nationality....It is true that among the 3,000,000 Poles in this country, there will be found undesirables, but the same is true of all nationalities; Americans of English descent not excepted."[24]

Wilson hastily replied to Piotrowski that the passage was misconstrued due to the necessity of condensation in publishing, and that it really referred only to contract labor, which drew "in many cases upon a class of people

---

[22] Ibid., 185–86, 213–14.

[23] James Duval Phelan to Woodrow Wilson, 20 April 1912, in Wilson, *Papers*, 24:351–53; and Wilson to Phelan, 3 May 1912, in ibid., 24:382–83. The telegram was a draft statement sent by Phelan. The statement was issued partly to win union votes. But there was a deeper equation of Asians and Blacks as not able to assimilate Wilson's mind. Phelan had warned Wilson that Asians might soon outvote Whites in Hawaii.

[24] Nicholas Piotrowski to Woodrow Wilson, 11 March 1912, in ibid., 24:241–42.

who would not have come of their own motion and who were not entirely representative of the finer elements of the countries from which they came." This became his stock-in-trade answer to irate ethnic groups. In addition, he agreed with Piotrowski that the Poles had a distinguished history in both Poland and the United States, and he declared that he certainly did not favor Chinese laborers over Polish ones. This reply apparently satisfied Piotrowski and many other Chicago Polish Americans, because Piotrowski was eventually very helpful in getting out the Polish vote for Wilson.[25]

The Democrats made every effort to win immigrant support.[26] The leaders of the Italian-American Association were invited to Sea Girt for a private reception at which Wilson offered similar apologies. Wilson praised their organization for resettling immigrants in the wholesome countryside, thus distributing the population more evenly and easing the overcrowding of the squalid port cities. The leaders of the Association reported afterwards that "we Italians may be certain that no man is less capable of damaging our interests even by a chance word, no man is better aware of the real position and importance of our countrymen in the United States, and no man is better disposed and more capable of viewing the Italo-American citizen as he really is."[27]

Most immigrant societies were dominated by middle-class immigrants who tended to vote Republican, however, and they remained hostile to Wilson. The United Polish Societies of Manhattan denounced him as "narrow and unjust in his attitude toward the Poles," while the Rev. John Strzelecki of St. Stanislaw's Church declared, "What he says is an insult to

---

[25] Woodrow Wilson to Nicholas Piotrowski, 13 March 1912, in ibid., 24:242–43; Link, *Road to the White House*, 386; Wilson to Piotrowski, 11 Dec. 1912, in Wilson, *Papers*, 25:586. Wilson also addressed two large Polish-American audiences in the South Side. Ibid., 24:299–303.

[26] Special bureaus were set up in the Chicago and New York headquarters to direct appeals to the immigrants. The New York headquarters spent $133,000 out of $828,122.79 on the foreign-born and Blacks, while the Chicago headquarters spent $13,000 out of $206,273. Link, *Road to the White House*, 486–87, 499.

[27] "Italians Get Wilson's Reply," *Newark Evening News* (17 May 1912) in Wilson, *Papers*, 24:404–407. The work of the I.A.A. in distributing immigrants around the country was strikingly similar to the efforts of the National Liberal Immigration League, of which Wilson had been a director until 1912. Wilson was a firm believer in the "agrarian myth," that virtue resided on the farm and vice reigned in the city. A more even distribution of immigrants would make assimilation easier, he believed, not only by breaking up the "Little Italys" of the cities, but also by exposing the immigrants to the ideal of American small-town democracy.

the white race!" Likewise, the Italian-American Civic Union of New York opposed his nomination due to his "prejudiced and narrow mind of very limited intelligence."[28] The United Polish Societies of South Brooklyn also remained opposed to his candidacy despite Wilson's promise to their leader, Ignatius Drobinski, to correct the offending passage in the next edition.[29] Hungarian Americans, too, remained hostile to Wilson despite his successful interview with Gezea Kende, editor of *Amerikar-Magyar Nepszava* (*American-Hungarian People's Voice*, the largest Hungarian newspaper in the United States), in which he gave a signed statement favoring only "responsible" restrictions on immigration that safeguarded health and morals but did not "exclude from the country honest, industrious men who are seeking what America has always offered—an asylum for those who seek a free field."[30]

The Roman Catholic Church was also upset by the publication of several anti-Catholic remarks by Wilson. A poll of 2,313 priests and monks from around the country revealed that while the majority of Irish and German clergy supported Wilson, the majority of Italian and Polish clergy opposed him. The Democratic Party enlisted a prominent Catholic layman, James Charles Monoghan, to write a pamphlet defending Wilson as a friend of Catholics. In his campaign speeches, Wilson paid his compliment to the Roman Church by praising it for keeping alive the flame of individual liberty and equality during the Dark Ages by allowing the humblest peasant the opportunity to become Pope through the priesthood. Wilson also

---

[28] *New York Sun*, 10 February 1912; *New York American*, 29 January 1912, and 10 February 1912, in Link, *Road to the White House*, 384–85.

[29] Francis Ignatius Drobinski to Woodrow Wilson, 2 February 1912, in Wilson, *Papers*, 24:131–32; Wilson to Drobinski, 7 February 1912, in ibid., 24:134–35; Drobinski to Wilson, 29 February 1912, in ibid., 24:219; and Wilson to Drobinski, 4 March 1912, in ibid., 24:223. Wilson's first reply stated, "I have received the greatest stimulation from my reading of Polish history," but it does not appear that Wilson had ever read Polish history, except for Piotrowski's letter. Wilson's second reply ignored Drobinski's other demands: an erratum slip for the present edition, and a public apology. He did, however, contact Harper & Brothers the same day about correcting the next edition. See also Link, *Road to the White House*, 386–87.

[30] "Wilson in Hiding to Write Speech," *New York Times* (23 July 1912) in Wilson, *Papers*, 24:563–64; and Link, *Road to the White House*, 384–85. This statement on what constituted acceptable and unacceptable immigration restrictions is almost identical to Wilson's later veto messages on the Burnett Bill.

accepted an honorary membership in the Knights of Columbus, ironically setting off a storm of anti-Catholic protest in Pittsburgh.[31]

The Hearst newspapers collaborated with the campaign staff of Wilson's rival for the Democratic nomination, Speaker of the House James Beauchamp "Champ" Clark. Hearst and Clark assailed Wilson's belated attempt to befriend immigrants as an about-face, trying to arouse nativist as well as immigrant anger. Hearst's editorials referred to Wilson as "a perfect jackrabbit of politics, perched upon his little hillock of expediency, with ears erect and nostrils distended, keenly alert to every scent or sound and ready to run and double in any direction." Hearst predicted that the only people who would vote for Wilson would be the railroad owners. "If the railroads could have Woodrow Wilson in the White House and a million Chinese laborers, as a starter, to work for them, it would be a very fine combination," Hearst declared, explaining, "Woodrow Wilson would, as President, protect them against legislation in favor of the people."[32]

Wilson tried to counter the impression that he was a nativist by describing the United States as an asylum for political and moral idealists. His campaign speeches in 1912 emphasized the desire for individual freedom and spiritual fulfillment as the force which motivated most immigrants to come to the United States. In part, Wilson was trying to mollify ethnic groups who were outraged over the infamous passage in his *History* by arguing that the quotation was taken out of context, and that it referred only to immigrants who were forced to come over as contract labor. By contrast, the majority of immigrants came over voluntarily, literally moved by the spirit.

---

[31] Link, *Road to the White House*, 499–500; James Charles Monoghan, *Is Woodrow Wilson A Bigot?* (New York: Democratic National Committee, 1912); and Wilson, *Papers*, 19:60; 20:329; 21:180. The exact figures of the poll were 60% of the Irish and 80% of the German clergy for Wilson, 90% of the Italians and 70% of the Polish clergy for Roosevelt. Wilson's compliment to the "democratic" Roman Catholic Church of the Middle Ages reveals something about Wilson's view of democracy: the theory was more important than the practice. As long as any peasant could technically become Pope (or President), it did not matter how many actually did so. Besides, noble sons (or mugwumps) made better Popes anyway.

[32] Link, *Road to the White House*, 382–84. Editorials taken from the 14 March 1912 *Washington Post* and the 27 May 1912 *New York Evening Journal*. Hearst was enraged because Wilson had rebuffed his earlier offer of support, literally telling him to "go to hell." Wilson's personal integrity would not allow him to accept the support of someone whom he considered irresponsible and corrupt. See also Link, *Road to the White House*, 382.

But this defense merged in his mind with what he considered to be the more important reason to emphasize the spiritual concept of America: the unity of believers which it implied. Woodrow Wilson believed that he could reunite the divided American people by teaching them that the past no longer mattered, save to teach them the necessity and inevitability of their being all as one now in the American spirit. It is as if Wilson was paraphrasing St. Paul again: "Here there is no Greek or Jew, immigrant or native, Pole, Italian, slave or free, but America is all, and is in all."[33] Wilson told a Polish-American crowd in Chicago's South Side, "When we speak of America, we speak not of a race; but of a people." He argued that the immigrants and their descendants probably outnumbered the descendants of the original colonial settlers. In any case, the nativists were wrong to distinguish between them because they were united in spirit. "The term America is bigger than the continent," he asserted, because "America lives in the hearts of every man everywhere who wishes to find a region somewhere where he will be free to work out his destiny as he chooses."[34]

Wilson began to protest wherever he spoke in the 1912 campaign against the very hyphenated terms used to label the immigrants. He realized that the use of such terms fostered the lack of unity felt by Americans of different ethnic backgrounds, and prevented the full flowering of united American power which he predicted for the twentieth century. He declared, "I am looking forward to an era of unprecedented national action. We are now coming to an era where there will be but one single expression and but one common thought." To establish this golden age, however, the vernacular of thought and expression had to be changed. Thus he continued, "I protest against speaking of German-Americans, or Irish-Americans or Jewish-Americans, for these nationalities are becoming indistinguishable in the general body of Americans. Drop out the first words, cut out the hyphens and call them all Americans."[35]

Wilson stressed the importance of language in communicating this spiritual concept of America to a group of approximately one hundred

---

[33] The original passage (Colossians 3:11, KJV) reads, "Here there is no Greek or Jew, circumcised or uncircumcised, barbarian, Scythian, slave or free, but Christ is all, and is in all."

[34] *Chicago Daily Tribune* (7 April 1912) in Wilson, *Papers,* 24:299–303. Despite his recognition of the fact that everyone in the United States (with the exception of the Indians) had immigrant roots, he still distinguished between "the settlers" and "the people of all the races of Europe."

[35] *Ann Arbor Daily Times-News* (19 January 1912) in ibid., 24:57–58.

editors of US foreign-language newspapers in 1912. He explained his view of America and stated that immigration laws should only exclude those who lacked the spirit of American idealism which caused people to emigrate voluntarily. He then protested against designating his audience as foreign-language editors, arguing that whatever language was used to convey American ideals, it was the language of America: "All my interest is that you shouldn't regard the language in which you print your periodicals as a foreign language when printed in America for the conveyance of American thinking."[36] True American faith, however, was limited to the elect. There were certain languages which simply could not convey the American spirit. Wilson thought that the key to a successful immigration policy was assimilation. Indeed, it was on this basis that Wilson supported the Chinese Exclusion Act. Wilson believed Asians, like African Americans, were simply incapable of conforming to the ideal. They were therefore obviously heathen intruders in the Kingdom of God who should be tolerated, but kept in their place.

Despite the fact that Europeans emigrated to the United States because they were already Americans at heart, Wilson held that assimilation was not an automatic experience. Immigrants needed to "work out their salvation with fear and trembling," and it was up to the native citizens to aid them. The key assistance was through education, and Wilson heartily approved of the naturalization classes and night schools started by progressive social workers. But, he believed that "the chief school that these people must attend after they get here is the school which all of us attend, which is furnished by the life of the communities in which we live and the Nation to which we belong." The ideal American community (i.e., small and rural) was the best school for instilling American ideals. The crowded cities, where political machines had corrupted those standards, could not teach the spiritual lessons that immigrants needed to learn in order to assimilate properly.[37]

---

[36] Wilson, Talk to approximately 100 Editors of Foreign-Language Newspapers in New York City, 4 September 1912, in ibid., 25:94–97. Very few of these editors endorsed Wilson, however, so it seems that they did not accept this as explanation enough of his statements in the *History*. Cf. Bragdon, *Academic Years*, 260–61, where he argues that Wilson's lecture notes show a belief that language differences had to be eliminated in order for a common media to be established. It is likely that Wilson's views on language changed along with his views on immigration.

[37] Philippians 2:12; Woodrow Wilson, "Loyalty Means Self-Sacrifice," Address on Citizenship to Conference on Americanization, Washington DC, 13 July 1916, in Wilson,

The chief lesson which immigrants needed to learn was proper American political behavior. Wilson was upset that the foreign-born sustained the urban political machines by exchanging votes for jobs and other favors because this process corrupted his ideal of the statesman. Although Wilson regarded the political party as a powerful tool, he demanded that elected officials act as individually responsible trustees, and not as mere delegates blindly following partisan dictates. In a 1912 campaign speech, Wilson cautioned his audience to distinguish between bosses and political leaders. He contended that parties were "absolutely legitimate and absolutely necessary," but only when the political leader used the party to serve the commonweal. "A boss," he explained "is a man who uses this splendid open force for the secret processes of selfish control."[38]

Wilson believed citizens must vote for the good of the nation as a whole; that politicians must serve that greater good. In his speech accepting the Democratic nomination in 1912, the man who had defeated the bosses in New Jersey called on his party to do the same nationwide. Politicians should not be lackeys of special interests, he declared, but "servants of the people, the whole people." He further lamented, *The nation has been unnecessarily, unreasonably at war within itself.* Interest has clashed with interest when there were common principles of right and of fair dealing which...should have bound them all together."[39] The Democratic candidate called once more on Americans to end this new Civil War and unite in patriotic homogeneity of belief and practice.

Wilson explicitly linked this homogeneity of American idealism to the assimilation of immigrants during the 1912 campaign. He argued that America had always opened its doors and extended hospitality to all the "modern civilized peoples," to share American ideals and enrich the melting

---

The New Democracy: Presidential Messages, Addresses, and Other Papers, 1913–1917, ed. Ray Stannard Baker and William E. Dodd, 2 vols. (New York: Harper & Brothers, 1926) 2:248; also in Wilson, *Papers,* 37:415. Note Wilson's belief in the "agrarian myth," as well as the "frontier thesis" of his former student, Henry Jackson Turner.

[38] Wilson, Campaign Speech at Carnegie Hall, New York, 19 October 1912, in Wilson, *Papers,* 25:446. Note the similarity between the call for parties to be an "open force" and Wilson's later demand in the Fourteen Points for "open" treaties. The American ideal was truly a world standard, in Wilson's mind, with the people of the world unifying to end the domination of the selfish special interests of groups called the European national governments.

[39] Wilson, Acceptance Speech, Sea Girt NJ, 7 August 1912, in ibid., 25:6 (emphasis mine).

pot. America had to be careful to live up to the ideals which persuaded the immigrants to come here, the vision of "a place of close-knit communities, where men think in terms of the common interest, where men do not organize selfish groups to dominate the fortunes of their fellow men, but where, on the contrary, they, by common conference, conceive the policies which are for the common benefit."[40] Once more, the image of special interest groups as an evil, divisive force emerged, as well as the image of small-town community life as the ideal force to Americanize and unify the diverse elements of the population.

In the end, the Hearst-Clark smear campaign failed. Wilson received the Democratic nomination in 1912 and defeated the divided Republican party to win the presidency. Wilson's immigration plank in his draft of the party platform declared, "Reasonable restrictions safeguarding the health, the morals, and the political integrity of the country, no one can object to, but regulation should not go to such an extent as to shut the doors of America against men and women looking for new opportunity and genuine political freedom." The final platform adopted by the convention, however, made no mention of the subject.[41] Despite Wilson's victory, the combined vote totals for William Howard Taft and Theodore Roosevelt exceeded his total. Roosevelt carried Pennsylvania, Michigan, Minnesota and South Dakota, all immigrant-rich states. Despite his insistence on fair treatment for Chinese and Japanese immigrants, Roosevelt also carried Washington and California with the help of his running mate, Hiram Johnson. Wilson won an outright majority in only twelve states, eleven of them in the South. Wilson received more votes than William Jennings Bryan had in 1908 in New England and the Pacific coast, but he ran behind the Great Commoner in several Midwestern states with large immigrant populations: Ohio, Indiana, Illinois, Michigan, Nebraska and Kansas.[42]

Woodrow Wilson's appointments, like those of his predecessors, showed an uncertain approach to the enforcement of immigration laws. He appointed California state senator Anthony Caminetti, who had led the fight

---

[40] Wilson, Campaign Speech at Carnegie Hall, New York, 19 October 1912, in ibid., 25:441–42. Note that the hospitality is limited to "modern civilized peoples," thus excluding non-Europeans.

[41] Ibid., 24:481; and Edward P. Hutchinson, *Legislative History of American Immigration Policy, 1798–1965* (Philadelphia: University of Pennsylvania Press, 1981) 631–32.

[42] Edgar Eugene Robinson, *The Presidential Vote, 1896–1932* (Palo Alto: Stanford University Press, 1934), 14–17.

for the golden state's anti-Japanese Alien Land Law of 1913, as Commissioner-General of Immigration. This appointment pleased Italian-Americans as well as restrictionists and shored up support for Wilson in California, which had given its electoral votes to Roosevelt in 1912. Caminetti strictly enforced the immigration laws, motivated in part by embarrassment over his son's conviction for violating the Mann White Slave Traffic Act in 1913.[43] The Secretary of Labor was William B. Wilson, a Pennsylvania Congressman and former Secretary-Treasurer of the United Mine Workers. Despite his union background, Secretary Wilson remained sympathetic to immigrants and insisted on their fair treatment, in part because he had emigrated from Scotland with his family as a boy.

Fredric C. Howe, President Wilson's former graduate student, became Commissioner at Ellis Island. Howe had been the liberal director of the People's Institute at Cooper Union in New York City. He reversed many of William Williams' harsh policies and tried to humanize the facility by adding an outdoor playground, benches, plants, and Sunday afternoon concerts. He also created a common social hall for detained families who had previously been allowed to reunite only at mealtimes. Howe was quoted in an October 1914 article in *The Outlook* as saying, "The only thing that is lacking over here is imagination. No one ever seemed to try to imagine what a detained immigrant must be feeling." Howe planned to encourage detainees to share their culture through folk dances, but he also desired to offer "Americanization" classes for both children and adults to instruct them in the English language.[44]

Woodrow Wilson certainly shared Commissioner-General Caminetti's hostility to Asian immigrants, and unlike Roosevelt, he refused to take a stand against California's attempts to legislate Japanese immigrants out of the state. When a reporter asked about the California anti-alien land ownership law at a press conference in April 1913, Wilson maintained that the 1911 Commercial Treaty negotiated by Taft and Secretary of State Philander C. Knox was unconstitutional because the federal government could not make a treaty which interfered with a state's right to pass local laws. "Nobody can for a moment challenge the constitutional right of

---

[43] Wilson, *Papers*, 28:99n4. Wilson refused to pardon Farley Drew Caminetti on the grounds that it would weaken the effectiveness of the Mann Act. Wilson to Key Pittman, 21 Feb. 1912, ibid, 41:261; and Wilson to Ella E. Martin, 22 March 1917, ibid., 453-54.

[44] Thomas M. Pitkin, *Keepers of the Gate: A History of Ellis Island* (New York: New York University Press, 1975) 112–15.

California to pass such land laws as she pleases," Wilson said. He argued that because the federal government had "gone beyond its powers" in making the treaty, it could not enforce the terms of the pact. The government nevertheless could be held liable for damages for failing to do so. When a reporter pointed out that this issue came up in the case of the lynching of eleven Italians in New Orleans in 1891, Wilson replied, "Yes, it did, and the federal government simply had to reimburse."[45] While he disapproved of the blatant discrimination in California's Alien Land Law, Wilson was too much of a Southerner to stand against state's rights.

The issue, of course, went beyond state's rights. Wilson tried to ignore anti-Asian racism and the trouble it posed for US–Japanese relations rather than confront it as Roosevelt had done. At a press conference on 12 May 1913, Wilson refused to discuss the Japanese Ambassador's protest against the California law and denied one reporter's insistent observations that the heart of the issue was the US government's denial of the right of naturalization to Japanese Americans. The following week he told the press off the record that the real problem was not the anti-alien land ownership law itself, but rather the wounded pride caused by its implication that Americans did not want to live with Japanese. He even made the dubious assertion that Roosevelt's negotiation of the Treaty of Portsmouth caused Japanese resentment of the United States. Wilson denied on 5 June he had instructed the Attorney General to pursue a test case about racial eligibility to citizenship. On 18 August he denied that the Justice Department could intervene in a court case. He expressed the willingness to indemnify Japanese if a loss under the treaty could be shown, but he said, "I can't imagine any basis for the indemnification."[46]

Behind the scenes, Wilson took a few tentative steps toward reigning in anti-Asian prejudice, but he never used the bully pulpit as Roosevelt had to denounce discrimination. Secretary of State William Jennings Bryan sent letters to Washington Governor Ernest Lister and Caminetti in 1913, urging them to reword the alien land laws so as to avoid the appearance of prejudice.[47] When Japanese diplomat Viscount Sutemi Chinda protested the California law in 1914, President Wilson replied that he could not interfere because it would be unconstitutional to do so and would only inflame anti-Asian prejudice. He did reassure Chinda, however, that Caminetti was

---

[45] Wilson, *Papers,* 50:16–17.

[46] Ibid., 54–57, 68, 99–100, 192–93.

[47] William Jennings Bryan to Wilson, 24 March 1913, in ibid., 27:220.

talking to California authorities behind the scenes.[48] In 1916 Wilson asked Secretary of Labor William B. Wilson to speak to Caminetti about the need "to change the attitude of mind of the immigration officials at San Francisco," suggesting that perhaps the officials were so imbued with prejudice that they did not realize how harshly they treated Chinese and Japanese Americans.[49] But he did not address the issue directly, as Roosevelt had with Victor Metcalf.

World War I, which broke out in August 1914, strongly influenced Wilson's attitude toward immigrants. It strengthened his conviction that all Americans—native and foreign-born—must unite as servants of God to build a peaceful "city on a hill" to set an example for the war-torn world. Wilson believed the oath of citizenship was sacred; immigrants who insisted on hyphens in their name and tried to fight old world battles in the new world violated their vows and betrayed America. He probably remembered his father pronouncing the judgment of Jesus from the pulpit: "No one who puts his hand to the plow and looks back is fit for service in the Kingdom of God."[50] Wilson used similar language when addressing a crowd of several thousand newly naturalized citizens in Philadelphia in 1915. He told the new Americans that they had not taken an oath of allegiance to people, but rather "to a great ideal, to a great body of principles, to a great hope of the human race." He explained that when they entered the United States they were free to bring their culture with them, but they had to leave their old loyalties and political ideas behind. "I certainly would not be one even to suggest that a man cease to love the home of his birth and the nation of his origin—these things are very sacred and ought not to be put out of our hearts," he said, "but it is one thing to love the place where you were born and it is another thing to dedicate yourself to the place to which you go." Most of all, naturalized citizens had to reject any ethnic group identity and embrace American individualism. "You cannot become thorough Americans if you think of yourselves in groups," Wilson argued, because "America does not consist of groups."[51]

---

[48] Viscount Sutemi Chinda to Baron Takaaki Kato, 29 October 1914, in ibid., 31:256–57, n3, n5.

[49] Woodrow Wilson to William B. Wilson, 20 April 1916, in ibid., 36:515–16.

[50] Luke 9:62.

[51] Woodrow Wilson, Address to several thousand naturalized citizens after ceremonies, Philadelphia PA, 10 May 1915, in Wilson, *New Democracy*, 1:318–19; also in Wilson, *Papers*, 33:147-48.

President Wilson desired unity of American spirit at all times. The efforts of hyphenated Americans—whether Irish, German, Italian, or English—to draw the United States into World War I on behalf of their homelands particularly infuriated him, since such activity violated his proclamation of neutrality. It was not by accident that in the same Philadelphia speech, Wilson made his famous declaration that America was "too proud to fight." Wilson's campaign against hyphenism coincided with ever-present nativism and the growing pro-Allied war movement to produce a backlash against immigration. This backlash again led Congress to promote the literacy test. Wilson opposed it as representing the restrictionist position of selfish trade unions, which to his mind was intolerable.

The champion of the renascent literacy test movement was Massachusetts Senator Henry Cabot Lodge, President Wilson's long-time political nemesis. Wilson and Lodge both held an idealistic, optimistic view of America's past and future greatness. Both men upheld the Puritan ideal of a public-spirited, homogenous society as the only salvation for the morass of self-serving urban politics. They disagreed, however, about how to achieve that homogeneity. Wilson sought American strength through unity, blending together the best characteristics of every nationality to create the ideal citizenry. Lodge, on the other hand, sought strength through racial purity, convinced that only the Anglo-American "race" could succeed in forging the bright national future. Lodge believed in assimilation, to be sure, but it could only be successful when immigrants abandoned their ethnic heritage entirely and became Anglo-Americans. While Wilson wanted the immigrants to share a common vision, Lodge wanted to admit only those who shared a common history, common language, and common genes as well.[52]

Like Roosevelt, Wilson advocated the distribution of immigrants away from the northeastern cities. Most Southerners were opposed to any immigrants being distributed in their states, however, and it is not surprising to find that most of the literacy test's supporters were Southern Democrats such as Alabama's Senator Oscar Underwood and Congressman John Burnett, the chair of the House Committee on Immigration and Naturalization. They wanted to end the admission of all non-"Teutonic" foreigners, and thought that the literacy test could accomplish this, just as it

---

[52] This subtle contrast between amalgamation and isolation was, of course, also at the heart of the battle over the League of Nations. See William Widenor, *Henry Cabot Lodge and the Search for an American Foreign Policy* (Berkeley: University of California Press, 1980) 16, 22–24, 27–28, 57–61.

kept Blacks from voting. Immigration restriction was also a golden opportunity for Southern Democrats to win back the farmers and union members who had bolted the party for the Populists in the 1890s.

On 15 December 1913 Burnett's committee reported out a bill which included a literacy test (with an exemption for religious refugees) and excluded persons who advocated the unlawful destruction of property.[53] While Wilson thought Southerners, White Californians, and the unions were guilty of promoting selfish special interests, Burnett attacked the foes of his bill as special interests: the "Ship Trust," the "Brewers' Trust." He argued that his bill did exactly what Wilson had advocated during the 1912 campaign: it restricted immigration to maintain American ideals. Burnett made sure his speeches cited the social science statistics that appealed to progressives. He established a connection between illiterate foreigners and crime by quoting experts such as New York Police Commissioner Theodore A. Bingham, who claimed that most crimes against women and children were committed "by fellows who can't talk the English language," were unfamiliar with American customs and were "in general the scum of Europe."[54]

The theme of racial superiority dominated Congressional debates nearly as much as did economic concerns about wages and jobs. Representative Everis Anson Hayes of California offered a motion in 1914 to amend the Burnett bill by excluding all "Hindoos [sic] and all persons of the Mongolian or yellow race, the Malay or brown race, the African or black race," but it was defeated handily. While Burnett was definitely a White supremacist, he successfully urged the House to reject Hayes' amendment because the amendment would insure the bill's defeat.[55] Senator James A. Reed of Missouri did get an amendment excluding all Blacks (carefully worded so as to bar even Black US citizens who traveled abroad from returning) to pass the Senate, but it was dropped by the conference committee of the House and Senate in 1915.[56] The 1917 bill that finally

---

[53] Hutchinson, *Legislative History*, 160–61.

[54] *Congressional Record,* 63d Cong., 3d sess., 1915, 52: 171–74. Burnett also quoted former New York Immigration Inspector Marcus Braun on the superiority of Northern European immigrants, including, one supposes, Hungarians such as himself.

[55] Hutchinson, *Legislative History*, 161; and *Congressional Record,* 63d Cong., 2d sess., 1914, 51:2781. The vote defeating the amendment was 54–203.

[56] Hutchinson, *Legislative History*, 163.

passed over Wilson's veto, however, did include an "Asiatic Barred Zone" that restricted immigration by longitude and latitude.[57]

The most outspoken opponent of the Burnett bill was Representative James A. Gallivan of Massachusetts. He denounced the new "holy wars" between Catholics and Protestants the debate on immigration was engendering. Gallivan also pointed out the hypocrisy of the Southern Democrats who supported the bill, noting that the majority of White Southerners, let alone Blacks, were as poor as the immigrants in question and themselves had much higher rates of illiteracy. In contrast, he observed that wealth and education had grown in the North along with immigration. Gallivan reminded his colleagues in the House that the Twelve Apostles were mostly illiterate when Jesus called them; and that the colonial ancestors of whom the representatives were so proud were also largely illiterate. "Then, as now, the men who faced the hazards of the tempestuous ocean and the perils of the savage continent were usually the bravest and most enterprising of their class," he said. While they lacked an education, "they had courage, strength, common sense, native ability, and a willingness to work out their own salvation in a new country." Gallivan pleaded for a true test of character, noting that a literacy test would not keep out the typically well-educated anarchists and socialists. He concluded, "We have grown fat and foolish in our progress; we forget our origins; we imagine that the eternal verities will change and that the letters and scripts that man has made have, by some curious alchemy, become greater and more worthy than the gifts God has given us."[58]

The House of Representatives was not moved by Gallivan's eloquence. In an apparent attempt to highlight the literacy test's origin as a device to bar African Americans from voting in the South, Edmund Platt of New York attempted to add a "grandfather clause" to the literacy test, but it was defeated. Illinois Congressman Adolph Sabath's effort to recommit the Burnett bill failed by almost one hundred votes on 4 February 1914. The House then passed the bill 253 to 126, a two-to-one margin. Burnett thanked his Republican colleague, Massachusetts Congressman Augustus Gardner, as well as Prescott F. Hall of the Immigration Restriction League for their

---

[57] Ibid., 162–63. Senator Reed opposed this, not because it excluded Asians, but because by drawing arbitrary lines, it overlooked some Asians who would still be able to enter the country.

[58] *Congressional Record,* 63d Cong., 3d sess., 1915, 52:1139–140; and ibid., 1915, 52:3016–017.

help and dismissed rumors of a presidential veto.[59] The possibility of a veto by the president, however, remained strong.

Wilson was reluctant to discuss pending legislation at his press conferences. When a reporter asked him in January 1914 if he had expressed any opinion about the merits of a literacy test, Wilson replied that he had not given it much thought. In response to a follow-up question Wilson was noncommittal about whether he would give hearings to opponents of the bill as had his predecessor, President Taft.[60] In December 1914, however, when pressed for his view of the literacy test, Wilson stated, "It is very well known that I think the literacy test is a bad test. I mean [it] is a test that does not test quality."[61] On 5 January 1915, Wilson denied that there would be hearings on the bill and cut off a reporter's question about lobbying by Louis Hammerling, president of the American Association of Foreign Language Newspapers. Pressed time and again to give his views on immigration restriction, the president continued to refuse to engage the matter publicly. At one point he dodged the issue by saying, "I feel I would have to hire a hall. It would take an hour."[62]

Despite his unwillingness to use the bully pulpit and discuss his opinions regarding immigration restriction with the press, Wilson was maneuvering to defeat the literacy test behind the scenes. He wrote to Senate Immigration Committee chairman Ellison D. Smith of South Carolina in March 1914, requesting that the literacy test be removed from the Senate version of the bill. He suggested that Congress create instead a commission to determine "the best plans for effecting an economic distribution of our immigrants after they arrive in this country," which would solve the problems of overcrowded cities filled with unskilled workmen.[63] Distribution was the proposal of the National Liberal Immigration League, of which Wilson had been a member prior to his 1912 campaign.[64] The

---

[59] Hutchinson, *Legislative History*, 160–61; and Robert Frederic Zeidel, "The Literacy Test for Immigrants: A Question of Progress" (Ph.D. diss., Marquette University, 1986), 323.

[60] Wilson, *Papers*, 50:357.

[61] Ibid., 655.

[62] Ibid., 668–70.

[63] Woodrow Wilson to Ellison D. Smith, 5 March 1914, in ibid., 29:310–11.

[64] See ibid., 24:89–90; 25:95; 27:75–78; and Link, *Road to the White House*, 387. Wilson resigned this and all similar positions when he ran for president, but Edward Lauterbach, President of the League, defended him to immigrant groups in the 1912 campaign.

creation of another commission, however, was interpreted as a delaying tactic by restrictionists who still resented the "Dilly-Dally Commission" promoted by Roosevelt.

Wilson also held private meetings with supporters of the Burnett bill. Edward Alsworth Ross, the University of Wisconsin professor of political economy who had been a graduate student with Wilson at Johns Hopkins, brought fellow restrictionists William Walter Husband, Henry Pratt Fairchild, Jeremiah Jenks, Joseph Lee and Robert Woods to the White House on 22 March 1914 to meet with the president. When Wilson objected to applying a literacy test to religious refugees, they suggested giving the Secretary of Labor discretion in such cases, rather than proclaiming an outright exemption for immigrants seeking religious asylum. They also tried to disabuse Wilson of the idea that the new immigrants wanted to own land and be farmers just as much as the old immigrants, claiming that only one out of every one hundred–thirty Poles, Italians or Magyars were farmers. Wilson was not convinced, but he did forward a memorandum they submitted after the meeting to Commissioner-General Caminetti.[65]

Smith's committee reported the Burnett bill out on 19 March 1914, noting that the literacy test was designed to be restrictive rather than selective. The Senators added amendments that raised the head tax to six dollars, denied citizenship to alien prostitutes who married citizens, and excluded Blacks. An amendment exempting political refugees was defeated. The Senate delayed action until after the 1914 elections, but on 2 January 1915 they passed the bill 50 to 7 (with 39 abstentions) despite the fact that Reed read a letter from Wilson opposing the literacy test. The House then passed it, 227 to 94.[66]

Wilson held a public meeting, as had Cleveland and Taft, on 22 January. Six days later, he followed their example and vetoed the bill. Wilson's veto message described the literacy test as "a radical departure from the traditional and long-established policy of this country...in which our people have conceived the very character of their government to be expressed, the very mission and spirit of the Nation," because it greatly curtailed the right to political asylum in the United States. Wilson also criticized the bill because it was a test of opportunity rather than character and quality. "Those who come seeking opportunity are not to be admitted

---

[65] Zeidel, "Literacy Test," 327–28.
[66] Hutchinson, *Legislative History*, 161–62; and Zeidel, "Literacy Test," 330–31.

unless they have already had one of the chief opportunities they seek, the opportunity of education," Wilson observed.[67]

The House failed to override the president's veto by four votes, 261 to 136. Although 34 more Congressman voted in favor of the bill than when it originally passed the House, 42 more voted against it. Still, 26 Congressmen failed to vote. Immigration Restriction League lobbyist James Patten accused Wilson and his secretary, Joe Tumulty, of using patronage to get thirteen Democrats to abandon the literacy test, including six who had voted to override Taft's veto two years before. The president told Mississippi Senator John Sharp Williams that he felt obliged to veto the bill because of his campaign promises to ethnic groups.[68]

The restrictionists did not give up. Burnett and Ellison Smith introduced identical bills in the House and Senate when Congress reconvened in December 1915. The head tax was increased to eight dollars, but waived for children. The literacy test would apply to all aliens over sixteen years old. Exemptions for those fleeing religious or political persecution were added, however, to preserve the tradition of asylum which Wilson had cited in his veto message. Aliens suffering from "constitutional psychopathic inferiority," chronic alcoholism, or tuberculosis, as well as vagrants, deportees returning within one year of deportation, and those advocating the unlawful destruction of property were added to the categories of excluded aliens. The original version of the bill also excluded "aliens ineligible to citizenship," but the Senate substituted an Asiatic Barred Zone which excluded Indians and most East and Southeast Asians, but not the Japanese. The House passed the bill 308 to 87 in March 1916, but the Senate did not take up the bill until August and then awaited the results of that year's elections before acting. In December the upper chamber passed the bill 64 to 7. The conference committee subsequently dropped two Senate amendments excluding "birds of passage" and aliens who had returned to Europe to fight in their nations' armies in World War I. Both houses approved the conference report by voice vote, so the support for an override could not be gauged.[69]

---

[67] Woodrow Wilson, Message to the House of Representatives, 28 January 1915, in Wilson, *New Democracy*, 1:252–54; also in Wilson, *Papers*, 32:142-44; and Zeidel, "Literacy Test," 331.

[68] Hutchinson, *Legislative History*, 162–63; Link, *Road to the White House*, 275–76; and Zeidel, "Literacy Test," 332–33.

[69] Hutchinson, *Legislative History*, 164–66; and Zeidel, "Literacy Test," 334–40.

This time the president held no public hearings before vetoing the bill on 29 January 1917. Wilson's second veto message essentially reiterated the first. He criticized the amendments exempting religious and political refugees from the literacy test, even though they were inserted to answer his objections about the elimination of asylum, because they would lead to "very delicate and hazardous diplomatic situations." Forcing immigration officials "to pass judgment upon the laws and practices of a foreign Government," Wilson warned, would be "a most invidious function for any officer of this Government to perform."[70] The ever-approaching war no doubt contributed to this seeming about-face, particularly the need to maintain good relations with Great Britain. Wilson probably anticipated trouble if Irish Catholics applied for religious asylum as part of their campaign to embarrass Great Britain and secure home rule or independence. Congress overrode the veto, 62 to 19 in the Senate and 287 to 106 in the House.[71]

These two vetoes fit in with Wilson's overall attitude towards immigration. He portrayed himself as another Lincoln or Cleveland, trying to heal the divisions of civil war and reunify the country to carry on its God-ordained mission. The Burnett Immigration Bill was a measure he had opposed from the start. Wilson deemed it unnecessary as he remained confident that the majority of immigrants were loyal Americans—and more importantly, he believed that it violated the foundational principles of the nation. The literacy test may have been useful in keeping African and Asian Americans out of American political life, because they were patently unassimilable in Wilson's view. It constituted, however, an arbitrary restriction on thousands of European immigrants who had the spirit of America in their hearts and could only help build the United States' empire in the twentieth century, spreading the gospel of political freedom to all the world.

More importantly, the rhetoric of Woodrow Wilson reveals the inherent tension within the concepts of the melting pot and asylum. The belief that Americans are the chosen people of God, building his Kingdom on Earth, rings forth in the religious imagery of Wilson. Like ancient Israel, America needed to be united in belief and practice to avoid being corrupted by the surrounding nations. Thus Wilson did not emphasize the cultural gifts the

---

[70] Woodrow Wilson, Message to the House of Representatives, 29 January 1917, in Wilson, *New Democracy*, 2:420–21; also in Wilson, *Papers*, 41:52–53.

[71] Hutchinson, *Legislative History*, 166–67; and Zeidel, "Literacy Test," 340–41.

immigrants brought to America as his predecessors had. Instead, he insisted that all cultural differences must blend away in the melting pot, and the United States must offer asylum only to the like-minded. As the old world was torn apart by war, the necessity of maintaining national unity and purity seemed even more obvious. *"E pluribus, unum"* thundered Wilson from the classroom and the bully pulpit of the Presidency. It is a tragic irony that the people responded by silencing all opposition to the war, staging race riots and abandoning the very ideals which Wilson had said unity would serve.

CHAPTER 5

THE MELTING POT AT ITS BOILING POINT

World War I was the turning point in the campaign to restrict immigration. Now government officials and prominent Americans regarded as treasonous all lobbying by immigrants on behalf of their old homelands. Even ethnic group pride was suspect. Hysterical denunciations of "hyphenate" political activity cowed immigrant leaders into either silence or abject cooperation with the campaign for "One Hundred Percent Americanism." Rumors of spying, sabotage and other disloyal activities convinced many middle-class Americans that the United States' multi-cultural society was not only undesirable, but downright dangerous. Nativist groups were able to convince millions of Americans that the melting pot concept had become inoperative, if indeed it had ever worked at all. The postwar Red Scare strengthened the impression that recent immigrants were failing to assimilate and made the traditional offer of asylum to political and religious refugees seem like an invitation to Communist revolutionaries. By 1920 Warren G. Harding and the Republicans swept to power with the slogan "America First!," committed to the virtual ending of immigration.

President Woodrow Wilson's role as a national leader during the growing hysteria was ambivalent. Like his predecessors Theodore Roosevelt and William Howard Taft, Wilson was outspoken in denouncing hyphenism and disloyalty while tempering his remarks with reassurances that most foreign-born Americans were wholeheartedly patriotic. Privately, he condemned many of the excesses of the campaign against German Americans and other ethnic groups. But he failed to use his presidential authority to curb lawlessness and abuse of civil liberties, and all too often he believed the paranoid rumors in circulation. Besieged by the demands of every nationality to achieve "self-determination" for their compatriots in the peace settlement, his frustration at his own inability to control the Paris conference was displaced onto the Irish whose desire for independence he had formerly supported. Stymied in his attempt to secure Senate ratification of the Versailles Treaty, he lashed out in the summer of 1919 at hyphenated Americans whose actions he considered disloyal, and desperately played upon racial and religious animosities as a final gambit. His pocket veto of the 1921 Emergency Quota Act was a sullen, and ultimately futile, act devoid of the noble sentiments of his earlier vetoes of the Burnett Bill.

From the moment the guns began firing in August 1914, many immigrant groups began to lobby on behalf of their homelands. Irish and German Americans realized that American intervention on the side of the Central Powers was impossible, so they worked instead to make sure that Wilson's proclaimed neutrality did not favor the British. Missouri Congressman Richard Bartholdt called fifty-eight Irish and German-American leaders to Washington in 1915 to organize the American Independence Union, dedicated to maintaining the absolute neutrality of the United States. Irish nationalists like Jeremiah O'Leary, the head of the American Truth Society, and his brother-in-law Daniel Cohalan, the head of Clan-na-Gael and the New York chapter of Sinn Fein, received assistance from German ambassador Count Johann von Bernstorff.[1] As long as the United States remained neutral such activities were tolerated, if just barely. But the more the Irish, and German Americans in particular, agitated on behalf of the Central Powers, the angrier Wilson grew with them. Wilson had indeed long supported the Irish nationalists in their struggle for independence, but not if it came at the expense of US neutrality—or, later on, the wartime alliance with Great Britain.[2]

Even before the fighting broke out "over there," the president insisted that immigrants must demonstrate that their primary loyalty was to their new homeland. Wilson most clearly enunciated his views on this subject when giving an address at the unveiling of a statue of Irish-American Commodore John Barry in May 1914. "This man was not an Irish-American; he was an Irishman who became an American," Wilson declared. "Some Americans

---

[1] Joseph Edward Cuddy, *Irish-America and National Isolationism, 1914–1920* (New York: Arno Press, 1976) 52–55, 79, 82–83. Irish and German Americans had first joined forces to oppose immigration restriction. They founded the Immigration Protective League in 1898 and the National Liberal Immigration League in 1906. Ibid., 41; and Rirka Shpak Lissak "The National Liberal Immigration League and Immigration Restriction, 1906-1914," American Jewish Archives 46/2 (1994): 205-06, 212-13.

[2] On the subject of Wilson's long-standing support for the Irish nationalists, see, e.g., Woodrow Wilson to Ellen Wilson, 27 February 1889, in Woodrow Wilson, *The Papers of Woodrow Wilson,* ed. Arthur S. Link et al., 69 vols. (Princeton: Princeton University Press, 1966–1994) 6:116, in which he expresses support for Charles Stuart Parnell.

need hyphens in their names, because only part of them has come over," he continued, "but when the whole man has come over, heart and thought and all, the hyphen drops of its own weight out of his name." The president called on all Americans to "assist in enabling America to live her separate and independent life, retaining our ancient affections, indeed, but determining everything that we do by the interests that exist on this side of the sea."[3]

Wilson continued to extol the effectiveness of the American melting pot. In an address to the Daughters of the American Revolution on 19 April 1915, Wilson told the members of that notoriously nativist organization that the United States was "reborn" and "renewed out of all the sources of human energy in the world." He declared, "There is here a great melting pot in which we must compound a precious metal," making a pun by saying that he meant both "the metal of nationality" and "the *mettle* of this nation."[4] Wilson believed that assimilation was the key to national unity, which strict neutrality required.

To assuage the fears of average Americans, he portrayed the "hyphenates" as a minor faction, comparable in their disloyalty to the most outspoken Allied supporters. Addressing the Daughters of the American Revolution again on 11 October 1915 in a speech titled "Be Not Afraid of Our Foreign-Born Citizens," Wilson cautioned the patriotic women: "There is too general an impression, I fear, that very large numbers of our fellow-citizens, born in other lands, have not entertained with sufficient intensity and affection the American ideal." He reassured them that there were only a few disloyal immigrants, who were more vocal than influential. Wilson went on to remind these women who were proud of their forefathers that "[s]ome of the best stuff of America has come out of foreign lands, and some of the best stuff in America is in the men who are naturalized citizens." He declared that "the vast majority of them came here because they believed in

---

[3] Woodrow Wilson, Address at unveiling of Commodore John Barry statue, Washington DC, 16 May 1914, in Woodrow Wilson, *The New Democracy: Presidential Messages, Addresses, and Other Papers, 1913–1917*, ed. Ray Stannard Baker and William E. Dodd, 2 vols. (New York: Harper & Brothers, 1926) 1:109; and Wilson, *Papers*, 30:35–36.

[4] Woodrow Wilson, Welcoming Address to the Daughters of the American Revolution, 19 April 1915, in Wilson, *New Democracy*, 1:299; and Wilson, *Papers*, 33:15.

America; and their belief in America has made them better citizens than some people who were born in America."[5]

Despite such assurances, the Wilson Administration also helped to create the impression that many Irish and German Americans were actively engaged in espionage and sabotage for the German government. US Treasury agents stole papers from German propagandist Dr. Heinrich Albert in 1915 that gave evidence of some German conspiracies. Treasury Secretary William G. McAdoo, Wilson's son-in-law, leaked the papers to loyal administration supporter Frank Cobb, who published them in his *New York World* four days before the August 1915 sinking of the *Arabic*.[6] While Wilson did not deliberately cultivate the growing paranoia, he did not prevent his government officials from so doing.

In a stump speech on preparedness in 1916, Wilson recognized that the immigrants' "intimate sympathies are with some of the places now most affected by this titanic struggle," and naturally "their affections are stirred, old memories awakened and old passions rekindled." He insisted, however, that "the majority of them are steadfast Americans, nevertheless." He noted that by contrast, many native Americans had been disloyal in seeking to draw the United States into the war on the Allied side, and he concluded that all disloyal favoritism must be put down.[7] This emphasis on loyalty and neutrality became the principal theme of his 1916 reelection campaign.

As in his first presidential campaign, Woodrow Wilson equated his struggle to bring unity to warring ethnic groups with Abraham Lincoln's struggle to unite to the warring states. On Memorial Day in 1916, President Wilson issued a proclamation that made Flag Day an official, nationwide celebration, seeking to use this obvious patriotic symbol to combat the "influences which have seemed to threaten to divide us in interest and sympathy." He called on all Americans to join together in pledging allegiance to the flag. "Let us on that day rededicate ourselves to the Nation, 'one and inseparable,' from which every thought that is not worthy of our fathers' first vows of independence, liberty, and right shall be excluded, and in which we shall stand with united hearts, for an America which no man

---

[5] Woodrow Wilson, "Be Not Afraid of Our Foreign Born Citizens," in Wilson, *New Democracy*, 1:379; and Wilson, *Papers*, 35:50.

[6] Frederick C. Luebke, *Bonds of Loyalty: German-Americans and World War I* (DeKalb IL: Northern Illinois University Press, 1974) 139.

[7] Woodrow Wilson, Stump speech on preparedness in Topeka KA, 2 February 1916, in Wilson, *New Democracy*, 2:83–84; and Wilson, *Papers*, 36:88.

can corrupt,... [and]no force divide against itself."[8] Here was an obvious reference to Jesus Christ's maxim that President Lincoln had quoted, "A house divided against itself cannot stand."[9] In his Flag Day address, Wilson explicitly compared the current test of unity to that of the Civil War and declared, "There is disloyalty active in the United States, and it must be absolutely crushed."[10] Unfortunately, in 1917 all dissent was indeed to be crushed under the weight of George Creel's Committee on Public Information and other wartime measures.

Wilson believed that many recent immigrants failed to understand what their new homeland required of them. He therefore endorsed the "Americanization" efforts begun by Frances Kellor and others to teach immigrants the English language and American political ideals. He told the Conference on Americanization in July 1916 that immigrants must be taught that idealism was not only allowed in the United States, it was mandatory. "Loyalty means that you ought to be ready to sacrifice every interest that you have, and your life itself, if your country calls upon you to do so. And that is the sort of loyalty which ought to be inculcated into these newcomers." He wanted naturalized citizens to realize "that, having once entered into this sacred relationship, they are bound to be loyal whether they are pleased or not; and that loyalty which is merely self-pleasing is only self-indulgence and selfishness."[11]

Many Irish Americans had come to believe by 1916 that Wilson was an anti-Catholic Anglophile, despite the reassurances offered by Joseph Tumulty, the president's Irish Catholic secretary (who today would be called chief of staff). They were first angered by Wilson's decision in 1914 to ask Congress to eliminate the exemption for United States ships from the Panama Canal tolls at the insistence of the British. Not only did this successful effort violate a Democratic platform promise in 1912, it seemed

---

[8] Woodrow Wilson, Flag Day Proclamation, 30 May 1916, in Wilson, *New Democracy*, 2:189–90; and Wilson, *Papers*, 37:122–23.

[9] Mark 3:25.

[10] Woodrow Wilson, Flag Day Address, 14 June 1916, in Wilson, *New Democracy*, 2:209; and Wilson, *Papers*, 37:223. Note the shift already to a more hostile, uncompromising stance on dissent. As Wilson became more and more convinced of the rightness of the Allied cause, he allowed himself to be pulled further and further towards the extremist position of Roosevelt and other "preparedness" advocates.

[11] Woodrow Wilson, "Loyalty Means Self-Sacrifice," address to Conference on Americanization, Washington DC, 13 July 1916, in Wilson, *New Democracy*, 2:249, 251; also in Wilson, *Papers*, 37:417.

to be a capitulation to meddling British imperialism. It was Wilson's handling of the 1916 Easter Rebellion in Ireland, however, which most enraged Irish Americans. Secret Service agents raided the German Consul-General's New York City office in April 1916 and the government passed along information to the British which allowed the Royal Navy to intercept a German munitions shipment to the Irish rebels. Then, despite a Congressional resolution and Tumulty's pleading, Wilson refused to lodge an official protest over the execution of Sir Roger Casement and other leading Irish rebels. His attacks on "hyphenates" and his support for the anti-Catholic General Venustiano Carranza in Mexico only confirmed the impression that the president was a bigot.[12]

Despite his desire for Irish independence, Tumulty claimed to share the president's anger at Irish Americans who wanted the United States to support Germany in forcing Great Britain to give Ireland her freedom. When Irish agitator Jeremiah O'Leary wrote to Wilson in 1916, threatening him with the loss of the Irish vote, Wilson replied angrily in a published letter, "I would feel deeply mortified to have you or anybody like you vote for me. Since you have access to many disloyal Americans and I have not, I will ask you to convey this message to them."[13] Although he thus repudiated the hyphenate vote in 1916, Wilson was not ready—as was Roosevelt—to silence all disloyal opposition completely. That would come one year later, however, with the United States' entry into the war.

Irish and German-American support for Republican candidate Charles Evans Hughes was tenuous because of fears that he would appoint Theodore Roosevelt, a staunch supporter of the Allies, as Secretary of State. Nevertheless, their support became an issue in the 1916 campaign, as Wilson and the Democrats attacked the Republicans for courting the "disloyal vote." Borrowing the same strategy used against Wilson in 1912, the Democrats linked Hughes to the jingoistic Roosevelt among German Americans while portraying Hughes as a pawn of the Kaiser to other Americans. On 23 October 1916 the Democratic National Committee published the minutes of

---

[12] Cuddy, *Irish-America*, 33–34, 107–122; John Morton Blum, *Joe Tumulty and the Wilson Era* (Boston: Houghton Mifflin Co., 1951) 107-08. and Charles C. Tansill, *America and the Fight for Irish Freedom* (New York: The Devin-Adair Co., 1957) 193–94, 198.

[13] Joseph Tumulty, *Woodrow Wilson as I Knew Him* (Garden City NY: Doubleday, Page & Co., 1921) 214. See also ibid., 4, 188–91, 208–09; and Henry C. F. Bell, *Woodrow Wilson and the People* (Garden City NY: Doubleday, Doran & Co., 1945) 156–57, 166–67, 202, 206.

the executive committee of the American Independence Union, a German and Irish-American group funded in part by the German government. The minutes revealed that Hughes had secretly met with the group in an attempt to win its support.[14] This strategy was dangerous because it alienated many Irish Americans who traditionally voted Democratic, as did Wilson's public denunciation of Jeremiah O'Leary.

Wilson, for the most part, remained above such unseemly partisanship. Asked to comment on the "hyphenate issue" at a 29 September 1916 press conference, Wilson put the onus on the hyphenates themselves for continually bringing up the issue. It would have disappeared, he stated, except "the damn fools that insist upon discussing the thing won't let it die, themselves." He denied the existence of a German-American conspiracy, however, pointing out that subscriptions to the *Milwaukee Journal* were up twenty percent despite that paper's editorializing against German intrigue and quoting Edmund Burke on the impossibility of indicting a whole people. "The great body of them are just as thoroughly American as we are, more thoroughly than some people born in the United States, because they chose to come here," he explained, pointing out that immigrants made "a definite choice of sovereignty that none of us who were born in this country has made."[15]

The differences between Theodore Roosevelt and Woodrow Wilson on the issues of wartime loyalty and "hyphenism" could easily be characterized as "that fantastic imaginary gulf that always has existed between Tweedledum and Tweedle-dee."[16] Despite the Rough Rider's martial hyperbole, his comments on these subjects did not differ greatly from Wilson's. Roosevelt simply arrived at his pro-Allies position much sooner than Wilson. Both paid tribute to the patriotism of the overwhelming majority of immigrants, while vociferously denouncing the disloyal few, particularly those of German and Irish origin.

Roosevelt's semi-retirement from politics after the 1912 campaign freed him to risk the displeasure of German-American voters. "Thank Heaven, I no longer have to consider the effect of my actions upon any

---

[14] Thomas J. Kerr, IV, "German-Americans and Neutrality in the 1916 Election," *Mid- America* 43:2 (April 1961): 101, 103; Arthur S. Link, *Woodrow Wilson and the Progressive Era* (New York: Harper & Row, 1954) 245–46; and Luebke, *Bonds of Loyalty*, 57–98.

[15] Wilson, *Papers*, 50:750–52.

[16] William Allen White, *Woodrow Wilson* (Boston: Little, Brown, 1924) 264.

party," he wrote with relief to Henry Cabot Lodge in 1915, "and accordingly I have temperately but with the strongest possible emphasis attacked the German-American propaganda."[17] Roosevelt did take great pains to emphasize to German Americans and others that his quarrel was only with "professional German-Americans"—that is, the disloyal few who championed a pro-German foreign policy. To Edmund Robert Otto von Mach he wrote, "On the whole, I think that I admire Germany more than any other nation," adding "that of all the elements that have come here during the past century the Germans have on the average represented the highest type." He insisted that in condemning Germany's invasion of Belgium he was "in no shape or way influenced by prejudice."[18]

Roosevelt also publicly repudiated the efforts of the English-Speaking Union and other Anglo-American groups who called on the United States to aid Great Britain in the war out of filial duty. He could not condone any appeal that accented rather than submerged ethnic cleavages in the country—after all, his credo was America First, not Britain First. In a letter printed in his October 1915 article in the *Metropolitan* and then again in his book, *Fear God and Take Your Own Part,* Roosevelt explained that he was opposed to all "hyphenates," including English Americans: "I do not believe in German-Americans or Irish-Americans, and I believe just as little in English-Americans." He offered himself as a product of the melting pot to model Americanism for the country, declaring, "England is not my motherland any more than Germany is my fatherland. My motherland and fatherland and my own land are all three of them the United States." Even in colonial times not all Americans had been English, he pointed out, and in the century and a quarter since the Revolution the number of immigrants from Germany and other countries exceeded the number from England. It was, therefore, absurd to pretend that most Americans were Anglo Americans. "We have a right to ask all of these immigrants and the sons of these immigrants that they become Americans and nothing else," he said, "but we

[17] Theodore Roosevelt to Henry Cabot Lodge, 18 February 1915, in Theodore Roosevelt, *The Letters of Theodore Roosevelt*, ed. Elting Morison and John Morton Blum, 8 vols. (Cambridge: Harvard University Press, 1951–1954) 8:892. See also Theodore Roosevelt to Rudyard Kipling, 4 November 1914, ibid., 830.

[18] Theodore Roosevelt to Edmund Robert Otto von Mach, 7 November 1914, in ibid., 834; see also Theodore Roosevelt to Bernhard Dernberg, 4 December 1914, ibid., 860.

have no right to ask that they become transplanted or second-rate Englishmen."[19]

Despite these caveats, Roosevelt's criticism of German Americans was harsh enough to embarrass the Republican party in 1916 which tried surreptitiously to woo German-American voters unhappy with the Wilson Administration's obvious partiality toward the Allies. In his letter to the Progressive National Committee on 22 June 1916, declining that party's nomination and endorsing instead Republican nominee Charles Evans Hughes, Roosevelt proclaimed that Hughes would "not merely stand for a programme of clean-cut straightout Americanism before election, but will resolutely and in good faith put it through if elected." Roosevelt explained that the German-American Alliance had only supported Hughes because they opposed his own nomination, and he took care to note that most German Americans were "precisely as good Americans as those of any other ancestry." He reassured the Progressives that "assuredly if I support a candidate it may be accepted as proof that I am certain that the candidate is incapable of being influenced by the evil intrigues of these hyphenated Americans."[20]

Hughes endorsed Roosevelt's vision of Americanism through preparedness. In his acceptance speech at Carnegie Hall, Hughes called for the Republican Party to be "the organ of the effective expression of dominant Americanism," which he defined as "a country loved by its citizens with a patriotic fervor permitting no division in their allegiance and no rivals in their affection—I mean America first and America efficient." Speaking of the need to defend American neutral rights in the war, he declared, "The greater the danger of divisive influences, the greater is the necessity for the unifying force of a just, strong and patriotic position. We countenance no covert policies, no intrigues, no secret schemes. We are unreservedly, devoutly, whole-heartedly, for the United States."[21] But Hughes, the son of a Welsh immigrant and a member of the National Liberal

---

[19] Theodore Roosevelt to Mrs. Ralph Sanger, 22 December 1914, in ibid., 867–68; and Theodore Roosevelt, *The Works of Theodore Roosevelt, National Edition*, 20 vols. (New York: Charles Scribner's Sons, 1926) 18:281–83.

[20] Theodore Roosevelt to Progressive National Committee, in Roosevelt, *Letters*, 8:1071–072; and Roosevelt, *Works*, 17:419–21.

[21] Charles Evans Hughes, advance copy of acceptance speech, Carnegie Hall, New York City, 31 July 1916, Warren G. Harding Papers, Series 5, Box 837 (reel 238), Ohio Historical Society, Columbus OH.

Immigration League and the Inter-Racial Council, was not as ardent a believer in "one-hundred percent Americanism" as Roosevelt.

Hughes and the Republican National Committee had to ask Roosevelt repeatedly to tone down his attacks on hyphenism. Roosevelt wrote to Hughes on 11 August 1916, promising to avoid using the phrases "hyphen" or "hyphenated American," admitting that "my method of stating the case seems to have lent itself to misunderstanding."[22] But the Republicans continued to use Roosevelt as a campaign speaker, in part because his hyperbolic patriotism offset Wilson's attempts to portray Hughes as the candidate of "disloyal hyphenates."

Wilson narrowly defeated Hughes in 1916, and California provided the crucial margin of victory. The Democratic president carried eighteen more counties in the golden state than he had in 1912, and Wilson's support for the anti-alien land law probably played as much a role in the election's outcome as had Hughes' infamous unintentional snub of Hiram Johnson. There does not appear to have been a mass defection of Irish-American voters to the Republican party, largely due to Tumulty's successful work among his fellow Irish Catholics. Hughes carried most of the immigrant-rich northeastern states, but he lost the key state of Ohio.[23] The Democrats successfully used the slogan, "He Kept Us Out of War" to set the tone for Wilson's reelection. Just one month after Wilson's second inauguration, however, Germany's resumption of unrestricted submarine warfare prompted the president to ask Congress to declare war on Germany.

Theodore Roosevelt believed that the war as an opportunity to heat up the melting pot and make it work more quickly. Remembering fondly his own experiences with the socially and ethnically diverse Rough Riders during the Spanish-American War, Roosevelt extolled army camps as "huge factories for turning out first-class American citizens," and urged the adoption of universal military service in peace as well as war. The military, at least in its ideal form, was the kind of America Roosevelt envisioned: heroic, disciplined, and egalitarian. "All are serving on a precise equality of privilege and of duty and are judged each only on his merits. The sons of the

---

[22] Theodore Roosevelt to Charles Evans Hughes, 11 August 1916, in Roosevelt, *Letters*, 8:1099. See also Theodore Roosevelt to William R. Willcox, 21 August 1916, ibid., 1101; and Theodore Roosevelt to Alvin T. Hert, 26 October 1916, ibid., 1121.

[23] Cuddy, *Irish-America*, 22–28; and Edgar Eugene Robinson, *The Presidential Vote, 1896–1932* (Palo Alto: Stanford University Press, 1934) 17–19.

foreign-born learn that they are exactly as good Americans as anyone else, and when they return to their homes their families will learn it, too."[24]

The Rough Rider refused to accept the results of the army intelligence tests or admit any differentiation in the fighting skills of the various ethnic groups. When his longtime friend Madison Grant, a notorious racist and nativist, passed along a correspondent's assessment that New Englanders and Southerners made the best soldiers because they were pure-blooded Anglo-Saxons, Roosevelt vehemently disagreed. He pointed out first that New England had a high rate of immigration, and therefore, could not be considered racially pure. Secondly, and more importantly, the First and Second Divisions of the American Expeditionary Force "exactly represent the melting-pot idea, about which he ignorantly prattles slander."[25]

Roosevelt showed no mercy to those with divided allegiance, comparing them to Lot's wife as "pillar-of-salt citizens" who destroyed themselves by looking back to their former homelands.[26] He singled out the German-American Alliance and supported the movement in Congress to revoke its charter. He also supported laws to ban the teaching of the German language in schools and called for the phasing out of the foreign-language press. While he acknowledged that most of the foreign-language press was loyal, and that some English-language newspapers were not, he reasoned that "treason in English is at least open, whereas in a foreign language it is hidden."[27]

Despite these attacks on "hyphenism," Roosevelt also reminded the American people that most German Americans were loyal and patriotic, even going so far as to identify himself publicly as a German American (apparently on the tenuous basis of his Dutch ancestry). He declared it "an outrage to discriminate against a good American in civil life because he is of German blood," and "an even worse outrage for the Government to permit such discrimination against him in the army or in any of the organizations

---

[24] Theodore Roosevelt, "Factories of Good Citizenship," *Kansas City Star*, 10 October 1917, in Theodore Roosevelt, *Roosevelt in the Kansas City Star: Wartime Editorials by Theodore Roosevelt* (Boston: Houghton Mifflin, 1921) 13–15.

[25] Theodore Roosevelt to Madison Grant, 30 December 1918, in Roosevelt, *Letters,* 8:1419.

[26] Theodore Roosevelt, "Pillar-of-Salt Citizenship," *Kansas City Star*, 12 October 1917, in Roosevelt, *Wartime Editorials,* 16.

[27] Theodore Roosevelt, "The Fruits of Fifty-Fifty Loyalty," *Kansas City Star*, 2 March 1918, in ibid., 110.

working under government supervision."[28] He pointed out that the anti-German hysteria was "profoundly anti-American in its effects, for it not only cruelly wounds brave and upright and loyal Americans, but tends to drive them back into segregation, away from the mass of American citizenship."[29] Roosevelt did not comprehend, however, that his own vitriolic language played a part in inciting the anti-German hysteria.

Roosevelt literally continued to champion Americanization until his death, and undoubtedly he would have made it the centerpiece of his 1920 presidential campaign to a far greater degree than did Warren Harding. In his last public message, which was read posthumously to the All-American Benefit Concert in New York on 5 January 1919, the former president declared: "There must be no sagging back in the fight for Americanism merely because the war is over." He insisted that fully assimilated immigrants must "be treated on an exact equality with everyone else, for it is an outrage to discriminate against any such man because of creed, or birthplace, or origin." But he warned immigrants that divided allegiance was unacceptable. He called on all Americans to embrace one flag, one language, and one loyalty for the melting pot to do its work successfully, "for we intend to see that the crucible turns our people out as Americans, of American nationality, and not as dwellers in a polyglot boardinghouse."[30]

The closer the United States came to entering the war, the closer Wilson's position came to Roosevelt's. In his second Inaugural Address in 1917, Wilson called for airtight unity in the face of the impending war. Speaking of the conflict raging in Europe, he admitted: "We are a composite and cosmopolitan people. We are of the blood of all the nations that are at war." Nevertheless, he asserted that most Americans, while emotionally moved, had remained neutral in thought and deed as he had requested, and "in that consciousness, despite many divisions, we have drawn closer together." He told the American people that "an America united in feeling, in purpose, and in its vision of duty, of opportunity, of service" was even

---

[28] Theodore Roosevelt, "To My Fellow Americans of German Blood," *Kansas City Star*, 16 April 1918, in ibid., 135–38 (quotation, 137). See also, "The Worst Enemies of Certain Loyal Americans," 10 March 1918, in ibid., 113–15; "An American Fourth of July," 23 June 1918, in ibid., 166–67; and "Every Man Has a Right to One Country," 15 July 1918, in ibid., 177–80.

[29] Theodore Roosevelt, "A Square Deal for All Americans," *Kansas City Star*, 27 April 1918, in ibid., 142–43.

[30] Theodore Roosevelt to Richard M. Hurd, 3 January 1919, in Roosevelt, *Letters*, 8:1422.

more important in war than it had been in peace. He warned them to "beware that no faction or disloyal intrigue break the harmony or embarrass the spirit of our people" and make sure "that our government be kept pure and incorrupt in all its parts."[31]

A month later, Wilson tried to praise loyal German Americans while condemning disloyalty in his war message to Congress. In asking Congress to declare war on Germany, he stated that "We have no quarrel with the German people. We have no feeling towards them but one of sympathy and friendship." He explained that such sympathy and friendship should also be extended to the German Americans in their midst. "They are, most of them, as true and loyal Americans as if they had never known any other fealty or allegiance. They will be prompt to stand with us in rebuking and restraining the few who may be of a different mind and purpose." He warned, "If there should be disloyalty, it will be dealt with with a firm hand of stern repression," but he reassured Congress and the American people that "if it lifts its head at all, it will lift it only here and there and without countenance except from a lawless and malignant few."[32] Wilson thus used both the carrot of praise and the stick of repression to win German-American support of the war against their erstwhile fatherland. Likewise, Wilson took advantage of Flag Day to condemn the work of German spies and propaganda in the United States, but he carefully blamed the war atrocities on the German army and government, rather than the German people.[33]

The difficulty for Wilson—as well as for Roosevelt—was that both underestimated the anti-German hysteria sweeping the land, in large part because both got caught up in it themselves. St. Louis Congressman Leonidas Dyer wrote to ask for help from the White House in combating the "slanderous attacks" on German Americans in July 1917. Wilson replied that he had repeatedly expressed his "confidence in the entire integrity and loyalty of the great body of our fellow-citizens of German blood," and he claimed that he was unwilling to express it again because it would indicate doubt as to whether the country had believed him to be sincere. He suggested instead that Dyer republish some of his earlier speeches "to offset

---

[31] Woodrow Wilson, "The Second Inaugural Address," 5 March 1917, in Wilson, *Papers*, 41:333, 335.

[32] Woodrow Wilson, "An Address to a Joint Session of Congress," 2 April 1917, in ibid., 41:523, 526.

[33] Woodrow Wilson, "A Flag Day Address," 14 June 1917, in ibid., 42:498–504.

the evil influences that are at work."[34] But his reluctance to repeat his earlier, more balanced remarks seems to show a willingness to believe many of the paranoid rumors swirling around the country.[35]

The Wilson Administration also did much to encourage the hysteria directed at Irish and German Americans. Although Irish nationalists like Jeremiah O'Leary and Daniel Cohalan supported the national war effort once open hostilities were engaged, their publications were banned from the mail by Postmaster General Albert Burleson. After O'Leary suspended operations of his American Truth Society for the duration of the conflict, he was arrested for violating the Espionage Act on the basis of rumors spread by the British. He languished in jail until March 1919, when a jury acquitted him of the charges.[36] Pacifist German Mennonites and Amish were subjected to severe persecution by their neighbors, who could not understand their unwillingness to buy Liberty Bonds, let alone serve in the US Army or Navy. The government also persecuted them. Secretary of War Newton D. Baker convinced the Mennonites to register for the draft, reassuring them that they would not be forced to violate their consciences by serving in military camps until President Wilson issued orders clarifying their duties as conscientious objectors. But the secretary subsequently issued orders to camp commanders to intimidate and harass them in a bid to persuade members of the pacifist religious communities to drop their status as conscientious objectors. Many such targets of the secretary's orders were subject to violence and abuse. A large number of Mennonites ultimately fled to Canada to avoid the draft.[37]

The Committee on Public Information, despite George Creel's best efforts to be fair to immigrants, often crossed the line with its anti-"hun" and anti-"hyphen" propaganda. One poster, showing a map of America with all of the major cities and landmarks renamed after a purported German

---

[34] Leonidas Dyer to Woodrow Wilson, 30 July 1917; and Wilson to Dyer, 1 August 1917, in ibid., 43:323–24, 336. Wilson's reply was printed in several newspapers, e.g., *New York Times*, 4 August 1917.

[35] For example, see Woodrow Wilson to William G. McAdoo, 16 January 1918, in ibid., 46:3–4, in which he informs the Treasury Secretary that he has received a letter warning of a plot by German and Irish-Americans to blow up all American and British shipping on 22 January of that year. This warning was also given to Attorney General Thomas W. Gregory.

[36] Cuddy, *Irish-America*, 134–51; Tansill, *Fight for Irish Freedom*, 269–70.

[37] Luebke, *Bonds of Loyalty*, 257–59, 274, 279, 289, 309, 315.

conquest, labeled New York City "Hyphenburg."[38] The Four Minute Men, volunteer public speakers who delivered short messages written for them by the Committee staff, were instructed to avoid adopting a patronizing attitude toward the foreign-born, and to balance appeals to them with appeals to the native-born. They were also instructed to emphasize that "America must come first in your heart."[39] The Committee's record on foreign languages was also mixed. The Division of Work with the Foreign Born made heavy use of the foreign-language press, and Creel defended this practice against those who wanted to ban the use of foreign languages (particularly German) altogether.[40] But the National School Service Bulletin—using the slogan, "One language and that the best!"—emphasized the need to Americanize immigrants and their children by teaching them the English language.[41]

Wilson himself privately condemned laws banning the teaching of the German language and other attempts to obliterate German culture, telling his Cabinet that they were "silly." He refused to answer letters on the subject, however, telling Tumulty that he did not wish to be drawn into such controversies. He sent vague, noncommittal replies to Otto Kahn of the Metropolitan Opera Company and Leopold Stokowski of the Philadelphia Orchestra when they asked about the propriety of playing German music.[42] Wilson felt overwhelmed by his responsibilities as Commander in Chief, and he doubtless thought that he had no time to fight against such misguided patriotism. Nevertheless, his silence only encouraged the zealots.

Wilson's greatest failure to use his presidential authority to curb wartime hysteria came with the circumstances surrounding the 5 April 1918 lynching of German immigrant Robert Prager in Collinsville, Illinois. Prager

---

[38] Stephen Vaughn, *Holding Fast the Inner Lines: Democracy, Nationalism, and the Committee on Public Information* (Chapel Hill: University of North Carolina Press, 1980) 89.

[39] Ibid., 124.

[40] Ibid., 200–01; Committee on Public Information, *The Creel Report: Complete Report of the Chairman of the Committee on Public Information, 1917:1918:1919*, reprint ed. (New York: Da Capo Press, 1972) 78–103; and George Creel to Wilson, 6 August 1918, in Wilson, *Papers,* 49:200–01. For Wilson's support of the foreign-language press, see Josephus Daniels' diary entry, 6 April 1917, in ibid., 41:556; and Woodrow Wilson to Thomas W. Gregory, 19 October 1917, in ibid., 44:405.

[41] Vaughn, *Holding Fast,* 105–06.

[42] Josephus Daniels' diary entry, 28 May 1918, in Wilson, *Papers,* 48:192; Woodrow Wilson to Joseph Tumulty, 12 October 1917, in ibid., 44:364–65; Wilson to Tumulty, 10 April 1918, in ibid., 47:311; Otto Kahn to Wilson, 6 April 1917 and Wilson to Tumulty, 6 April 1917, in ibid., 42:7–9; and Wilson to Tumulty, 27 August 1918, in ibid., 49:360.

recently had begun work in area coal mines and had applied to join the local miners union. For reasons not clear, although certainly related to the anti-German immigrant hysteria, he was suspected by many of being a spy. Although Prager repeatedly professed his loyalty to the United States and willingly kissed the flag, a mob was incited to murder him by Joseph Riegel, an alcoholic ex-soldier. Republican Illinois Governor Frank Lowden was outraged and promised a thorough investigation. Collinsville Mayor John Siegel, who had done little to stop the lynch mob, tried to divert attention by writing to US Senator Lee Overman of the Judiciary Committee, blaming the act of lawlessness on congressional failure to pass a more stringent sedition law.

At Wilson's 6 April cabinet meeting the consensus was to follow the mayor's lead and blame Congress, reasoning that tougher sedition laws would make the American people feel more secure and hence make them less likely to murder their fellow citizens. Attorney General Thomas Gregory urged Wilson to issue a statement calming the nation and publicly condemning mob violence, but the president failed to do so until 26 July. His 12 April letter to Otto Butz of the Chicago chapter of the Society of Friends of German Democracy—a Committee on Public Information group—was widely printed in the newspapers, but it did not specifically condemn the Collinsville atrocity.[43] By contrast, on 11 April William Howard Taft wrote an editorial in the *Philadelphia Public Ledger* denouncing Prager's murder. Taft urged the passage of stronger Sedition and Espionage Acts, but he also insisted, "Mob violence is disgraceful to American civilization. Lynching is dreadful and there is no justification for it."[44] Doubtless political considerations played a role in restraining Wilson, as neither superpatriots nor Southern Democrats would have appreciated an attack on lynching.

The president expressed confidence in the loyalty of the foreign-born in a public message to the various ethnic societies in recognition of their Indipendence Day celebrations in 1918, coordinated by the Committee on Public Information. "Nothing in this war has been more gratifying than the

---

[43] Luebke, *Bonds of Loyalty*, 3–26; and Woodrow Wilson to Otto H. Butz, 12 April 1918, in Wilson, *Papers,* 47:324. Wilson wrote to Butz, "It distresses me beyond measure that suspicion should attach to those who do not deserve it and that acts of injustice and even of violence should be based upon the suspicion," but he did not mention Prager or the Collinsville incident specifically.

[44] William Howard Taft, *Collected Editorials, 1917–1921*, ed. James F. Vivian (New York: Praeger, 1990) 49–51.

manner in which our foreign-born fellow citizens and the sons and daughters of the foreign-born, have risen to this greatest of all national emergencies," Wilson declared. He praised them for demonstrating their loyalty by their willingness to sacrifice their lives for the nation: "Before such devotion as you have shown, all distinctions of race vanish, and we feel ourselves citizens in a republic of free spirits." Like Lincoln at Gettysburg, he urged all Americans, foreign and native-born, to rededicate themselves and the nation to unity. "As July 4, 1776 was the dawn of democracy for this nation, let us on July 4, 1918, celebrate the birth of a new and greater spirit of democracy," he said, by which freedom "shall be fulfilled for all mankind."[45]

Wilson also continued to champion America's place as an asylum for political and religious refugees, despite the stronger provisions for deporting radicals contained in the Burnett Bill that had become law over his veto in 1917. In his 1918 Independence Day speech at Mount Vernon, Wilson explained to representatives of thirty-three ethnic groups that the Founding Fathers "were consciously planning that men of every class should be free and America a place to which men out of every nation might resort who wished to share with them the rights and privileges of free men."[46] His continued belief that America was the asylum of the world was only made possible by his abiding faith in the melting pot's power to assimilate and homogenize newcomers from Europe. Refugees from Asia, however, were still not welcome. Furthermore, such occasional uses of the bully pulpit failed to offset the drastic curtailment of civil liberties the president countenanced during the war.

Despite Wilson's affirmation of the United States as an asylum, his administration began to expel unwanted refugees. The war changed the primary function of the Immigration Bureau from screening immigrants to detaining and deporting "undesirable" aliens. Even before the United States entered the war, the rate of immigration declined dramatically as a result of the difficulty of wartime travel. The Bureau held those awaiting deportation because it was not safe to send them back to Europe. Ellis Island

---

[45] Wilson, "To Various Ethnic Societies," (printed in the C.P.I.'s *Official Bulletin*) 23 May 1918, in Wilson, *Papers,* 48:117. Wilson also told British diplomat Sir Cecil Arthur Spring Rice that as the war continued, he had become reassured of the nation's unity and loyalty. See Spring Rice to Arthur Balfour, 4 January 1918, ibid., 45:455.

[46] Wilson, "An Address at Mount Vernon," 4 July 1918, in ibid., 48:515; Committee on Public Information, *Creel Report*, 83–84.

Commissioner Frederick C. Howe had always disliked deportation hearings that did not follow the normal judicial standards of due process, and he acted to parole many women who clearly were not professional prostitutes. After the United States declared war in April 1917, Wilson used the 1798 Alien Enemy Act to hold thousands of German aliens at Ellis Island during the first few months of the war until new internment camps were ready in Hot Springs, North Carolina, and other places. Most of the buildings at the immigration station were then taken over by the Army and Navy.[47]

Secretary of State Robert Lansing and Secretary of Labor William B. Wilson issued a joint order on 26 July 1917 that required all aliens to have a passport viséed by a United States consular office in order to enter the country. On 22 May 1918 Congress passed a law formalizing this requirement.[48] The State Department resisted assuming the responsibility of determining whether or not prospective immigrants would meet all the legal requirements, so for the time being the Bureau of Immigration continued to inspect immigrants at the ports of arrival. In 1924, however, the National Origins Act mandated overseas inspection by the consular officers. The entire process of selecting and rejecting immigrants was thereby removed from the watchful eyes of the courts and the press.

At the same time that the Wilson Administration was making entry to the United States more difficult from Europe, it was simplifying the process from Mexico. On 12 June 1918 the Secretary of Labor suspended the literacy test, head tax, and contract labor law to admit 73,000 Mexican laborers. This *braceros* program was designed to meet the wartime labor shortage. It was officially ended on 2 March 1921.[49] Nevertheless, the program presaged the immigration policies of the 1920s, which all but shut the "front door" to Europe while leaving the "back door" wide open to Mexico and Canada.

---

[47] Thomas M. Pitkin, *Keepers of the Gate: A History of Ellis Island* (New York: New York University Press, 1975) 117, 119–20.

[48] Patricia Russell Evans, "'Likely to Become a Public Charge:' Immigration in the Backwaters of Administrative Law, 1882–1933" (Ph.D. diss., George Washington University, 1987) 165; Darrell Hevenor Smith and H. Guy Herring, *The Bureau of Immigration: Its History, Activities and Organization* (Baltimore: Johns Hopkins University Press, 1924) 31; and Peter H. Wang, *Legislating Normalcy: The Immigration Act of 1924* (San Francisco: R. & E. Research Associates, 1975) 3.

[49] Smith and Herring, *Bureau of Immigration*, 32 n. 60. As of 1 July 1921, 35,000 workers had returned to Mexico, 400 had died, 500 had become US citizens, 21,000 had disappeared, and 15,000 were still employed in the US.

While the federal government curtailed European immigration, it also took steps to encourage the assimilation of those Europeans already in the United States. Both the Labor Department's Bureau of Naturalization and the Interior Department's Bureau of Education conducted "Americanization" programs during the war to inculcate immigrants with patriotic devotion. Wilson supported the proposed Smith-Bankhead Americanization Bill to provide federal matching funds to the states through the Bureau of Education for teacher salaries and training programs to eliminate illiteracy and teach the English language. Interior Secretary Franklin K. Lane had endorsed the bill, warning the president that the current immigrants were "not fit melting-pot metal and if they were ready to be, we, the native-born, have generally forgotten our duty as fire-tenders."[50] Congress did not pass the bill, but Wilson continued to tout education as the most powerful tool for assimilation. His brother-in-law, Stockton Axson, delivered the president's message to teachers' groups across the country in 1918: "It is now more than ever a duty to teach a burning, uncompromising patriotism which will admit of no divided allegiance but demands all that the heat and energy of the citizen can give."[51] There was plenty of patriotism both in and out of schools in 1918, and Wilson, while deploring its excesses, appealed to it in the belief that he was thereby assisting the melting pot process.

Whatever renewed optimism Wilson felt about American unity during the war was severely shaken by the intense pressures brought to bear on him as he sought to negotiate the peace settlement after the war. In addition to dealing with David Lloyd George, Georges Clemenceau, Vittorio Orlando and other European leaders, Wilson faced constant, often conflicting demands from various American ethnic groups intent on securing "self-determination" for their compatriots in Europe. In the case of the various peoples subject to the Austro-Hungarian Empire, the Wilson administration had deliberately built up their hopes as part of a duplicitous scheme to pressure the Habsburgs into making a separate peace. Southeastern European immigrants had begun to lobby for independence for their

---

[50] Franklin K. Lane to Woodrow Wilson, 26 February 1919, in Wilson, *Papers,* 55:284–88; and Wilson to William Bankhead, 27 February 1919, ibid., 302. The money would have been allocated proportionally, based on the number of illiterate or non-English-literate people in each state—an arrangement which would have benefitted Hoke Smith's Georgia and William Bankhead's Alabama. Lane, however, emphasized the immigrant angle in his memo to Wilson.

[51] Theodore Wilson, "A Message to Teachers," 28 June 1918, in ibid., 48:455–56. The message was drafted by Axson and revised and approved by Wilson.

respective nationalities even before Wilson sought to use them, and they expected him to fulfill his promises. The creation of Czechoslovakia, Yugoslavia, and Poland did much to meet those demands, although the Italians felt betrayed by Wilson's unwillingness to abide by the secret Treaty of London provisions giving Italy Dalmatia, which became instead part of Yugoslavia.[52]

German Americans, beaten into submission during the war, maintained a sullen silence for the most part during the postwar period. Their only overt reaction against the Wilson war-years administration was to vote overwhelmingly for Warren G. Harding and the Republican party in the 1920 election.[53] Some undaunted German Americans organized the Steuben Society, which provided evidence of loyal German-American service in all wars from the Revolution to World War I, while protesting the Treaty of Versailles and the "League of Damnations."[54]

Any unfavorable comments the German Americans made about the peace process, however, were met with swift and severe criticism. Charles Nagel, Taft's Secretary of Commerce and Labor, had proclaimed during the war, "There is no room for the hyphen." When he dared to publish an article in *The Nation* criticizing the Treaty of Versailles for failing to implement Wilson's Fourteen Points, George Creel and other pro-administration figures attacked him as a hyphenate who was part of a disloyal German propaganda campaign.[55]

Other groups, in particular the Irish and the Jews, were highly organized and vocal in their attempts to secure independent homelands. Jewish efforts met with much greater favor from Wilson, in large part due to Wilson's friendship with Zionist leader Louis Brandeis. Wilson supported

---

[52] John B. Duff, "The Italians," in Joseph P. O'Grady, ed., *The Immigrants' Influence on Wilson's Peace Policies* (Lexington: University of Kentucky Press, 1967) 111–39; George Barany, "The Magyars," in ibid., 140–72; George J. Prpic, "The South Slavs," in ibid., 173–203; Otakar Odlozilik, "The Czechs," in ibid., 204–223; Victor S. Mamatey, "The Slovaks and Carpatho-Ruthenians," in ibid., 224–49; Arthur J. May, "The Mid-European Union," in ibid., 250–71; and Louis L. Gerson, "The Poles," in ibid., 272–86.

[53] Luebke, *Bonds of Loyalty*, 323–27; and Austin J. App, "The Germans," in O'Grady, *Immigrants' Influence*, 30–55.

[54] Cuddy, *Irish-America*, 188; Carl Wittke, *German-Americans and the World War (with Special Emphasis on Ohio's German-Language Press)* (Columbus: Ohio Archaeological and Historical Society, 1936) 200–206; and Thomas A. Bailey, *Woodrow Wilson and the Great Betrayal* (New York: Macmillan Co., 1945) 23.

[55] App, "The Germans," in O'Grady, *Immigrants' Influence*, 44–46.

the Balfour Declaration, despite the opposition of Secretary of State Robert Lansing.[56] Edith Benham, Edith Wilson's private secretary, recorded in her diary that Wilson was "much interested" in Zionism. "He doesn't expect all Jews will want to return naturally, but it would give them as a race the same nationality they have lacked for centuries," she wrote.[57] He also publicly condemned antisemitism at home and abroad, and may have secretly tried to get Henry Ford to end his antisemitic campaign in the *Dearborn Independent*.[58] William Howard Taft likewise supported Zionism and attacked anti-semitism in his editorials.[59]

Irish-American attempts to secure independence for Ireland, despite his earlier support for their cause, drove Wilson into a fury. Earlier, in April 1917, the president had made discreet suggestions to the British government encouraging home rule for Ireland. He and Lansing resisted British attempts to highlight the link between Sinn Fein and Germany.[60] The Committee on Public Information may also have secretly channeled funds to Irish nationalist Thomas Power O'Connor.[61] Despite the importance of the Irish-American vote to the Democratic party, Wilson was unwilling to do more than engage in these sorts of behind-the-scenes maneuvers. For example,

---

[56] Morton Tenzer, "The Jews," in O'Grady, *Immigrants' Influence*, 287–317; Robert Lansing to Woodrow Wilson, 13 December 1917, in Wilson, *Papers,* 45:286, n. 1; Wilson to Stephen S. Wise, 31 August 1918, in ibid., 49:403; and "President Gives Hope to Zionists," *New York Times*, 3 March 1919, in ibid., 55:386.

[57] Edith Benham's diary entry, 2 February 1919, in Wilson, *Papers,* 54:432–33.

[58] Stephen S. Wise to Woodrow Wilson, 9 September 1920, in ibid., 66:108–110, n. 1; and Isaac Landman to Wilson, 20 September 1920, in ibid., 77:130–31, n. 1. According to the editors, there is some evidence to suggest that Wilson sent Edward N. Hurley on such a mission, although it was unsuccessful. The entire Henry Ford file in the Wilson Papers has been destroyed, so verification is impossible.

[59] Taft, *Collected Editorials*, 140–41, 202–03.

[60] Woodrow Wilson to Robert Lansing, 10 April 1917, in Wilson, *Papers,* 42:24–25; Wilson to Joseph Tumulty, 5 May 1917, and Tumulty to John D. Crimmins, 5 May 1917 (published in *New York World*, 12 May 1917, as part of news report on Wilson's meeting with Arthur Balfour), in ibid., 42:223, n. 1; Robert Lansing to Wilson, 19 May 1918, in ibid., 48:63–66; Josephus Daniels' diary entry, 28 May 1918, in ibid., 48:192; William Wiseman to Eric Drummond, 30 May 1918, in ibid., 48:206; and Cuddy, *Irish-America*, 151–57.

[61] Newton D. Baker to Woodrow Wilson, 21 June 1920, in Wilson, *Papers,* 65:442–43. Baker wrote that Josephus Daniels did not think it wise to allow George Creel to give a full accounting of C.P.I. expenditures to Congress because "certain disbursements," including those to O'Connor, would be subject to unfavorable comment. If such payments were made, they were omitted from Creel's official accounting.

Senator James Phelan of California led a committee to present Wilson with a small bronze replica of a statue of Irish rebel Robert Emmet. Phelan hailed the president as a spokesman for all oppressed peoples, including the Irish, in their quest for independence. Wilson, however, refused to take the bait. He had high words of praise for Emmet, but he stated that "it would not be in good taste" for him to comment on current Irish efforts to throw off British rule.[62]

By August 1918 Wilson's displeasure with the constant pressure from Irish Americans was evident. Colonel Edward M. House recorded in his diary that the president declared privately "that he did not intend to appoint another Irishman to anything; that they were untrustworthy and uncertain," although he made an exception for Tumulty.[63] The end of the war and the start of the Paris Peace Conference only intensified Irish-American pressure and concomitantly, Wilson's ire. On 4 March 1919, after a speech at the Metropolitan Opera House in New York and just before he returned to Paris, Wilson met with Governor Alfred Smith and the delegates of the Irish Race Convention, but only after they eliminated Daniel Cohalan from the group. The delegates wanted Wilson to promise to work for the creation of an independent Irish republic in Paris. The president declined, calling it "a domestic affair for Great Britain and Ireland to settle themselves, and not a matter for outside interference." When Bishop Peter J. Muldoon of Illinois compared the Irish to the Slavic peoples granted independence at Versailles, Wilson snapped back, "These nations, Bishop, fell into our lap!"[64] Discussing the meeting the next night aboard ship with Dr. Cary Grayson, Wilson said that "the Irish as a race are very hard to deal with owing to their inconsiderateness, their unreasonable demands and their jealousies," and he

---

[62] Woodrow Wilson, "An Address and Reply," 10 January 1918, in ibid., 45:559–61. Phelan had been an early supporter of Wilson's nomination in 1912, so no doubt he felt that a political debt was due.

[63] Edward M. House, diary entry, 16 August 1918, in ibid., 49:275. House commented that "he does the Irish an injustice," although he thought it "curious" that Wilson regarded Tumulty as an exception.

[64] Cary T. Grayson, diary entry, 4 March 1919, in ibid., 55:411–12; "Wilson Won't Meet Cohalan With Irish," New York Times, 5 March 1919, in ibid., 55:421–22; Ray S. Baker, diary entry, 8 March 1919, in ibid., 55:463; Cuddy, Irish-America, 174–77; and Tansill, Fight for Irish Freedom, 302. Wilson told Baker that he refused to see Cohalan "in language so plain & loud that it could be heard by the Tammany policemen who stood about," and that the delegates were so insistent in making their case that he "had hard work keeping [his] temper."

feared that Irish and German Americans would work to defeat the Democratic party in 1920.[65]

Of course, from the Irish-American point of view, Wilson was being inconsiderate and unreasonable to the most loyal Democrats in the land. They resented being shunted aside while newer immigrants saw their nationalist aspirations fulfilled. They understood that there was a difference between liberating peoples subject to the defeated Central Powers and the subjects of Allied nations, but they pointed out that the principle of "self-determination" should apply equally to all people. John Devoy, editor and publisher of the New York *Gaelic-American*, cogently declared that the "one fatal defect" in Wilson's Fourteen Points was that they applied "only to a portion of the world—that controlled by Germany and her allies—and utterly ignore the rest."[66] Party leaders urged Wilson to advocate publicly the Irish cause and put as much pressure as possible on the British government. Senators Peter Gerry, David Walsh, Key Pittman, John Kendrick and Thomas Walsh warned him that failure to do so would not only jeopardize the Democratic party, but also seriously diminish the chances for Senate ratification of the peace treaty.[67] Wilson, however, refused to be stampeded.

The president's sympathy for the British increased as he tried to unite his own divided party and country. At lunch with Lloyd George in Paris, Wilson explained to the British prime minister how Abraham Lincoln had not approved of social equality between the races even though he opposed slavery. Lloyd George, perhaps seeing a parallel, then congratulated Wilson on his handling of the "impossible" Irish. Wilson quipped that if it were up to him, he would grant home rule but reserve the movie rights, implying that the Irish would be no more capable of self-government than he imagined

---

[65] Cary T. Grayson, diary entry, 5 March 1919, in Wilson, *Papers,* 55:443. Wilson's fears were no doubt prompted by the publication of Lodge's "Round Robin" a few days before, signaling Republican opposition to the League.

[66] Joseph P. O'Grady, "The Irish," in O'Grady, *Immigrants' Influence,* 58; and Cuddy, *Irish-America,* 134–36, 151–57, 190–212. In a gubernatorial campaign speech in New Brunswick NJ on 26 October 1910, Wilson had linked the Irish struggle for home rule with the struggle for human rights around the world, as well as the struggle for accountable government in the United States. But Wilson was often blind to the gulf between the idealism of his rhetoric and the realism of his actions. Wilson, *Papers,* 21:439.

[67] Peter Gerry, David Walsh, Key Pittman, John Kendrick and Thomas Walsh to Woodrow Wilson, 28 March 1919, in Wilson, *Papers,* 56:397–98.

Southern Blacks had been during Reconstruction. Wilson's wrath was notorious for turning into personal hatred, and in the case of the Irish it seems to have stirred up racial and religious prejudices which the president had long kept buried.[68]

Irish-American lobbyists followed Wilson to Paris. The Irish Race Convention appointed as commissioners to plead their cause in France with anyone who would listen: Francis P. Walsh, joint chairman of the War Labor Board and a member of the executive committee of the League to Enforce Peace; former Chicago mayor and Illinois governor Edward F. Dunne; and Michael J. Ryan, the former city solicitor for Philadelphia and president of the United Irish League.[69] Frank L. Polk, a State Department official working to prevent the House of Representatives from considering the Gallagher Resolution supporting Irish independence, asked if he should deny passports to these commissioners. Wilson told him only to deny one to Cohalan.[70] Wilson met with Walsh in Paris on 17 April 1919, at least partially at the urging of George Creel, but again the president made no promises. Secretary Lansing drafted a cumbersome and bureaucratic reply to the commissioners' plea that the US government request safe passage for Eamon De Valera and other representatives of the newly declared Irish republic. Wilson rejected Lansing's draft and substituted a much harsher letter blaming the IrishAmericans' inflammatory rhetoric for creating a situation in which Britain refused to grant safe passage.[71]

Not only did Wilson's latent prejudice surface in 1919, but he also expressed his willingness to arouse the hatred of his fellow Protestants. He told journalist Ray Stannard Baker that he would unleash anti-Catholic bigotry if the Irish-Americans did not relent: "I have one weapon which I can use against them—one terrible weapon, which I shall not use unless I am driven to it ... I have only to warn our people of the attempt of the Roman

---

[68] Cary T. Grayson, diary entry, 31 March 1919, in ibid., 56:438. On Wilson's youthful anti- Catholic prejudice, see his three "Anti-Sham" letters to the editor of the *North Carolina Presbyterian*, 25 January, 15 February, and 22 March 1882, in ibid., 2:97–102, 113–16.

[69] Cuddy, *Irish-America,* 171, n3; and Tansill, *Fight for Irish Freedom*, 313, n3, 4.

[70] Frank L. Polk to Woodrow Wilson, 1 March 1919, and Gilbert F. Close to Polk, 3 March 1919, in Wilson, *Papers,* 55:406–07.

[71] George Creel to Woodrow Wilson, 31 March 1919, in ibid., 56:486; Cary T. Grayson, diary entry, 17 April 1919, in ibid., 57:426–27; and Wilson to Robert Lansing, 22 May 1919, in ibid., 59:394.

Catholic hierarchy to dominate our public opinion, and there is no doubt about what America will do."[72]

The Irish issue unavoidably entered partisan politics, with the Republicans gleefully seizing the opportunity to drive a wedge between the Democrats and one of their core constituencies. Henry Cabot Lodge, despite the fact that he personally despised them, cultivated Irish-American discontent as a means, not only of winning votes in Massachusetts, but also rallying support for his opposition to the Versailles Treaty and the League of Nations. Republican Senator William Borah forged a coalition of Irish, German, and Italian Americans dissatisfied with the treaty.[73] He offered a resolution requesting the United States Peace Commission to secure safe conduct from Ireland to Paris for De Valera and the other Irish delegates. It passed the Senate 60 to 1 on 6 June 1919, with only John Sharp Williams opposed. Republican Albert Fall of New Mexico warned that the League would inevitably summon American soldiers to help put down an Irish rebellion. Democrat James Phelan of California argued that Article 10 only applied to external attacks on member states, but Republican Medill McCormick of Illinois countered that Wilson himself had declared that the League would use armed might to protect the rights of minorities. One way or the other, he concluded, the League would be dragged into the conflict.[74]

Denied safe passage to France, Eamon De Valera came instead to the United States to rally Irish-American support. Tumulty warned his boss that this could be the rock on which the treaty would founder. He urged the president to give public support to Irish independence, but to no avail.[75] The Irish Catholic secretary was able to avoid becoming a target of the Scots-Irish president's wrath, always framing his arguments in terms of Wilson's political goals and avoiding anything that smacked of dictating to the strong-willed man. Although he pushed Wilson as hard as anyone on behalf of the Irish cause, Tumulty's loyalty to the president and the nation was never in question.

---

[72] Ray S. Baker, diary entry, 31 May 1919, in ibid., 59:646.

[73] Cuddy, *Irish-America*, 181–85.

[74] *Congressional Record*, 66th Cong., 1st sess., 1919, 58:729; O'Grady, *Immigrants' Influence*, 74–78. Wilson had told Ray Stannard Baker in Paris that contrary to Irish claims, Article 10 safeguarded the right of revolution, by guaranteeing the integrity of member states only against external attack. Ray S. Baker, diary entry, 29 May 1919, in Wilson, *Papers,* 59:604.

[75] Joseph Tumulty to Woodrow Wilson, 25 June 1919, in Wilson, *Papers,* 61:182–83.

As Wilson began his fateful cross-country speaking tour to appeal to the American people for ratification of the Treaty of Versailles and acceptance of the League of Nations, he met with opposition from Irish Americans. Daniel Cohalan and the Friends of Irish Freedom raised over one million dollars to distribute pamphlets and publish rebuttals to Wilson's pro-League speeches.[76] Such actions only stoked the fire of Wilson's fury and convinced him that the disloyal wartime propaganda of hyphenated Americans had once again reared its ugly head. In an all-out effort to save his League and treaty, Wilson gradually lost all restraint as he lashed out with increasingly venomous rhetoric against his enemies.[77]

To the crowd in St. Paul, Minnesota, he pleaded for unity based on American ideals, which he claimed were embodied in the League of Nations. He acknowledged, in the heavily German and Scandinavian-populated Midwest, that "a great many millions of our people carry in their hearts the traditions of other peoples, the traditions of races never bred in America." But, he asserted, the melting pot had made them "all unmistakably and even in appearance American, and nothing else." Indeed, it was the very multiethnic character of America, coupled with its democratic ideals, that made it God's chosen instrument to lead this new world era of peace. Because Americans came "from every civilized stock in the world," Wilson reasoned they were ready by sympathy ... to understand the peoples of the world" and thus become "the predestined mediators of mankind."

Wilson followed this celebration of America's multiethnic heritage with a caution: "There are a great many hyphens left in America." More explicitly, he warned of a renewed German menace that threatened the League. "That intrigue which we universally condemn—that hyphen which looked to us like a snake, the hyphen between 'German' and 'American'—has reared its head again. And you hear the 'his-s-s' of its purpose," he declared. The sinister plan, Wilson explained, was "to keep America out of the concert of nations, in order that America and Germany, being out of that concert, may some time, in their mistaken dream, unite to

---

[76] Tansill, *Fight for Irish Freedom*, 332; O'Grady, *Immigrants' Influence*, 78.

[77] Taft also blamed hyphenates for the defeat of the Treaty, writing in the 21 November 1919 *Philadelphia Public Ledger*, "The Irish and pro-Germans in their hostility thronged the meetings of the 'Bitter-End' senators and gave an impression of strong popular opposition to the pact." Taft, *Collected Editorials,* 311.

dominate the world."[78] He did not explicitly link the Irish and German Americans together, but he hardly needed to do so, as they were already indelibly intertwined in the public mind.

He hinted at the Irish connection more strongly in Cheyenne, Wyoming: "It is the pro-German forces, *and the other forces that showed their hyphen during the war*, that are now organized against this treaty. And we can please nobody in America except these people by rejecting it or qualifying it in our acceptance of it." As he had in the 1916 electoral campaign, Wilson tried to link the Republicans to "disloyal" German and Irish Americans. He also appealed to nativists by reassuring them that the League could never "say that our immigration laws were too rigorous and wrong; that our laws of naturalization were too strict and severe," because "the Covenant expressly excludes interference with domestic questions."[79]

In Pueblo, Colorado, just before he fell ill and collapsed, Wilson warned again that the "organized propaganda" against the treaty and the League of Nations came from exactly the same source as the anti-war propaganda. He portrayed these hyphenated Americans in sinister tones, using the stereotype of the violent, knife-wielding immigrant. He declared that "any man who carries a hyphen about with him carries a dagger that he is ready to plunge into the vitals of this republic whenever he gets the chance," and such a man was "an enemy of the republic." He told the crowds it was only "certain bodies of sympathy with foreign nations that are organized against this great document, which the American representatives have brought back from Paris."[80]

How far Wilson would have pursued this strategy—whether he would have made good his threatened use of anti-Catholic prejudice to silence the Irish Americans—cannot be known; his collapse and subsequent stroke

---

[78] Wilson, "An Address in St. Paul Auditorium," 9 September 1919, in Wilson, *Papers,* 63:139–143. Wilson was able to assert that all Americans were alike in appearance because he saw only those with European backgrounds as being truly Americans, explaining, "We come from all the great Caucasian races of the world." Wilson repeated the argument that only America, as a result of the melting pot, could lead the world into peace in his luncheon addresses in Portland and San Francisco, in ibid., 280, 282, 313.

[79] Woodrow Wilson, "An Address in the Princess Theater in Cheyenne," 24 September 1919, in ibid., 469–70, 475–76 (emphasis mine).

[80] Woodrow Wilson, "An Address in the City Auditorium in Pueblo, Colorado," 25 September 1919, in ibid., 500–501. See also his Denver speech on the same date, in ibid., 493, where he declared, "Hyphen is the knife that is being stuck into this document."

ended the national tour, and the losing battle for the League would henceforth be fought by proxy. When Wilson insisted that the 1920 presidential election be made a "solemn referendum" on the treaty and the League, he ensured Irish and German-American hostility to the Democratic ticket of Governor James Cox of Ohio and Franklin D. Roosevelt of New York. Despite the silence of the Republican platform on the "Irish question" and Senator Warren G. Harding's insistence (echoing Wilson) that it was a domestic British problem, Irish Americans joined German Americans in supporting the Republican candidate. Harding won Boston by a large majority and carried all five boroughs of New York handily.[81]

Wilson succeeded in branding the vocally anti-treaty and anti-League of Nations Irish and German Americans as dangerously disloyal. In this respect he unwittingly gave great assistance to those pushing for further immigration restriction. By marginalizing the two largest immigrant populations, Wilson paved the way for the 1924 National Origins Act that would set drastic quotas on all immigration except that from Great Britain. The Irish and German Americans bitterly protested this law as a continuation of wartime prejudice but their arguments were dismissed as more treasonous propaganda, like that which had threatened the war effort and defeated the peace treaty.

World War I had all but halted immigration from Europe. The numbers of Southern and Eastern European immigrants, who made up the overwhelming majority of the prewar influx, declined steadily from 127,545 in 1917 to 27,991 in 1918 and 17,628 in 1919. When the armistice was signed in November 1918, government officials predicted a massive new influx of immigrants from ravaged Europe as soon as wartime travel restrictions were lifted. Efforts to halt all immigration began almost as soon as the war ended. Alabama Congressman John L. Burnett introduced a bill to suspend all immigration for four years in January 1919, and Mississippi Senator Patrick Harrison proposed a five-year suspension in May. Montana Senator Henry Lee Myers introduced legislation to ban immigration from the former Central Powers for fifty years, and from all other countries for twenty-five years.[82] None of these bills passed, but Myers' two-tier proposal clearly shows the influence of lingering wartime animosities on postwar restrictive legislation.

---

[81] Cuddy, *Irish-America*, 224, 231–32.
[82] Wang, *Legislating Normalcy*, 4, 6, 14-15.

Woodrow Wilson certainly did not favor the renewed restrictions on all immigration. But he was too embittered to defend the concepts of the melting pot and asylum with lofty rhetoric, and he remained deeply suspicious of disloyal hyphenates. When Commerce and Labor Secretary William B. Wilson brought up Albert Johnson's bill suspending all immigration for one year, President Wilson replied that he wished he had an x-ray to determine where each immigrant's heart lay so that he could send back those who were not Americans.[83] Many were indeed sent back by Caminetti and Wilson's new Attorney General, A. Mitchell Palmer, during the Red Scare.

A. Mitchell Palmer grew up in rural Monroe County, Pennsylvania, where less than four percent of the population was foreign-born in 1900. He had a lifelong distrust of the newer immigrants. In his commencement address when graduating from Swarthmore College, he defended the mob which had lynched eleven Italian Americans in New Orleans in 1891. In 1912, Palmer had chaired the Pennsylvania delegation to the Democratic national convention, and he had remained loyal to Wilson despite offers to become Champ Clark's running mate or a dark-horse candidate in his own right. Palmer had hoped to be named Attorney General, but was instead offered the post of Secretary of War, which he declined due to his own (or his wife's) Quaker convictions. In 1915 the New York *World* had accused him of using his influence on behalf of German agents, and while he denied it at the time, he was very anxious afterwards to prove his loyalty. Palmer was overzealous and hostile toward foreigners as Alien Property Custodian, taking advantage of the war to try to "Americanize" all German-owned businesses. Wilson had to order him to cease his efforts to sell the Busch brewery, whose owner was an American citizen.[84]

Wilson's decision to appoint Palmer in Thomas Gregory's stead on 5 March 1919 reveals much about the president's frame of mind, given Palmer's record as Alien Property Custodian. Tumulty, a personal friend of Palmer, suggested him for Attorney General and often pleaded the Pennsylvanian's case to the stricken president. In addition to Tumulty, Secretary of State Robert Lansing and Postmaster General Albert Burleson

---

[83] Josephus Daniels, diary entry, 28 December 1920, in Wilson, *Papers,* 67:9.

[84] Stanley Coben, *A. Mitchell Palmer: Politician* (New York: Columbia University Press, 1963) 7, 55–63, 67–72, 118–22, 136–38, 149–50, 197. Palmer later admitted to Congress that he was involved in the scheme uncovered by the *World*, but he denied knowing that he had been working for German agents.

supported Palmer's aggressive tactics. Navy Secretary Josephus Daniels, Agricultural Secretary David Houston, Interior Secretary Franklin K. Lane and Labor Secretary William B. Wilson opposed Palmer, but only Wilson did so openly.[85]

Even before Palmer became the Attorney General, the Immigration Bureau began to more actively deport "disloyal" immigrants. In January 1918 Seattle Immigration Commissioner Henry C. White began to round up alien radicals, including members of the Industrial Workers of the World. Secretary Wilson, supported by then-Attorney General Gregory and the president, refused to sanction White's standard of guilt by association. Commissioner-General Caminetti sided with White, however, and wrote to Wilson in March 1918 that the antiradical provisions of the 1917 Burnett Act were "intended to reach the word as well as the deed, and in some respects, to reach the underlying thought as well."[86] To gain legal sanction for that viewpoint, the Justice Department and the Bureau of Immigration drafted and secured the passage of the Immigration Act of October 1918, broadening the definition of anarchism and removing the five-year time limit for deportations. White then sent thirty-six alien Wobblies on a "Red Special" train to New York for deportation in February 1919. Still, the Labor Secretary insisted on carefully reviewing each case, and as a result only twelve were deported. Wilson also promulgated "Rule 22" in March, allowing aliens to have legal counsel at deportation hearings for the first time.[87]

Woodrow Wilson's new Attorney General initially tried to continue Attorney-General Gregory's moderate ways. But Palmer was badly frightened when a suicide bomber dynamited his house on 2 June 1919, following attempted May Day mail bombings of Secretary Wilson, Commissioner-General Caminetti, and Ellis Island Commissioner Frederic C. Howe.[88] When Congress failed to pass the peacetime sedition law Palmer and the president had requested, the Attorney General decided to use

---

[85] Blum, *Joe Tumulty and the Wilson Era,* 187, 191, 197, 217–21; and Robert K. Murray, *Red Scare: A Study in National Hysteria, 1919– 1920* (Minneapolis: University of Minnesota Press, 1955) 192 n3, 203–205.

[86] William Preston, Jr., *Aliens and Dissenters: Federal Suppression of Radicals, 1903–1933* (Cambridge: Harvard University Press, 1963) 84, 163–72.

[87] Hutchinson, *Legislative History,* 168–69; Preston, *Aliens and Dissenters,* 182–83, 198–207. Only thirty-eight anarchists were excluded between 1903–1921, and only fourteen were deported between 1911–1919. Ibid., 33.

[88] Coben, *A. Mitchell Palmer,* 198–206; Murray, *Red Scare,* 71, 78–79, 192–93.

deportation to prevent what he believed to be an incipient Communist revolution. The Supreme Court had ruled several times that deportation hearings were administrative rather than judicial proceedings, so Immigration Bureau officials were not required to follow the usual standards of due process of law.[89] Caminetti cooperated with J. Edgar Hoover, head of the General Intelligence Division of the Federal Bureau of Investigation, in planning the notorious "Palmer Raids." On 30 December—in Secretary Wilson's absence—the acting-Secretary, department solicitor John W. Abercrombie, reversed the new "Rule 22." He and his supporters hoped that alien radicals, often arrested on the basis of little evidence, would thereby more easily incriminate themselves and be deported.[90]

On 2 January 1920 over four thousand alleged alien radicals were arrested in thirty-three cities in twenty-three states, many without warrants and with physical abuse. Using the language of the nativists and eugenicists, Palmer told the press that "their lopsided faces, sloping brows, and misshapen features" proved that these aliens were of "the unmistakable criminal type."[91] These alien "reds" were sent to Ellis Island, where Commissioner Howe, a former graduate student of President Wilson's, tried to treat them fairly and secure due process of law. Howe's conduct was investigated by the House Immigration Committee, vilified by Utah Senator William King, and faulted by liberal New York Congressmen Fiorello LaGuardia and Isaac Siegel. After a stormy meeting with Caminetti, Howe resigned in protest and burned all of his papers relating to Ellis Island. His assistant, Byron H. Uhl, became acting commissioner and cooperated with Caminetti and Palmer.[92]

When William B. Wilson returned on 26 January, he reversed Abercrombie's rule change and once more allowed aliens to be represented by lawyers. Illness, however, prevented him from devoting his attention to the Palmer Raids. Instead, Under Secretary Louis F. Post reviewed each case and dismissed 2,202 of them because of violations of due process, or because the people were "unconscious" members of the Communist party who had no idea of its doctrines. In the end, only five hundred fifty-six alien

---

[89] *Eiku v. United States*, 142 US 651, 660 (1892); *Bugajewitz v. Adams*, 228 US 585, 591 (1913); and Evans, "Likely to Become a Public Charge," 34, 125–27.

[90] Murray, *Red Scare*, 193–94, 211, 247; and Preston, *Aliens and Dissenters*, 208–22.

[91] Murray, *Red Scare*, 213–19.

[92] *Congressional Record*, 66th Cong., 1st sess., 1919, 58:1522–523; Pitkin, *Keepers of the Gate*, 121-28.

Communists were deported. Post's courageous decision was greeted with outrage by many observers. Kansas Congressman Homer Hoch introduced a resolution to impeach Post, but the latter defended himself so brilliantly before the House Rules Committee that Congress and the press were forced to cease their attacks.[93]

Woodrow Wilson allowed his Attorney General to violate the rights of radical aliens because he shared in the lingering post-war anti-immigrant hysteria. When Secretary Wilson and Attorney General Palmer argued about the raids at a cabinet meeting in April, the president simply made a joke of it, telling Palmer "not to let the country see red."[94] This was Wilson's first cabinet meeting since his stroke, so his ability to focus on the issue may be questioned. On the other hand, Wilson had endorsed Palmer's drastic Sedition Bill in his 1919 State of the Union message and in 1920 he signed two pieces of legislation introduced by Albert Johnson making it easier to deport aliens. The first allowed the deportation of enemy aliens who had been convicted of violating the Espionage and Sedition Acts. The second broadened the definition of "anarchist" to include all members of any organization promoting revolution, assaulting officers, destroying private property, or anyone who possessed literature from such groups. Both laws, however, left discretionary power in the hands of the Secretary of Labor who had already shown his unwillingness to use it.[95]

The continued postwar hysteria cast suspicion on all immigrants and paved the way for the general restriction of immigration. In December 1920, the House of Representatives passed Albert Johnson's bill suspending all immigration for fourteen months by a vote of 293 to 41. The Senate Immigration Committee substituted William Dillingham's bill, which set annual quotas for each nationality representing five percent of their numbers in the 1910 census. The Vermont Senator noted that the majority of the 592,436 immigrants allowed to enter each year in his plan would be from Northern and Western Europe. The Senate lowered the quotas to three percent of the 1910 census, and passed the bill 62 to 2 in February 1921,

---

[93] John Higham, *Strangers in the Land: Patterns in American Nativism, 1860—1925*, 2nd ed. (New Brunswick: Rutgers University Press, 1988) 222–33; Murray, *Red Scare*, 247–51; Preston, *Aliens and Dissenters*, 222–24, 226-29. Cf. Dominic Candeloro, "Louis F. Post and the Red Scare of 1920," *Prologue* 11 (Spring 1979): 41–55.

[94] Josephus Daniels, diary entry, 14 April 1920, in Wilson, *Papers,* 65:187.

[95] Ibid., 64:81, n. 5, 111; Hutchinson, *Legislative History*, 172–74; and Preston, *Aliens and Dissenters*, 226–29, 238–39.

with only James A. Reed of Missouri and Joseph France of Maryland opposed. The joint House and Senate conference committee subsequently approved the Senate version of the Emergency Quota bill, as it was called..[96]

William B. Wilson wrote a memorandum to the president outlining his objections to the bill, noting first of all that there was no emergency. The total number of aliens admitted during the first eight months of the current fiscal year was 547,000, which projected to 821,000 for the year, well below the 1,012,000 average per year between 1905–1914. He pointed out that the current law had not been in operation long enough to gauge its effectiveness, and that the provision for sending immigration inspectors overseas had not yet been attempted. The secretary thought overseas inspections "would be much more useful in restricting immigration on a selective basis than the plan proposed in this bill on a percentage basis." The alleged health emergency the bill's supporters cited could be met by the Public Health Service's quarantine and disinfection procedures. Furthermore, the president already had the power to halt all immigration due to health concerns under the 1893 immigration law.

Lastly, Secretary Wilson argued that the quota plan would be "extremely difficult, if not impossible" to administer. He concluded it would only exacerbate the "great tragedy... [that] grows out of the necessity of detaining aliens when they have arrived in port or sending them back to the countries from which they came." He also pointed out that leaving open the nation's "back door" to Canada, Mexico and Latin America would have the effect of transferring immigration from the current ports to the Canadian and Mexican borders, where the Immigration Bureau lacked the resources to examine immigrants adequately, and thus "would make our Canadian and Mexican Borders an easy means of access to the United States without running the chance of being disbarred on account of the allotments having been exhausted."[97]

Whether the president concurred with the analysis of his Secretary of Commerce and Labor is difficult to say. He chose to kill the bill by pocket veto, thus avoiding public comment or confrontation. Wilson failed to employ his usual lofty rhetoric defending the role of America as the asylum of the oppressed peoples of the world (or at least Europe), no doubt a

---

[96] Hutchinson, *Legislative History*, 174–76; and Wang, *Legislating Normalcy*, 16–19.

[97] William B. Wilson to Woodrow Wilson, 1 March 1921, in Wilson, *Papers,* 67:178–80. Secretary Wilson also noted that the provision exempting tourists on temporary business or pleasure trips could also easily be abused.

reflection of his anger at earlier Irish and German-American opposition to the Treaty of Versailles. The absence of an eloquent presidential defense favoring a more open immigration policy was ultimately irrelevant; the newly-elected Congress wasted little time in re-passing the legislation and President Wilson's successor did not hesitate to sign it into law.

Perhaps it was inevitable that Wilson's idealistic vision of a national melting pot creating both American unity and world peace would be destroyed by the war and the ensuing peace process. Having built up his own expectations—and those of the nation—to unreasonably high levels, Wilson set himself up for disaster. He also unwittingly paved the way for the racist quota restriction laws of the 1920s by demonizing the two largest American ethnic groups. As the Paris Peace Conference and the Senate battle played out, Wilson refused to admit his own folly. He instead lashed out at the immigrants whose hopes he had raised. German and Irish Americans may have briefly enjoyed the sweet revenge of defeating Wilson's League of Nations in the Senate and the Democrats at the polls in 1920. They soon discovered, however, that the Republican cure was far worse than the Democratic disease. Having been pushed to the margins and labeled disloyal hyphenates, German and Irish Americans had little room to maneuver against the rising tide of restriction.

CHAPTER 6

WARREN G. HARDING AND
AMERICANIZATION REVISED

The Republican administration of Warren G. Harding faced a tidal wave of restrictionist sentiment, fueled by memories of alleged disloyalty by immigrants during the World War I years. This sentiment also was sustained by fears that a new influx of cheap immigrant labor would reduce wages and intensify the overcrowding of slums. It would have taken an extraordinarily courageous politician to stand up to the vocal elements of public opinion demanding restriction, and Harding was not such a public servant. He had a keen sense of what it was possible to accomplish politically, and he did not travel beyond the limits his pragmatic political intuition set. As a United States senator, Harding had been largely passive when it came to initiating legislation—a fact that contributed to his attractiveness to fellow senators as the 1920 Republican presidential nominee. He was also the product of small-town, rural America: Blooming Grove and Marion, Ohio, were far removed from the polyglot industrial cities. He had a middle-class background and believed in the American Dream because he had realized it. He did not, however, see the "poor, huddled masses, yearning to breathe free" as participants, but as threats to that dream.

Warren Harding had not always viewed immigration so pessimistically. During his early political career in Ohio he gave scant attention to immigration matters, but by and large viewed the phenomenon as proof of the goodness of America's promises of freedom and prosperity. He also expressed confidence that the melting pot not only blended different nationalities, but different classes, ultimately making of America a classless society. Addressing the Canton and Massilon Boards of Trade in 1907, Harding told them of his return from a trip to Europe on a ship with immigrants. He said that the "motley" steerage passengers pouring out onto the main deck as the ship reached quarantine left him fearing that the class barrier between him and them was permanently fixed. But a fellow cabin traveler, who claimed to have arrived in the United States as a steerage passenger nine years before, reassured him that these new immigrants would soon realize the American dream. Harding's faith in the melting pot was renewed by the man's words and he declared to his Ohio audience: "With resources incalculable, with freedom unrestrained, with hopes unhampered, with rewards unlimited, we have attracted the human stream from all the countries of the earth...We have assimilated the adopted citizen and inspired the native born, and of them both we have made an exalted citizenship."[1] Harding's idealism held that in America, all class divisions were only temporary. Impoverished immigrants who worked hard and lived a morally upright life would succeed and be assimilated into American society. Today's steerage passengers would be tomorrow's first-class voyagers.

Of course, Harding was not always so sanguine about the effects of immigration, and his editorials in the Marion *Star* occasionally expressed that hostility toward outsiders common in small-town America. In 1885 he wished that a recent tornado had struck the Mormon settlements instead of a nearby Washington Courthouse. Following the 1886 Haymarket Riot, he denounced alien anarchists and John Peter Altgeld, the German-American Governor of Illinois, writing that immigration, having built the United States, "now threatened to ruin it."[2] But these negative outbursts were infrequent and seemed to express popular sentiment more than personal opinion.

As a loyal Republican moving up the party ranks, Harding had additional reason to laud the prosperity of the United States: it showed the wisdom of the party's economic policies. In a 1910 gubernatorial campaign speech, Harding used the record immigration of the period as proof of the success of the Republican party's policy of a protective tariff. "If protection and its alleged robbery is leading to oppression," he said, "let some knowing opponent tell us why the incoming trans-Atlantic liners are bringing one hundred thousand emigrants monthly from the low-tariff or free trade countries of the old world and landing them on our shores." He assured his audience that immigrants "keep pouring into this new-world haven of liberty

---

[1] Warren G.Harding, "Address to Canton and Massilon (Ohio) Boards of Trade," 1907, Warren G. Harding Papers, Series 5, Box 835 (reel 238), Ohio Historical Society, Columbus OH. Harding reused this story many times.

[2] Marion (Ohio) *Star*, 27 May 1886; and Francis Russell, *The Shadow of Blooming Grove: Warren G. Harding in His Times* (New York: McGraw-Hill, 1968) 70.

and hope, to find equal rights, the reward of industry and merit and opportunity to mount the plane of exalted American citizenship."[3] In his 1912 campaign speeches on behalf of President William Howard Taft, and as late as 1915, Harding sounded the same theme: the protective tariff kept the wages and standard of living of American workers much higher than that of their counterparts in Europe, and so Europeans flocked to the United States to take advantage of its benefits. Harding argued that return migration to the old world occurred in Democratic administrations, while immigration to America—with immigrants from Northern and Western Europe especially in mind—reached its peak during years of "Republican good fortune."[4]

Harding's optimism about immigration and assimilation weakened as he served in the United States Senate during World War I. The conflicting loyalties demonstrated by many Americans, torn between President Woodrow Wilson's insistence on neutrality and their continued emotional attachment to their old homeland, troubled Harding. After the usual humorous remarks at the Gridiron Club Dinner in February 1916, the senator from Ohio turned serious about what he called the "submergence" of Americanism: "It has seemed to me that the qualities of our Americanism are rapidly approaching the great test, and popular government and patriotism must weigh in the same balance." Harding, echoing Theodore Roosevelt, offered military preparedness as a solution for this lack of Americanism. Not only would military service instill patriotism, but also America could fulfill its God-given destiny to elevate the rest of the world to a higher plane of civilization.[5] Ultimately, his views on immigration and citizenship reflected the prevailing Republican party stances.

Harding's call for "One-Hundred Percent Americanism" became stronger in his April 1916 Hamilton Club speech in Chicago. He previously had regarded immigration as a positive bellwether of national prosperity. Now he saw it as a threat. He quoted Abraham Lincoln's stance on behalf of "a fair start and an unfettered chance in the race for life," and then suggested that cheap foreign labor threatened that equality of opportunity. Harding began to argue for "an unfettered chance of an American with an American

---

[3] Warren G. Harding, "Gubernatorial Campaign Speech (to Stamina League)," 1910, Harding Papers, Series 5, Box 836 (reel 238), Ohio Historical Society, Columbus OH..

[4] Warren G. Harding, "Taft Campaign Speech," 1912; and "Grant Birthday Dinner Address," Boston, 27 April 1915, ibid.

[5] Warren G. Harding, "Gridiron Dinner Address," Washington DC, 26 February 1916, ibid.

in the race for American achievement." Harding continued to support the neutrality of the United States in the war in Europe, and he asked that his fellow Americans "ignore the unavoidable and pardonable sympathies of the millions of our people whose derivation or ties of kinship make them partisans." But he argued that such old world connections must not stand in the way of a united American citizenry any longer. He thundered, "We must be a people with one great ideal, one all-encompassing aspiration, one guiding hope, one American interest, one people and one flag."[6]

By June of that year, Harding's budding nationalism reached full flower in his keynote address at the Chicago Republican National Convention. Speaking of the patriots who fought for American freedom at Bunker Hill, he argued that their dedication to the common cause of the Revolutionary War—despite their diverse backgrounds—had united them as American citizens. "They were not all Americans by birth," he explained, "but they were dedicated Americans in the baptismal rites of a new republic and a new patriotism." He described the patriot soldiers as men who "came from oppression and stood erect in the freedom of the republic." Fighting to protect their asylum created ties deeper between them than those of race, according to Harding. "There was lack of homogeneity of race," he admitted, "but there was kinship of soul, and that soul was American."

The Revolutionary War heated the melting pot, and caused it to forge a new nationality. As it was in the fateful days of the 1770s, so it could be—must be—in the twentieth century, Harding argued. He understood the immigrants' anguish over the conflict that was engulfing their homes of origin. "It is not surprising that in their hearts there is sympathy or partiality for the land of their nativity when it is involved in a life and death struggle like that which saturates Europe with the blood of their kinsmen," he said, echoing President Wilson. But he declared divided loyalties no longer pardonable. "This is the hour for the blazing soul of American allegiance," he proclaimed, "a plain, simple, glad and unalterable Americanism." This Americanism had less to do with teaching aliens the English language than recruiting them to fight and die for the United States. Military service was the best way for immigrants to prove their loyalty. Harding argued that the United States "must have a citizenship less concerned about what the

---

[6] Warren G. Harding, "Hamilton Club Address," Chicago IL, 8 April 1916, ibid., Box 837.

government can do for it and more anxious about what it can do for the nation."[7]

Harding could not be classified as a nativist. He was, however, more than willing to pander to nativist sentiment when it furthered his political career. In his 1916 US Senate campaign, he did not repudiate a nativist smear campaign against his Irish Catholic Democratic opponent, Timothy Hogan, featuring a graffiti slogan inviting voters to read a scurrilous nativist newspaper: "Read the *Menace* and get the dope, Go to the polls and beat the Pope."[8] On the other hand, he was careful to assuage the large foreign-born population in Ohio's cities, particularly the politically powerful German Americans. Addressing the Cincinnati Businessmen's Club at the end of March 1917, he expressed sympathy with German Americans who felt torn between the old world and the new, lauding the accomplishments of the German nation. Nevertheless, he suggested that entering the war in Europe might help to unify the nation. Harding denied he wanted war, "but if it comes and our American people are thereby reconsecrated and made one people, with undivided allegiance and distinctively and exclusively American ideals, there will be some fit compensation for the awful cost, and the republic will endure."[9]

Harding's own wife and father-in-law were of German heritage, and his lover, Carrie Phillips, threatened to expose their affair if he voted to declare war on Germany. Nevertheless, Harding endured the personal cost to vote in favor of war against Germany in April 1917. He was careful to praise the loyalty of Germans to their government, but he called on all Americans— including those of German birth—to show the same loyalty to the United States. He argued once again that the war would be an opportunity to forge a more unified citizenry, quoting a letter from a constituent that claimed there was no "distinctly American nationality." Harding replied: "If there is no one who is distinctly American, then, in the name of the Republic, it is time that we find [such a nationality]." Harding insisted that his decision in favor of war was not "in response to the alleged hysteria of a subsidized or

---

[7] Warren G. Harding, "Keynote Address, Republican National Convention," Chicago IL, 7 June 1916, ibid. Note that this last phrase bears remarkable similarity to one made famous by President John F. Kennedy.

[8] Andrew Sinclair, *The Available Man: The Life Behind the Masks of Warren Gamaliel Harding* (New York: Macmillan Co., 1965) 54–55.

[9] Warren G. Harding, "Address to the Cincinnati Business Men's Club," 31 March 1917, Harding Papers, Series 5, Box 837 (reel 238).

English-owned press," but rather "for the maintenance of just American rights."[10] Later, he supported an amendment to the Sedition Bill to permit foreign-language religious publications. He defended the German press of Ohio for printing "the finest utterances of American devotion and loyalty," although he looked forward to the day "when the making of a really American Republic demands that we have a one-language Republic."[11]

Like Wilson, Harding compared the perceived threat of immigrant disloyalty in the United States during World War I to the disunity resulting from the American Civil War. In the 1850s and 1860s, the United States had been split along sectional lines; now the division was along racial and ethnic lines. In his Memorial Day speech at Columbus in 1917, Senator Harding argued that just as the Civil War was fought to maintain the union, the current war was being fought to maintain American rights and "reconsecrate" American citizens. The war exposed the innate threat that any asylum posed: "It is the pitiable truth, under the banners of our boasted freedom, with open gates to the oppressed of the world, we were becoming the haven of a polyglot people instead of the treasured home of a patriotic people." Thus the nation faced "the test of making the preserved nation of 1865 the patriotic nation of 1917 and forever thereafter." Harding asked his fellow citizens to resolve that "Henceforth the man who dons the habiliaments [sic] of an American and dwells in American opportunity, must be an American in his heart and be committed to every American cause."[12] He never explained how one could tell what was in another person's heart.

The demands for "One-Hundred Percent Americanism" did not end with the armistice signed in November 1918. The postwar Red Scare again fueled suspicions of dangerously disloyal foreigners threatening the unity and stability of the United States. Harding returned to the Civil War analogy in his 11 September 1919 Senate speech, paraphrasing Abraham Lincoln's memorable phrase about a house divided: "No republic can endure half loyal and half disloyal; no citizenship is of permanent value whose heart is not in

---

[10] Warren G. Harding, "Address (before Senate) on Declaration of War with Germany," Washington DC, 4 April 1917, ibid.; *Congressional Record*, 65th Cong., 1st sess., 1917, 253–54; Russell, *Shadow of Blooming Grove*, 281, 283–84; and Sinclair, *Available Man*, 85–88.

[11] *Congressional Record*, 65th Cong., 2d sess., 1918, 4890; and Sinclair, *Available Man*, 88.

[12] Warren G. Harding, "Memorial Day Address," Columbus OH, 30 May 1917, Harding Papers, Series 5, Box 837 (reel 238).

America."[13] Speaking in 1920 in Portland, Maine, Harding even went so far as to put words in Lincoln's mouth concerning the current situation: "I can fancy him crying out that there are no privileges of American citizenship except for those who assume its duties, and there is no room anywhere in free America except for those who subscribe to orderly government under the law."[14] While he defended the practice of deporting aliens found guilty of treason, he also condemned as "terrorism" the overreaction against aliens in general by government officials.[15]

Harding argued that the root of the dilemma faced by the recent immigrants to the United States was their failure to put America first. Speaking about the need for postwar reorganization in 1918, Harding argued that the melting pot needed to work more effectively in order to create a stable new citizenry: "In the great crucible we shall burn the dross of indifference and disloyalty and reveal the pure gold of a proud and loyal American citizenship." Without such complete assimilation, the United States' place as an asylum to the world was too dangerous. Harding insisted that America must be "more than a temporary haven for the oppressed, who would bring oppression here; more than a convenient camp for the ungrateful and a conspiring spot for the hostile."[16]

Although he originally had hoped that the war would unite all Americans, Harding began to fear that such was not the case. Borrowing language from Lincoln's Gettysburg Address, he spoke frequently in 1919 about the need to "dedicate" and "reconsecrate" all Americans. This need applied especially to the foreign-born, as Harding described at length in his America Day speech that year: "The United States is 100 percent American today, and we mean to hold it so henceforth and forever." Like Roosevelt, Harding was careful to insist that Americanism was not limited to certain races or religions: "We demand no distinction by birth, no advantages of origin, but we do demand the obligations of loyal citizenship, and devotion to law and order." He did, however, accept the nativists' distinction between

---

[13] Warren G. Harding, "Safeguarding America," US Senate speech, 11 September 1919, ibid., Box 838 (reel 238); *Congressional Record*, 66th Cong., 1st sess., 1919, 8791–792; and Sinclair, *Available Man*, 97.

[14] Warren G. Harding, "Lincoln Club Address," Portland ME, 13 February 1920, Harding Papers, Series 5, Box 838 (reel 238).

[15] Warren G. Harding, "Platform Address," Omaha NE, 7 October 1920, ibid., Box 841 (reel 239).

[16] Warren G. Harding, "Speech on US Role in World War I, and on Post-War Problems," ca. 1918, ibid., Box 837 (reel 238).

the motives of the old and new immigrants, arguing that the Founding Fathers had encouraged immigration to develop the land without worrying about assimilating the immigrants "because the early comers soon became an interested and inseparable part of American life....Men came to embrace American liberty, not to abuse it, not to profit by it temporarily and then defile and denounce it." Harding was of the opinion that more recent immigrants to America had little desire to assimilate.

Unlike the Dillingham Commission, however, Harding did not cast all the blame on the new immigrants. Instead, he blamed the native-born for failing to educate the immigrants properly: "We left the ignorant and unfortunate to be schooled by the agitator and the enemy of orderly government when we ought to have been pointing out the unfailing way to advancement and achievement." Like Wilson, he emphasized the need to teach immigrants how to participate properly in political life, because "men born to class conditions of the old world cannot understand representative democracy until they are taught their part in the reign of intelligent and thoughtful public opinion." Furthermore, education in the public schools was crucial in the assimilation process and helped to create America's classless society. He said that no one who watched children walking to school in the morning could discern "from varied garb, or burdened walk, or discordant music in their laughter, which is the daughter of the humblest citizen, which is the pride of the worker's home, which is the pet of home, of captain of industry or commander of capital."[17]

Warren Harding consistently argued for the Americanization of immigrants but had little to say on the subject of immigration restriction. During the 1920 presidential campaign, he tried to avoid an outright endorsement of the Republican party's platform in this regard. The plank called for the elevation of the standard of citizenship by immigration restriction based on eugenics. "The selective tests that are at present applied," it stated, "should be improved by requiring a higher physical standard, a more complete exclusion of mental defectives and of criminals, and a more effective inspection applied as near the source of immigration as possible, as well as at the port of entry." It went on to call for distribution and registration of aliens and to endorse the existing methods of Asian

---

[17] Warren G. Harding, "America Day," ca. 1919, ibid., Box 838 (reel 238).

exclusion.[18] In his acceptance speech at Marion on 22 July, however, Harding said merely: "I believe in establishing standards for immigration, which are concerned with the future citizenship of the republic, not of mere manpower in industry." He reiterated the call for every immigrant to "become an American in heart and soul."[19] Listeners were left to figure out for themselves whether Harding's standards were the same as those of the party platform.

Harding followed Roosevelt's 1912 campaign strategy as his own presidential campaign developed. He stressed assimilation and Americanization rather than immigration restriction. He frequently told the story of the competing claims made by representatives of various ethnic groups on behalf of their former countries before the Senate Foreign Relations Committee when it held hearings on the Treaty of Versailles in 1919. Harding used the story to justify the United States' rejection of the League of Nations, arguing that it would drag the various foreign-born groups into endless contentions and hamper the salubrious work of the American melting pot. "It is folly to think of blending Greek and Bulgarian, Italian and Slovak, or making any of them rejoicingly American when the land of adoption sits in judgment on the land from which he [sic] came."[20] His call to put America first thus reinforced his anti-League stance.

The Republican candidate emphasized the positive aspects of immigration more than the negative. He told an audience in Oklahoma City that the immigrants who had helped to build America "blended themselves in our American life, and, for the most part, they became devoted American citizens." But while immigrants "drank of the waters of American political life," native Americans had occasionally forgotten to teach the foreign-born "the duties and obligations of citizenship which go with the privileges..." The solution to this problem was to Americanize the immigrants. "So from this time on, my countrymen," he declared, "I want an America that is 100

---

[18] Edward P. Hutchinson, *Legislative History of American Immigration Policy, 1798–1965* (Philadelphia: University of Pennsylvania Press, 1981) 633. By contrast, the Democratic platform only endorsed Asian exclusion.

[19] Warren G. Harding, "Acceptance Speech," Marion OH, 22 July 1920, Harding Papers, Series 5, Box 839 (reel 238).

[20] Warren G. Harding, "Address to Wayne County Delegation," Marion OH, 4 August 1920, ibid., Box 839 (reel 239). See also Warren G. Harding, "Speech at State Fair Grounds," Oklahoma City, 9 October 1920, ibid., Box 841 (reel 239).

per cent American."[21] While the phrase "one-hundred percent Americanism" carried the repressive overtones of the war years, Harding clearly downplayed the danger of a disloyal foreign-born population. This was in part because he wished to capitalize on German and Irish-American anger about Wilson's peace treaty in the 1920 election.[22]

Conversely, Harding wooed Californians—whose support for Wilson in 1916 had cost Charles Evans Hughes the election—with his firm support for Asian exclusion. On 31 August, when he addressed the Republican governors, he held a special conference with California Governor William D. Stephens concerning Japanese exclusion. Harding's attitude on this issue had changed over the years, no doubt in response to political pressures. In 1905, Harding had spoken favorably, if condescendingly, about the bravery of Japanese soldiers in the Russo-Japanese War. The original version of his Chautauqua speech on Alexander Hamilton, written in 1908, contained a passage condemning California for defying the federal government and risking a war with Japan over the exclusion issue, but he struck it out in later years.[23] Now, in September 1920, Harding listened to Governor Stephens defend "Oriental exclusion" as necessary to protect the White race, and then agreed in his own speech that "there is abundant evidence of the dangers which lurk in racial differences."

Although he carefully distinguished these differences from "racial inequalities," recognizing that "the civilization of the Orient is older than ours, that her peoples have their proud and honorable traditions," there was no doubt in Harding's mind that Asians could not be assimilated in the American way of life. They were, he was certain, too different from European immigrants to be accepted into American society, or to become Americans at heart. He spoke proudly of the nation's history as "a haven to the oppressed and the aspiring from all the nations of the earth."[24] Harding nevertheless argued that keeping out immigrants who could not be assimilated into society, or who resisted Americanization was not a violation of the tradition of asylum but a means of restoring "normalcy."

---

[21] Warren G. Harding, "Speech at State Fair Grounds," Oklahoma City, 9 October 1920, ibid.

[22] Warren G. Harding, "Campaign Speech," DesMoines IA, 7 October 1920, ibid.

[23] Warren G. Harding, "The Complete Counterpart, the American Soldier," n.d. [1905]; and "Alexander Hamilton," 1908 [pencilled notations at top: "original 1908, used again in 1913," and "1908, 1914, 1916."], ibid., Box 835 (reel 238).

[24] Warren G. Harding, "Address to California Delegation," Marion OH, 14 September 1920, ibid., Box 840 (reel 239).

Harding, like Woodrow Wilson, thus excluded Asians from the melting pot. He did not however, suggest that African Americans were also unassimilable, as Wilson had. In part this was because the Republican party sought the votes of the thousands of Blacks moving to Northern cities. But it also had to do with the fact that Harding had his own ancestry called into question during the campaign. William E. Chancellor, an Economics and Political Science professor at Wooster College, published broadsides repeating the old rumors of "Negro blood" in Harding's family. Harding's campaign staff sent out lily-white family trees to disprove the rumor. Campaign manager Harry Daugherty boasted, "No family in the state has a clearer or more honorable record than the Hardings, a blue-eyed stock from New England and Pennsylvania, the finest pioneer blood, Anglo-Saxon, German, Scotch-Irish, and Dutch."[25] In fact, Harding was descended from an English Puritan, Richard Harding, who settled in Braintree, Massachusetts in 1623. The legend of African American ancestry was attributed by Harding's great-great-grandfather, Amos Harding, to a vindictive neighbor whom he had caught stealing corn. Nevertheless, Warren Harding had endured the taunts all his life, even from his father-in-law, and he was never entirely certain that the rumor was false.[26]

The Republican slogan, "America First," could be interpreted in several ways. It summarized the party's isolationist opposition to the League of Nations and its support for immigration restriction. Harding also used it, however, to appeal to ethnic groups disgusted with the repression of the Wilson administration and eager to demonstrate their patriotism. Many such foreign-born delegations came to Marion, Ohio, on 18 September 1920. The delegations, wearing red, white and blue arm bands and waving small flags, next paraded down the streets of Marion to Harding's house, led by Gugliotta's Military Concert Band of Cleveland. They carried banners

---

[25] Russell, *Shadow of Blooming Grove*, 372, 403–405, 413–15 (quotation, 404). For Harding's appeal to black voters, see Harding, "Address to Colored Delegation, "Marion OH, 10 Sept. 1920, Harding Papers, Series 5, Box 840 (reel 239). In an August 1921 speech in Birmingham AL, Harding demanded political, economic and educational equality for Blacks, although he left unchallenged segregation. Russell, *Shadow of Blooming Grove*, 470-72; and Sinclair, *Available Man*, 230-35.

[26] Ibid., 17, 27, 40, 85. He said to Cincinnati *Enquirer* reporter James M. Faulkner, "How do I know, Jim? One of my ancestors may have jumped the fence." Russell argues that Harding's deep-seated need to be liked, his conformity and conservatism, sprang from insecurity about his racial identity reinforced by childhood taunting. While this seems an extravagant claim, such insecurity no doubt had some influence on Harding.

emblazoned with slogans such as, "Thirty Races but Only One Country and One Flag," and "Americans All; For America First."[27] They surrounded Harding's front porch, where the delegates and the candidate used patriotic rhetoric to proclaim a united, indivisible America.

The Ohio Senator made a point of addressing the delegates not as foreign-born, but as Americans: "We are all Americans, and all true Americans will say, as I say, America First!" Harding described the national discord among ethnic and racial groups caused by World War I as an "awakening" to the reality that many immigrants had not been assimilated. "We talked of the American melting pot over the fires of freedom," he said, "but we did not apply that fierce flame of patriotic devotion needed to fuse all into the pure metal of Americanism." He was careful not to blame the foreign-born, saying, "Charge it to American neglect." Harding also explained that he did not want immigrants to abandon completely their cultures or their ethnic pride. He did want them to put America first through "the consecrations of citizenship."

Harding declared himself "unalterably against any present or future hyphenated Americanism," and demanded that politicians—seeking only their own political self-interests rather than what was best for the country—stop appealing to people along such lines. Once again he told his tale of the Senate Foreign Relations Committee hearings, and argued that involvement in the League was dangerous because it "tends to drive into groups seeking to make themselves felt in our political life men and women whose hearts are led away from 'America First!' to 'Hyphen First!'" He further warned that if an "organized hyphenated vote" became the balance of power in American politics, "America would be delivered out of the hands of her citizenship, and her control might be transferred to a foreign capital abroad."

"America First" did not mean ignoring the needs of humanity at home and abroad, Harding reassured his audience, and he urged all Americans to serve the common good and seek social justice. For the immigrants, he specifically suggested distribution away from the overcrowded cities. Resettlement in rural areas would allow them "to know the best America and give their best to America."[28] Thus Harding laid out his vision of "America

---

[27] Warren G. Harding, "Address to Foreign Born," Marion OH, 18 September 1920, Harding Papers, Series 5, Box 840 (reel 239).

[28] Ibid.

First" to the foreign-born members of the Republican party, and received their approval.

In fact, most voting Americans approved of the Republican candidate. Warren Harding won the election of 1920 in a landslide. The election was the first since 1896 to feature two new presidential candidates. The total vote increased by eight million over 1916, mostly due to the passage of the nineteenth amendment giving women the right to vote. Governor James Cox of Ohio received slightly more votes than Wilson had in 1916, but he carried only eleven Southern states and received fewer electoral votes than Alton B. Parker had in 1904. Cox's strident denunciation of disloyal "hyphenates" and his support for Wilson's peace treaty did not seem to deter some Irish or Italian American voters, but German, Scandinavian, Russian, and British Americans (including British Canadians) voted overwhelmingly for the Republican candidate. Harding won nearly twice as many votes as Hughes had, and swept the immigrant-rich Northeast and Midwest. He won all but one county in New England, all but three counties in the middle Atlantic states, and all but twenty-five in the eastern north-central states. He also swept every county in the Pacific coast states, at least partially due to his strategy of endorsing Asian exclusion.[29]

Harding did not refer to immigration or Americanization at all in his inaugural address, and he made no suggestions about restriction legislation in addressing Congress shortly thereafter. Nevertheless, the Emergency Quota Restriction Bill that President Wilson had pocket-vetoed in the last days of his term was passed again. Albert Johnson, chairman of the House Immigration Committee, introduced a bill on 21 April 1921 that set quotas at three percent of the number of foreign-born of each nationality according to the 1910 census. The minimum quota for each nation was 400, and the total of all the quotas was 387,803. Professionals, domestic servants, religious refugees and citizens of Western Hemisphere countries who had lived in those countries for at least one year were exempt. Wives and minor children of alien residents and citizens had preference, but they were not exempt from the quotas, and even the exempt classes were charged against the quotas until they were filled. Congressman Isaac Siegel of New York tried in vain to amend the bill so that the 1920 census would be the basis for the quotas.

---

[29] Allan J. Lichtman, *Prejudice and the Old Politics: The Presidential Election of 1928* (Chapel Hill: University of North Carolina Press, 1979) 98–104; and Edgar Eugene Robinson, *The Presidential Vote, 1896–1932* (Palo Alto: Stanford University Press, 1936) 19–21.

The Senate substituted a similar bill and passed it 78 to 1, with 17 abstentions. The exemption for religious refugees, originally intended to mollify President Wilson, was dropped by the conference committee.[30]

Hulbert Taft, editor of the Cincinnati *Times-Star* and brother of William Howard Taft, wrote a letter to the new president urging him to sign the bill; Harding replied that he would.[31] On 6 May 1921, a delegation from the Inter-Racial Council met at the White House with Harding to discuss issues of concern to the foreign-born. They denied any political stance with regard to immigration, but Senator Frank B. Willis forwarded a letter from James H. Patten, lobbyist for the Immigration Restriction League and the Patriotic Order Sons of America, warning Harding that they were really lobbying against the bill.[32]

Since Harding did not hold a public hearing as Taft and Wilson had done, Louis Marshall of the American Jewish Committee took the liberty of sending the president a lengthy brief opposing the Emergency Quota Act. He argued that there was no emergency that called for further restriction, as the current restriction of the physically, mentally, morally, and educationally undesirable immigrants was sufficient. He pointed out that Cleveland, Roosevelt, Taft and Wilson all opposed harsh restriction laws, and that immigrants had contributed both to the industrialization of America and the recent victory in war. In addition, the quota system embodied in the legislation was arbitrary and discriminatory. Allied Belgium and France would be entitled to only 5,000 together, while enemy Germany would get 75,000. The quotas were obviously designed to discriminate against Southern and Eastern Europeans, including Jews, manifesting an ugly racial prejudice. The exemption for Canadians, Mexicans, and Central and South Americans was also unfair, allowing certain regions (like the agricultural Southwest) to use immigrant labor, while denying it to other regions and industries.[33]

George B. Christian, Harding's secretary, responded to Marshall that "after very careful consideration, in view of all the circumstances, [Harding]

---

[30] Hutchinson *Legislative History*, 178-81, 185.

[31] Hulbert Taft to Warren G. Harding, 2 May 1921; and Harding to Taft, 6 May 1921, Harding Papers, Series 4, President's Executive Office File 114, Folder 1, Box 558 (reel 178).

[32] Frances Kellor to George B. Christian, 2 May 1921; and Frank B. Willis to Warren G. Harding, 10 May 1921, ibid.

[33] Louis Marshall to Warren G. Harding, 17 May 1921, ibid.

felt constrained to approve the bill."[34] Congressman Adolph Sabath of Illinois sent the president a similar brief, and received like response.[35] Harding signed the Emergency Quota Act into law on 19 May 1921 and appears to have done so without reservation.[36] This was no surprise, as he had supported restriction legislation as a US Senator. Harding had voted for the Literacy Test Bill in 1917, although he told Ohio manufacturers that he had done so "as one takes a dose of castor oil."[37] The bad taste came not from conviction, however, but from fear of losing the political support of big business.

Harding explained his stance in an "interview" (actually an old speech written for him by Alexander Wolcott and reworked by Christian and Harding into an interview format) for the *American Legion Weekly* in 1921. While he criticized some of the foreign-born for being led astray by socialist propaganda, Harding once again blamed the native-born for their failure to teach immigrants the English language and American political ideals. "Therein has been the real un-Americanism, therein the great treason," he said. But while native Americans had to do more to welcome and Americanize immigrants, Harding believed it was only common sense that "we must not take any more of these strangers in a given time than we can make comfortable." Harding also reiterated the Dillingham Commission's assertion that many of the new immigrants sought not asylum, but temporary employment. In any case, he rejected the right of asylum: "It is rubbish to suggest that the gates of America should stand wide to all the world. We want only those who come in the spirit of the old pioneers, seeking home and freedom." He denied that protecting national interests was selfish, because the United States was leading the rest of the world by example and the American image presented must always remain unblemished.[38]

The hardships created by the immediate enforcement of the Emergency Quota Act created a storm of bad publicity for the Harding Administration. The act took effect on 3 June 1921, only fifteen days after Harding signed it.

---

[34] [George B. Christian] to Louis Marshall, 19 May 1921, ibid.

[35] Adolph Sabath to Warren G. Harding, 17 May 1921; and [George B. Christian] to Sabath, 19 May 1921, ibid.

[36] Hutchinson, *Legislative History*, 181.

[37] Warren G. Harding to Malcolm Jennings, 10 February 1917, Jennings MSS, Ohio Historical Society, Columbus OH; Sinclair, *Available Man*, 215.

[38] [George B. Christian] to Harold W. Rosem, ed., *The American Legion Weekly*, 21 July 1921, Harding Papers, Series 4, President's Executive Office File 139, Folder 1, Box 565 (reel 180).

At Ellis Island, 10,000 immigrants above the new monthly quota landed in June. They were admitted temporarily under bond, and their numbers charged against future quotas. Thereafter, steamships raced to enter a port the first few days of each month before the quotas were filled.[39] Mayor Andrew Peters of Boston, the second largest port of entry, wrote to the president seven days after the quota law took effect urging remedial legislation to alleviate the plight of immigrants who set sail before the bill was passed and now faced deportation upon arrival because the quotas were already filled. Dr. W. John Harris of St. Louis sent two heartbreaking tales of immigrants facing deportation taken from the St. Louis *Post-Dispatch,* warning Harding that "such bad publicity is costing the administration dearly with voters." The Federal Council of Churches weighed in with a resolution demanding asylum without regard to quota restrictions for Greek and Armenian refugees fleeing Turkish persecution.[40]

Harding replied to a critical letter from New York Congressman Isaac Siegel: "I haven't any doubt in the world but the enforcement of the Immigration Laws is working many a hardship. My own distress has been very great over some of the specific instances which have been reported to me." He blamed the steamship companies for bringing "innocent immigrants" and attempting to take advantage of "the government agents who have been disposed to be sympathetic and more than generous in carrying out the law." He expressed great confidence in the Commissioner of Immigration and called Secretary of Labor James J. Davis, "one of the most humane and sympathetic men in all the land."[41] If indeed Harding's distress was very great, it was probably due more to the political than to the human cost.

That same day Harding wrote to Secretary Davis, forwarding Siegel's letter and asking if there was any additional information he could give the Congressman. Davis, clearly defensive due to all of the negative press, explained that he had admitted thousands in excess of the quotas in June and

---

[39] Thomas M. Pitkin, *Keepers of the Gate: A History of Ellis Island* (New York: New York University Press, 1975) 136–37. No more than twenty percent of the yearly quota was supposed to be admitted in any month.

[40] Andrew J. Peters to Warren G. Harding, 10 June 1921, Harding Papers, Series 4, President's Executive Office File 114, Folder 1, Box 558 (reel 178); W. John Harris to George B. Christian, 30 June 1922; and Federal Council of the Churches of Christ in America to Harding, 10 November 1922, ibid., Folder 2, Box 558 (reel 178).

[41] Warren G. Harding to Isaac Siegel, 9 September 1921, ibid., Folder 1, Box 558 (reel 178).

August "with much doubt in my mind as to the strict legality of it solely in the interest of humanity and against the advice of men occupying important positions in the Bureau of Immigration." Davis denied Congressman Siegel's charge that families were being deliberately separated by the enforcement of the new law. He admitted that often one or more members of a family were legally inadmissible. He went on, however, to reassure the president: "In every case of this kind the aliens were told what the rule is and the admissible alien was urged to return with the other members of the family rather than separate them. This Department in no case has separated families." He also pointed out that if he had enforced the law strictly, the family separations of which Siegel complained would not have occurred at all, because all would have been barred. Davis considered himself duty-bound to enforce the laws Congress passed, but he instructed immigration officials to "remember the human element and to enforce the law with all possible consideration for all people affected."[42]

Both Davis and Harding supported restriction, but they intervened frequently and bent the law to prevent deportations for humanitarian reasons. Harding ordered one thousand immigrants to be spared in December 1921, and he granted New York Congressman Fiorello LaGuardia's request to delay the deportation of three hundred Jewish immigrants who had come in after the quota. Davis created a Board of Review, which included former Commissioner General of Immigration Terence V. Powderly, to screen individual hardship cases.[43] The Secretary of Labor, however, was not as sympathetic to the immigrants as he might appear from such actions. In an article in the *American Review of Reviews*, he lashed out at the "insidious propaganda" of humanitarian groups.[44] Unlike previous Secretaries Oscar Straus, Charles Nagel and William B. Wilson, Davis firmly supported immigration restriction. Despite belonging to a family of Welsh immigrants who had come to the United States poor and illiterate, he despised

---

[42] James J. Davis to Warren G. Harding, 26 September 1921, ibid. Davis wrote that 95 percent of all aliens came to relatives already in the United States, and over 50 percent came with families, so that the potential for family separation could not be avoided. Allowing immigrants to remain at Ellis Island until the next month was not an option, because then steamship companies would never know how many passengers to take, and the operation of the Bureau would be hopelessly complicated.

[43] Robert K. Murray, *The Harding Era: Warren G. Harding and His Administration* (Minneapolis: University of Minnesota Press, 1969) 269–70.

[44] James J. Davis, "How the Immigration Laws are Working," *American Review of Reviews* 65/5(1922): 515; and Murray, *Harding Era*, 270.

particularly the immigrants from Southern and Eastern Europe who came through Ellis Island and the other ports during his tenure.

Harding commissioned actress and singer Lillian Russell Moore as a special agent to investigate conditions in Europe. She recommended a five-year suspension of all immigration, sounding very much like a nativist. "The higher civilizations of past ages, history teaches us, succumbed to such foreign invasions as now threaten us," she wrote. Congress did not follow Moore's recommendation. Instead, in May 1922 it passed an act that extended the quotas for two more years, increased the Western Hemisphere residency requirement to five years and imposed a two-hundred-dollar fine on the steamship companies for each inadmissible immigrant they brought, unless they could prove that they could not reasonably have known that the person would be inadmissible.[45]

In the face of pressure from both restrictionists and liberals, the Bureau of Immigration renewed its request to move inspection overseas. Ellis Island Commissioner Frederick A. Wallis resigned in 1921, warning that the nation was committing "a gross injustice" by sending back immigrants who had already left everything behind to come to America. He urged consular inspection abroad to spare inadmissible immigrants the unnecessary and expensive transatlantic trip. His successor, New York investment banker and Scottish immigrant Robert E. Tod, turned his European vacation into a fact-finding mission in the summer of 1921. Tod reported that the consuls were unwilling to inspect immigrants, but they would accept immigration inspectors as "vice consuls" under their authority.[46]

Harding wrote to Secretary of State Charles Evans Hughes in September 1921 requesting that the consuls handle the quota problems to avoid further embarrassment to the administration. Hughes had already issued an order on 31 August telling the consuls not to issue visas in excess of the quotas. The Director of the Consular Service, Wilbur Carr, reiterated his bureau's willingness to accept immigration inspectors as vice consuls. At a meeting with top State Department officials early in 1922, Davis and Assistant Labor Secretary Edward J. Henning tried to give the Bureau of Immigration to the State Department, saying that they found it distasteful to

---

[45] Hutchinson, *Legislative History*, 182–85.
[46] Pitkin, *Keepers of the Gate*, 137, 139–40.

enforce the new law. Carr and Hughes, however, did not want that responsibility.[47]

Unlike his predecessors Oscar Straus, Charles Nagel and William B. Wilson, James Davis believed in the need for immigration restriction. The Labor secretary outlined his views on immigration reform in a letter to the president in April 1923. He lamented that too much attention was focused on "bootlegged" immigrants (whose numbers he estimated at between 100 and 1,000 a day) and inadmissible aliens who plied friends, relatives, and public sympathy to gain admission. He noted that eugenicist Harry H. Laughlin had testified before the House Immigration Committee that over forty-five percent of all immigrants in the last thirty years would have been barred if the wartime Army intelligence tests were used. Davis proposed "strict, but just tests of physical and mental health" to screen out immigrants, to be administered abroad in order to avoid the "heartrending scenes" at Ellis Island that made administration of the law so difficult. He pointed out, "we could end all of these horrors if we could make our selections on the other side, and transform our immigrant stations at the ports into gateways of welcome, devoid of the harshness of official delays and pains, of sorrows and disappointments." Although he did not mention it, Davis no doubt had realized that screening in Europe would also be freer from routine scrutiny by the American press and the courts.

In addition to mental testing and consular inspection, the Secretary of Labor proposed the registration of all immigrants, not as an anti-espionage measure, but to offer the opportunities of education and Americanization necessary for citizenship. He called for the deportation of those whose records indicated that they were unfit for citizenship, but denied that he was advocating compulsory naturalization. "Merely forcing an alien to go through the formal legal ceremony of naturalization will not make him an American. True citizenship must come from the mind and the heart," he wrote. Davis recalled his own family's arrival in America, and commented that he believed his proposals would have given his uneducated, although patriotic, father "a better chance to absorb the spirit of America." He reassured Harding that "no racial group which is honestly American and which thoroughly understands these proposals will reject them," and he blamed opposition to his plan on anarchists, Communists and criminals, as well as

---

[47] Patricia Russell Evans, "'Likely to Become a Public Charge': Immigration in the Backwaters of Administrative Law, 1882–1933" (Ph.D. diss., George Washington University, 1987) 172–74.

businessmen who sought cheap labor and threatened the nation's prosperity.[48]

James Davis was greatly impressed by Laughlin's eugenics research and his testimony before the House Immigration Committee. The secretary asked A. E. Hamilton, who worked at the Carnegie Institution's Station for Experimental Evolution with Laughlin and Charles B. Davenport, to prepare a series of thirty-seven explanatory "press letters" for release as articles under the collective title, "Selective Immigration or None." In April 1923 Arthur E. Clark, Davis' private secretary, forwarded drafts of all thirty-seven releases to George B. Christian. It is unclear if Harding ever read these articles before his death. There is no recorded reply from either the president or his secretary. Nevertheless, Harding had the responsibility to approve or disown political statements made by his cabinet members. Harding never disavowed the articles. In 1925 they were edited and published in book form.[49]

The articles proposed to make eugenics the basis for "selective immigration," rather than arbitrary quotas assigned from percentiles of census rolls. The initial release lauded the immigrants who built America, comparing them to industrious beavers, but then warned "the rat type has also begun to come." The "rats" included both those unable and those unwilling to work, the "feeble-minded, imbeciles, insane, psychopathically inferior, reds, anarchists and communists." When the "rats" outnumbered the "beavers," Davis warned, American civilization would fall.[50]

Turning to a puddling analogy, dear to his heart as a former iron puddler, Davis compared the "rat-men" to misshapen nails and pig iron—they were too brittle to use in construction. Then he mixed the metaphors of

---

[48] James J. Davis to Warren G. Harding, 16 April 1923, Harding Papers, Series 4, President's Executive Office File 15, Folder 5, Box 435 (reel 140). He argued that Mexican immigrants in particular were unsuitable, and that the immigration laws were based on the principle that only the Caucasian and "African negro" race were eligible for naturalization, so all others should be excluded.

[49] James J. Davis, "Selective Immigration or None: Forward," n.d. [1923], ibid., Folder 6, Box 435 (reel 140). This, like the rest of the articles, was toned down considerably when it was published in book form in 1925. See Davis, *Selective Immigration* (St. Paul: Scott-Mitchell, 1925). Although ghost-written by Hamilton, Davis was listed as the author, and he claimed the opinions were his own.

[50] James J. Davis, "Selective Immigration or None: Forward," n.d. [1923], Harding Papers, Series 4, President's Executive Office File 15, Folder 6, Box 435 (reel 140). Davis used this rat and beaver analogy earlier in his autobiography. See Davis, *The Iron Puddler: My Life in the Rolling Mills and What Came of It* (Indianapolis: Bobbs-Merrill Co., 1922) 60–61.

the melting pot and the puddling furnace to present his vision of his own destiny as a "master puddler of humanity" who would "gather thousands of men into a melting-pot and boil out the envy, greed and malice as much as possible, and purify the good metal of human sympathy." He explained that "the task of civilization, the task of America is to purify men as we have purified metals."[51] The melting pot concept could work, in other words, if the proper ingredients were used and a scientific recipe followed. Davis offered himself to the nation as that master puddler who would set the immigration policy on the sure foundation of genetics research.

The Secretary of Labor offered his readers examples from history, arguing that the ancient civilization of Egypt was gradually weakened and finally destroyed when inferior races (probably a veiled reference to the Jewish slaves who built the pyramids) were admitted to the country and allowed to amalgamate with the natives.[52] In America's own history, Davis stated, there was a decline in the quality of immigration, as the pioneers from Great Britain, Ireland and Germany were gradually replaced in the late nineteenth century by cheap labor from Southern and Eastern Europe. These new immigrants not only lowered wage scales and standards of living, their arrival dissuaded further immigration from the Northern and Western parts of Europe (the points of origin Davis claimed for his family). "Labor that valued itself, labor that required a certain higher standard of living," he explained, "stayed at home rather than come to America to compete with slum-boarding-house conditions created by our impatient demand for quantity production at any cost."[53]

Davis wholeheartedly accepted the invidious distinctions between old and new immigrants drawn by the Dillingham Commission. He used Harry Laughlin's statistics to argue that Southern and Eastern Europeans were taking a frightful toll on society through crime and tax money used to care for the insane and "feeble-minded."[54] Davis argued, however, that the

---

[51] James J. Davis, "Selective Immigration or None: Forward," n.d. [1923], Harding Papers, Series 4, President's Executive Office File 15, Folder 6, Box 435 (reel 140). Davis used similar words in his autobiography, *Iron Puddler*, 275.

[52] James J. Davis, "Selective Immigration or None: Letter No. 22X: Historical Migrations of Mankind," n.d. [1923], Harding Papers, Series 4, President's Executive Office File 15, Folder 6, Box 435 (reel 140).

[53] James J. Davis, "Selective Immigration or None: Letter No. 22B: Historical Background of Immigration (The Major Migrations)," n.d. [1923], ibid.

[54] James J. Davis, "Selective Immigration or None: Letter No. 3: Our Alien Insane"; Davis, "Selective Immigration or None: Letter No. 4: Our Criminalistic Aliens"; and

quality of immigrants was determined by their physical and mental qualities, not their racial backgrounds: "We must learn to think, not in terms of race or religion or nationality so much as in terms of civic worth from the standpoint of potential, of possibility." The immigrants' potential, measured by their physical and mental qualities, would be determined by eugenics, "the dawning science of mankind."[55]

Secretary Davis' proposed policy called for scrapping the old ideal of the United States as an asylum for the poor and oppressed of the Western world. He asserted that most refugees "were oppressed and persecuted because they were found unsocial and impossible citizens at home."[56] Eugenics, he believed, showed that the Declaration of Independence was wrong: All men were not created as equals. Americans had to learn to distinguish between "bad stock and good stock, weak blood and strong blood, sound heredity and sickly human stuff." Davis also suggested that a mental test would be more fair than the current literacy test, quoting Wilson's veto message about the need for tests of quality and not of opportunity.[57]

The secretary's two main proposals were registration of aliens to track their progress toward citizenship and give them aid, and scientific testing of would-be immigrants in their own countries. Davis denied that registration of aliens would be used for the government to spy on card-holders, but he pointed out that registration would make it much easier to identify and deport illegal aliens.[58] As for scientifically screening immigrants before they embarked for America, Davis defended such testing as a more humane alternative to the current policy of deporting those who failed to pass inspection at Ellis Island. Immigrants who were still feeling seasick and faced a daunting gauntlet of officials speaking a foreign language were not in a proper frame of mind to take a psychological battery of examinations. If they were tested in the comfort of their own homes in their homelands, Davis believed, the results would likely be more accurate. Inspections

---

Davis, "Selective Immigration or None: Letter No. 11b: Dumping of Criminal Aliens," n.d. [1923], ibid., Folder 7, Box 435 (reel 140).

[55] James J. Davis, "Selective Immigration or None: Letter No. 22A: Historical Setting of Immigration," n.d. [1923], ibid., Folder 6, Box 435 (reel 140).

[56] James J. Davis, "Selective Immigration or None: Letter No. 25B: The Immigration Faith and Policy of the American People," n.d. [1923], ibid.

[57] James J. Davis, "Selective Immigration or None: Letter No. 1: Our National Intellectual Stamina," n.d. [1923], ibid.

[58] James J. Davis, "Selective Immigration or None: Letter No. 15: The Enrollment of Aliens," n.d. [1923], ibid., folder 8, Box 435 (reel 140).

overseas would also avoid the heartbreaking scenes of deportations and relieve the sorrow caused to US immigration officials who were doing their best to provide humane enforcement of the law.[59]

To be fair, Secretary of Labor James J. Davis was not a hard-hearted despot. He was well-known for establishing Mooseheart, a vocational school for orphans supported by the Loyal Order of Moose, an organization which he led. But like many progressive-minded leaders of charities and settlement houses, Davis believed that exclusion of "unfit" immigrants based on the "science" of eugenics would be more humane than the existing system. In 1922 he wrote in his autobiography: "Tenderness and human sympathy to the aliens passing through Ellis Island does not mean that we are weak, or that the unfit alien is welcome...He who is tenderest toward the members of his own household is bravest in beating back him who would destroy that house."[60] Davis avoided the outright racist language of Laughlin and other eugenicists, despite relying on their research, and was always careful to emphasize the benefits of immigration. Having gone to work in the mills at the age of eleven, however, Davis lacked a college education and was easily awed by scientists and other educated men. Later, he joined Secretary of Commerce Herbert Hoover and Secretary of State Frank Kellogg in opposing the national origins quotas.

Harding agreed with Davis' proposals and began to put them into practice. Robe C. White, who was named Second Assistant Secretary of Labor to oversee immigration laws, and Meyer Bloomfield went to Europe in 1922 to lay the groundwork for overseas screening of immigrants. Davis himself went to Europe the following summer.[61] When both Tod and Commissioner General William Walter Husband requested money to expand the overcrowded facilities at Ellis Island, Davis instead used overcrowding as a reason for overseas inspection. Tod resigned his post in frustration in 1923.[62] The difficulty with overseas inspection was that under current law, the Labor Department was forbidden to spend money outside of the US to enforce the immigration laws. Secretary of State Charles Evans Hughes made it clear

---

[59] James J. Davis, "Selective Immigration or None: Letter No. 24: Deportation," n.d. [1923], ibid., folder 7, Box 435 (reel 140).

[60] Davis, *Iron Puddler*, 48–49.

[61] James J. Davis to Warren G. Harding, 10 July 1922, Harding Papers, Series 4, President's Executive Office File 15, Folder 4, Box 435 (reel 140); Davis to Harding, 2 July 1923, ibid., folder 6, Box 435 (reel 140); and Murray, *Harding Era*, 269.

[62] Pitkin, *Keepers of the Gate*, 145–46.

that he and his State Department staff were already unhappy with their role in enforcing the quotas by limiting the number of visas they issued.[63]

Harding addressed the resurgent immigration issue in his annual message to Congress on 8 December 1922. To create the impetus for reform he warned Congress of a renewed threat of radicalism and hyphenism, just as Woodrow Wilson had done in campaigning for the Treaty of Versailles in 1919. "Abusing the hospitality of our shores are the advocates of revolution, finding their deluded followers among those who take on the habiliments of an American without knowing an American soul," Harding declared. In addition to such anarchists, the president decried "the recrudescence of hyphenated Americanism which we thought to have been stamped out when we committed the Nation, life and soul, to the World War."[64] The president formally endorsed Secretary Davis' proposals for registration of all aliens to combat this threat, asserting: "The Nation has the right to know who are citizens in the making or who live among us and share our advantages while seeking to undermine our cherished institutions." He also recommended that the government "establish our examination boards abroad, to be sure of desirables only" and to "end the pathos at our ports."[65] Noting the link between illiteracy and immigration, Harding also called for Federal funding of education for immigrants.[66]

Albert Johnson wrote Harding a memorandum the day before the address, informing the president that the House Committee had drawn up amendments to make the Quota Act "more workable and more humane," including one to deny admission to Asian aliens ineligible for citizenship. This "anti-Oriental" amendment was not introduced earlier when the Quota Act was extended, he explained, because the US Senate and Japanese Diet had been considering the naval arms limitation treaty. Johnson opined that "the great bulk of the public if not directly interested in securing cheap alien labor, or in securing admission of refugees for racial or family reasons, desires the Three Per Cent Law continued or even tightened," and that there

---

[63] James J. Davis to Harding, 7 June 1923, Harding Papers, Series 4, President's Executive Office File 114, Folder 2, Box 558 (reel 178); and Evans, "Likely to Become a Public Charge," 165.

[64] Warren G. Harding, "Address to Congress," 22 November 1922, pp. 32–33, Harding Papers, Series 5, Box 844 (reel 239).

[65] Ibid., 36–38.

[66] Ibid., 38–39. The argument that illiteracy in the United States was due to immigrants was false: the statistics Harding cited showed that illiteracy ranged from 0.2 to 2% in Europe, while it was 6% in the United States.

was instead much support for his own proposal to use the 1890 census as a base. He noted that several Congressmen reported that immigration restriction drew the most applause in the recent campaign. In a slap at Davis, Johnson argued that those who favored "selective immigration" could not define it when pressed and "admit that the melting pot has broken down," while plans to distribute aliens would lead to "serfdom." His only concern about the Quota Act was that while it kept out great numbers of refugees, "the number of Jews who have come in the various quotas seems to cause alarm—particularly in New York."[67]

While restrictionists like Johnson lobbied Harding, the president also was under pressure to liberalize immigration—not only from liberal opponents of the new quotas, but also from big business. As the United States' economy came out of its postwar recession, a tightening labor market once more made executives long for cheap foreign labor. Hulbert Taft wrote Harding in November 1922 that he was concerned about big business' "growing determination" to "break down the immigration law." He urged the president not to yield to such pressure. Harding's response showed both his support for Davis' "selective immigration" and his unwillingness to challenge Congressional leadership. Congress was unlikely to end restriction, but it was also unlikely to accept Davis' proposals. Harding agreed with his Labor Secretary that it would be "altogether desirable to invite an increased coming from certain sections of Europe," but "because of the political crosscurrents, we are not likely to adopt a policy of choosing, and, therefore, continued restriction is our nearest approach to proper safeguard[sic]."[68]

Whenever possible, Harding avoided challenging Congressional Republicans, whose leaders were quick to rein him if he expressed contrary opinions. After the *New York Times* said in April 1923 that Harding agreed with US Steel executive Elbert Gary about the existence of a labor shortage and the need to increase immigration, Albert Johnson wrote to George Christian, asking if he would be "justified in saying that the President stands by his Immigration statements in his message to Congress of last fall; that he does not wish an *excess* of labor, or an excess of immigrants, and that he wants all hardships removed from quota law as far as possible." Christian

---

[67] Albert Johnson to Warren G. Harding, 7 December 1922, Harding Papers, Series 4, President's Executive Office File 114, Folder 2, Box 558 (reel 178). Whatever effect this letter had on Harding, it did not cause him to alter the text of his speech at all, which was drafted on 22 November 1922.

[68] Warren G. Harding to Hulbert Taft, 6 November 1922, ibid.

meekly replied that Johnson would be justified in making such a statement to the press.[69]

Harding's last extended public comments on the subject of immigration were made in 1923 during an Independence Day speech in Portland, Oregon. His words suggested no change of outlook. He repeated material from his earlier speeches in 1918–1920, speaking of World War I as the turning point in the "reconsecration" of American citizenship. Then he addressed the current situation. He acknowledged that the growing economy was creating a tight labor market, but he declared, "I prefer waiting jobs to idle men, and I choose quality rather than quantity in future immigration." He also condemned illegal immigration. Finally, he warned the people to be always on guard against foreign agitators "who work within our borders to destroy the very institutions which have given them hospitality."[70]

Warren Harding, had he lived, would undoubtedly have signed the National Origins Act of 1924.[71] While he favored James Davis' eugenic proposals for "selective immigration," he lacked Roosevelt's ability to influence Congressional action on the issue. The brief indications that he favored relaxing the quotas in the spring of 1923 were due to pressure from big business, rather than any change of heart on the issue. Harding did object, however, to the coercive Americanization programs begun during World War I. He urged native-born Americans to welcome and educate the foreign-born in a more tolerant manner. He consistently supported the concept of the melting pot, but he did not share Taft and Wilson's commitment to the ideal of asylum. His political instincts told him that the majority of the American people no longer believed that the United States should be the asylum of the world, and he never opposed the majority.

---

[69] Albert Johnson to George B. Christian, 2 May 1923 (emphasis in the original); and George B. Christian, telegram to Albert Johnson, 5 May 1923; ibid.

[70] Warren G. Harding, "Cross-Country Speech (fragment)," Portland OR, 4 July 1923, Harding Papers, Series 5, Box 845 (reel 239).

[71] Sinclair, *Available Man*, 215–17; and Murray, *Harding Era*, 394–95.

CHAPTER 7

CALVIN COOLIDGE AND
THE PROSPEROUS MELTING POT

Calvin Coolidge grew up in the tiny Vermont hamlet of Plymouth Notch, about as homogeneous a place as could be found anywhere in the United States. But he spent his adult life in Massachusetts, a state with one of the heaviest concentrations of immigrant populations. From the beginning of his political career in the city of Northampton, through his tenures in the Massachusetts state legislature and governor's office in Boston, Coolidge had faced the issues surrounding immigration far more directly than Warren G. Harding. He appealed to Irish Catholics and other immigrants with the rhetoric of the melting pot. He believed in the need for immigration restriction, however, and he did not challenge the basic premise of the 1924 National Origins Act that he signed into law.

The 1924 presidential campaign literature and oratory emphasized Coolidge's "all-American" roots, especially that he was born on the fourth of July in a town named Plymouth. A biographical article in *Success* magazine in July 1924 said, "No one could take Calvin Coolidge for anything but an American—an American not of the melting pot but of the forefathers. There is a peculiar appropriateness in the fact that he was born on the fourth of July."[1] Coolidge was descended from the Puritan John Coolidge, who came to Massachusetts Bay about 1630. His family had lived in Plymouth Notch since the 1770s, and both his father and grandfather had served briefly in the Vermont state legislature.[2]

---

[1] *Success*, July 1924, 12, enclosed in Walter Hoff Seely to Calvin Coolidge, 12 June 1925, Calvin Coolidge Papers, President's Personal File (PPF) 166 (reel 7), Forbes Library, Northampton MA.

[2] Claude M. Fuess, *Calvin Coolidge: The Man from Vermont* (Boston: Little, Brown & Co., 1940) 12–16; and Donald R. McCoy, *Calvin Coolidge: The Quiet President* (New York: Macmillan, 1967; reprint, Lawrence: University Press of Kansas, 1988) 4–6.

Coolidge had a highly idealistic view of America and the duties of American citizenship, heavily influenced by Charles Garman, one of his professors at Amherst College. Garman's class imbued Coolidge with the idea that all men were brothers, with God as their common Father, and therefore all men were equal in kind if not in degree.[3] To a Johns Hopkins University audience in February 1922, then Vice President Coolidge explained that the purpose of America was to be a shining example of this kind of Christian brotherhood to the rest of the world: "In the fullness of time America was called into being under the most favoring circumstances, to work out the problem of a more perfect relationship among mankind that government and society might be brought into harmony with reason and conscience."[4] Such brotherhood required acceptance of, and equality among, the different racial and ethnic groups that made up the American citizenry.

Coolidge rejected Social Darwinism as contrary to the American rights of liberty and equality under the law. Addressing the Roxbury Historical Society as lieutenant governor of Massachusetts on Bunker Hill Day in 1918, he said: "There has been much talk in recent years of the survival of the fittest and of efficiency. We are beginning to hear of the development of the super-man and the claim that he has of right dominion over the rest of his inferiors on earth." He argued that such a philosophy did not lead to progress, because those who were the best and brightest were called to self-sacrifice on behalf of others, rather than self-preservation or aggrandizement. "The law of progress and civilization is not the law of the jungle," he insisted, but rather "a divine law. It does not mean survival of the fittest, it means the sacrifice of the fittest." He noted that American heroes like Nathan Hale and Abraham Lincoln had laid down their lives for their country, while the traitor Benedict Arnold had survived. "The example above all others," he said, "takes us back to Jerusalem some nineteen hundred years ago."[5] Coolidge had learned about public service from his father and grandfather. But his ultimate example of a public servant was Jesus Christ, the Suffering Servant who died to redeem the whole world.

---

[3] Calvin Coolidge, *The Autobiography of Calvin Coolidge* (New York: Cosmopolitan Book Corp., 1929) 66.

[4] Calvin Coolidge, *The Price of Freedom: Speeches and Addresses* (New York: Charles Scribner's Sons, 1924) 136.

[5] Calvin Coolidge, *Have Faith in Massachusetts: A Collection of Speeches and Messages*, 2nd ed. (Boston/New York: Houghton Mifflin Co., 1919) 117–18.

Coolidge's call to sacrifice for one's country had added power in the throes of World War I. Like Warren Harding and Woodrow Wilson, Coolidge saw in the darkness of war an opportunity to unify America. He declared to the Somerville Republican City Committee in 1918, "Out of our sacrifice and suffering, out of our blood and tears, America shall have a new awakening, a rededication to the cause of Washington and Lincoln, a firmer conviction for the right."[6] To the Essex County Club he explained that this rededication involved the elimination of ethnic and class division: "We entered the war a people of many nationalities. We are united now; every one is first an American." Echoing Theodore Roosevelt, Coolidge declared that military service had contributed greatly to this Americanization.[7]

Any division of America into hostile groups, whether based on ethnicity or class, was an unacceptable violation of the American ideals of individualism and equality. As vice president in 1921, Coolidge told an American Legion convention in Kansas City that while previous wars had left America still divided, World War I had left it united. "The opportunity to make this nation one, the sacrifice which made this nation one," he told the veterans, "was of your day alone." The veterans were not the only ones who had sacrificed themselves, for "the American people presented themselves at the altar of their country with the offering of their every dollar and their every life." He continued, with rhetoric strongly reminiscent of Harding: "The flame of patriotism swept over the whole land, consuming away the dross of all past differences, and fusing the entire people into one common national unity."[8]

Although Coolidge showed concern over the postwar Red Scare, blaming it in part on unrest in the immigrant community, he avoided the hysteria of many of his fellow politicians. Giving the commencement address at Holy Cross College in Worcester in June 1919, the governor said that Communist agitators had swayed recent immigrants by telling them that "men of their race and ideas had no hand in the making of our country, and that it was formed by those who were hostile to them and therefore they owe it no support." But Coolidge denied that it was true, at least for his largely Irish Catholic audience. "Whatever ignorance and bigotry may imagine, such arguments do not apply to those of the race and blood so prominent in

---

[6] Ibid., 131.

[7] Ibid., 143–44.

[8] Coolidge, *The Price of Freedom*, 85–86.

this assemblage," he declared.[9] While Woodrow Wilson lashed out at Irish-Americans, Calvin Coolidge cultivated their support.

He did not blame some of the immigrants for falling victim to radical propaganda. They had not been raised to believe in American ideals, so they could not be expected to view American politics in a favorable light. "They are disposed and inclined to think our institutions partake of the same nature as these they have left behind," he explained, adding, "They must be shown they are wrong."[10] He believed that the way to show them was through sacrificial service to immigrants, which would prove the reality of American ideals.

In his inaugural address as governor of Massachusetts, Coolidge said, "There are among us many recent arrivals who are entitled to some consideration and assistance." While he admitted that assistance for the immigrants was mostly the responsibility of the federal government, he urged Massachusetts citizens to demonstrate "an interest in their welfare, a desire to protect them from imposition, a respect for their own national spirit, and an effort to have them use that spirit in appreciating our own citizenship and supporting our own institutions." Like Harding, Coolidge blamed the American-born populace for not making the foreign-born feel welcome. He recommended Americanization through education, "to assist in teaching all up to middle age to speak, read, and write our language, and come in that way to an understanding of our institutions."[11] Coolidge called on his fellow citizens to make the sacrifice of time and money to teach American ideals to the new immigrants. Like most others of his time, Coolidge believed that understanding the English language was essential in order to comprehend American politics and society.

As Theodore Roosevelt had done, Coolidge shrewdly appealed to ethnic pride to win votes. Many Irish-American voters supported him, and he went out of his way to court Roman Catholics. One of his first acts as a Northampton city councilman in 1898–1899 was to introduce a resolution honoring a recently deceased Irish-American Democrat. His fellow Massachusetts politicians spoke of "Coolidge Democrats" who crossed party

---

[9] Coolidge, *Have Faith in Massachusetts*, 232–33.

[10] Ibid., 265.

[11] Henry F. Long, "Public Record of Coolidge," 5 January 1924, Coolidge Papers, PPF 247B (reel 7), Forbes Library.

lines to vote for the taciturn Republican.[12] Writing to his father in 1909 about his election as mayor of Northampton, Coolidge broke down the wards and explained, "I got all the Italians, Jews, Polish, most of the French and hundreds of Irish."[13] The *Daily Hampshire Gazette* interviewed Coolidge after his election to the state senate in 1911 and reported, "He said he never made any distinction between American citizens of different nationality [sic]. He had always found the Irish people good Americans and good citizens. He had appointed about 75 of them to responsible positions because he had found them good American citizens and well qualified for public service."[14] His appointments as governor show the usual effort to distribute patronage among the various ethnic groups: in 1919 he appointed fifty-five Catholics, seven Jews, two Swedes, three Italians, one Pole and eight Frenchmen; while in 1920 he found jobs for forty-two Catholics, eight Jews, three Swedes, three Italians, one Portuguese, one Pole and two Frenchmen.[15]

In addition to appointments, Coolidge made symbolic gestures to win ethnic support. Governor Coolidge addressed the annual convention of the Massachusetts State Council of the Knights of Columbus in 1919, praising the Catholic fraternal order for its patriotism and devotion to American ideals. This came back to haunt him in 1923 when the head of the Massachusetts delegation to the international convention in Montreal wired Coolidge to express sympathy on the death of Harding and Coolidge responded with a brief note of thanks. Somehow, his reply was confused with the earlier 1919 statement and released to the press, where it caused a sensation. It appeared that the new president's first official action was a statement praising the Catholic fraternal order and nativists were outraged. The Knights apologized to Coolidge and issued a public denial.[16] The story,

---

[12] Robert Sobel, *Coolidge: An American Enigma* (Washington DC: Regnery, 1998), 51–52.

[13] Calvin Coolidge, *Your Son, Calvin Coolidge: A Selection of Letters from Calvin Coolidge to his Father*, ed. Edward Connery Lathem (Montpelier: Vermont Historical Society, 1968) 111.

[14] *Daily Hampshire Gazette*, 8 November 1911, 1–2; and Coolidge, *Your Son*, 119.

[15] Long, "Public Record of Coolidge."

[16] "President Praises Principles of K.C.," *Washington Post*, 6 August 1923; William C. Prout telegram to Calvin Coolidge, 5 August 1923; Coolidge to Prout, 6 August 1923; James A. Flaherty to Coolidge, 19 August 1923; Henry F. Long to Ted ____, 21 August 1923; and [Long] to James C. White, 14 October 1924; Coolidge Papers, PPF 3 (reel 1), Forbes Library.

however, continued to circulate through the fall and during the 1924 campaign with additional rumors spread by the Ku Klux Klan that Grace Coolidge was secretly a Catholic and that the president's two sons were being sent to a private Catholic boarding school.[17]

Coolidge's idealism was practical in its application. Writing to his father from college in 1892, Coolidge explained, "Genius is the ability to harmonize with circumstances," and such genius could accomplish great things "when it directs itself along the right channels and not in opposition to some force that is uncontrollable."[18] Three years later he wrote in a similar vein, "It is more true than you thought you that the common people decide. They decide everything and it is the man who is quick enough to see before they do what they will decide upon [who] is the man who can succeed."[19] Coolidge's idealism led him to call for equality among all citizens and to promote sacrificial service as the best exemplar of American ideals to immigrants. He did not try to oppose the people, however, when they decided to drastically curtail immigration in the 1920s. Instead, he "harmonized with circumstances," while trying to direct the flow of those circumstances toward the furtherance of American ideals.

A month after assuming office following the death of President Harding, Coolidge requested a meeting at the White House with Samuel Gompers, longtime president of the American Federation of Labor and his foil in the notorious Boston Police Strike.[20] According to Gompers, the labor

---

[17] J. M. Wolfe to G. Bascom Slemp, 27 September 1923; [Henry F. Long] to Wolfe, 1 October 1923; C.A. Walsh to Slemp, 17 November 1923; [Long] to Walsh, 21 November 1923; Rush W. Kidd to F. P. Litzebert, 24 July 1924; and [Long] to Kidd, 31 July 1924; ibid., PPF 2 (reel 1), Forbes Library. Calvin and Grace Coolidge were both members of the Congregational Church, and their children attended Mercersburg Academy, a nonsectarian school.

[18] Coolidge, *Your Son*, 42.

[19] Ibid., 73.

[20] The Boston Police went on strike in September 1919 to protest Police Commissioner Edwin Curtis' refusal to recognize their formation of a union affiliated with the American Federation of Labor. After two nights of looting and rioting, Governor Coolidge called out the state guard and publicly supported Curtis' decision to fire those who had deserted their posts. When Gompers telegraphed the governor to ask that the striking police officers be reinstated and the dispute mediated, Coolidge refused, declaring: "There is no right to strike against the public safety by anybody, anywhere, anytime." (Coolidge, *Have Faith in Massachusetts*, 222-23.) His handling of the police strike made him a hero nationwide and led to his nomination as Harding's running mate

leader explained to the president that the three biggest concerns of working men were child labor, the abuse of injunctions and immigration. No doubt desiring to get back into Labor's good graces after the conflict in Boston, Coolidge "expressed himself as greatly concerned regarding the immigration problem and recognized that the standards of America should not be lowered by the influx of immigrants not easily assimilable."[21]

In his first annual message to Congress in December 1923, the president—known for his economy of speech—had quite a lot to say on the subject of immigration. He framed his recommendations with regard to this controversial issue in terms of good citizenship. He accepted the theory that democracy was of "Anglo-Saxon" origin and agreed with the nativists that immigrants should not differ too much from that racial or cultural type. Coolidge believed that "new arrivals should be limited to our capacity to absorb them into the ranks of good citizenship," so he supported a policy of immigration restriction "of a selective nature with some inspection at the source, and based either on a prior census or upon the record of naturalization." Despite the burgeoning economy, Coolidge remained "convinced that our present economic and social conditions warrant a limitation of those to be admitted." He also called for a law requiring the immediate registration of all aliens. The president warned alien radicals: "Those who do not want to be partakers of the American spirit ought not to settle in America."[22]

Having attended cabinet meetings at Harding's invitation, Coolidge was doubtless familiar with Secretary of Labor Davis' selective immigration scheme. The new president was pledged to continue his predecessor's policies, at least until he was elected in his own right. But Coolidge's message to Congress did not endorse Davis' eugenics-based proposals. He suggested making either the census or the naturalization records the basis for quotas, rather than any test of mental or physical capacity. His suggestion to use the naturalization records fit his own emphasis on good citizenship, as it rewarded immigrant groups which had demonstrated the greatest willingness

---

in 1920. At the time, however, Collidge hesitated to act, certain that he was commiting political suicide. See Coolidge, *Autobiography*, 128; and McCoy, *Quite President*, 83-94.

[21] Samuel Gompers, *Seventy Years of Life and Labor: An Autobiography*, 2 vols. (New York: E. P. Dutton & Co., 1925) 1:557.

[22] *Congressional Record*, 65th Cong., 1st sess., 1923, 96, 99; McCoy, *Quiet President*, 200; and Robert Washburn, *Calvin Coolidge: Farmer - Mayor - Governor - President: His Life - Its Lesson* (Boston: n.p., 1924) 43–44.

to become citizens. Of course, its effect would be the same as any other basis for it would operate against the most recent arrivals, many of whom had not yet had time to become naturalized—but it avoided the taint of prejudice.

Coolidge would not endorse Davis and Laughlin's call for eugenic testing because he did not believe in the definitiveness of the results. In a December 1922 speech in Reynoldsville, Pennsylvania, Coolidge suggested that the results of mental testing reflected the test-takers' lack of education rather than their innate ability. In any case, such tests could not measure "the possibilities of human soul." Furthermore, he argued that intelligence was not, as many eugenicists assumed, necessarily related to character: "It is not only what men know but what they are disposed to do with that which they know that will determine the rise and fall of civilization."[23]

Coolidge believed that education was the key to assimilating the immigrants and helping them to grasp, and believe in, American ideals. Addressing the National Education Association on the nation's birthday (and his) in 1924, Coolidge declared: "Education should be the handmaid of citizenship." He noted that the 1920 census showed that almost fourteen million foreign-born White people lived in the United States, and even though many of them were beyond traditional school age, they "nevertheless need the opportunity to learn to read and write the English language, that they may come into more direct contact with the ideals and standards of our life, political and social."[24]

Education was particularly crucial to political participation. In a national broadcast from the White House the night before the 1924 election, President Coolidge explained that democracy functioned only when citizens cast informed ballots. "To live up to the full measure of citizenship in this nation requires not only action, but it requires intelligent action," he explained. Such education came not only from the classroom, but from the pulpit as well, because "the background of our citizenship is the meeting house and the school house, the place of religious worship and the place of intellectual training."[25] While Coolidge believed in the separation of church and state, he believed that religion provided the moral basis for American ideals that the political system was supposed to put into practice. Religion

---

[23] Coolidge, *The Price of Freedom*, 223.

[24] Calvin Coolidge, *Foundations of the Republic: Speeches and Addresses* (New York: Charles Scribner's Sons, 1926) 58, 60.

[25] Ibid., 176.

and education were thus mutually reinforcing, rather than antagonistic, forces.

Coolidge was not disposed to lobby Congress publicly on legislation as Theodore Roosevelt had done, especially as the inherited scandals of the Harding Administration threatened to ruin him. In response to a reporter's question at a 9 November 1923 press conference, Coolidge said: "I have no doubt that the incoming Congress will extend the [quota] law...Just what provisions will be adopted, of course, I can't tell. It is perfectly apparent I think, however, that we shall have very careful restriction of immigration."[26] Two weeks later he explained to the reporters that there were no general arrangements for admitting aliens once the quotas were exhausted. He admitted that some of the cases reported in the newspapers were "quite distressing," but he said that the Labor Department assured him that it tried to take care of all "worthy cases." The State Department stood by its insistence that passports were issued with the express understanding that they did not guarantee admittance to the United States.[27]

It became apparent early on in the 1924 legislative session that Japanese immigration would be one of the most controversial issues surrounding the new law. Coolidge had no intention of altering in any way the longstanding Gentlemen's Agreement.[28] But Congress resented what they considered an unconstitutional attempt by the executive to bypass both the legislative power to pass immigration laws and the Senate's power to ratify treaties. In November 1922 the Supreme Court ruled in the case of *Ozawa v. United States* that Japanese immigrants were not eligible to become citizens because they belonged to neither the White nor the Black race, reaffirming state and federal court rulings. The House Committee, borrowing from California's Alien Land Law, inserted a clause into the 1924 bill to prohibit all "aliens ineligible to citizenship" from entering the United States as immigrants.[29]

---

[26] Calvin Coolidge, *The Talkative President: The Off-the-Record Press Conferences of Calvin Coolidge,* ed. Howard H. Quint and Robert H. Ferrell (Amherst: University of Massachusetts Press, 1964) 88.

[27] Ibid., 88–89.

[28] Ibid., 89.

[29] Ozawa v. US, 260 US 178(1922); Robert A. Divine, *American Immigration Policy, 1924–1952* (New Haven: Yale University Press, 1957) 21–22; and Peter H. Wang *Legislating Normalcy: The Immigration Act of 1924* (San Francisco: R&E Research Associates, 1975) 89.

Coolidge opposed the explicit exclusion of Japanese immigrants, but as usual, he worked behind the scenes to defeat it. He had no comment on Japanese exclusion for reporters on 15 April, but ten days later he admitted that he was "attempting to see if there is any way that the question can be solved so as to satisfy those that want to have restriction and at the same time prevent giving any affront to the Japanese Government."[30] As in the earlier crisis during Roosevelt's presidency, the issue was not whether to exclude the Japanese, but how. Coolidge, like Roosevelt, wished to avoid offending a militarily strong nation that could threaten American interests and possessions in the Pacific.

Coolidge and Secretary of State Charles Evans Hughes fought to remove the clause barring aliens ineligible to citizenship and retain the Gentleman's Agreement. They appear to have been succeeding until the secretary made a fatal error. Hughes got the Senate to write a quota of 250 into its version of the bill, which was more than the token 100 to which Japan would be entitled under the two percent formula based on the 1890 census. This posed little difficulty, especially since the chairman of the Senate Immigration Committee, LeBaron Colt of Rhode Island, was opposed to the discriminatory quotas in the first place. Hughes also asked the Senate formally to endorse the Gentlemen's Agreement, thereby reminding the senators that the agreement had never been submitted as a treaty for ratification. The ensuing heated debate in the Senate, nevertheless, initially favored the administration's policy hopes. Hughes, however, forwarded a letter from the Japanese ambassador, Masano Hanihara, that warned of "grave consequences" if the agreement was broken. The Senate, led by ardent nativists Henry Cabot Lodge and Hiram Johnson, bristled at what the former called a "veiled threat" and voted down not only the endorsement of the Gentlemen's Agreement, but also the Japanese quota. Only Colt stood by the administration.[31]

President Coolidge talked with Senators Lodge and Frank B. Willis of Ohio about the possibility of vetoing the bill, but they warned him that such action would be overridden—an unpleasant prospect in an election year.[32] He asked the conference committee seeking to reconcile the House and Senate versions of the bill for a two-year delay, then a one-year delay, to

---

[30] Coolidge, *Talkative President*, 91.
[31] Divine, *American Immigration Policy*, 22–23; and McCoy, *Quiet President*, 229–30.
[32] Ibid., 230–31.

negotiate a new treaty with Japan, but he was turned down. At a 24 May press conference, the president told the reporters that he had not yet decided whether to sign it.[33]

In the end, Coolidge signed the 1924 Immigration Act into law on May 26. But he was understandably furious with Congressional Republicans for humiliating both the Japanese government and himself. He issued a statement which explained that while he supported the exclusion of Japanese immigrants, "this method of securing it is unnecessary and deplorable at this time." Nevertheless, Coolidge decided that the other provisions of the bill, including the national origins quotas, outweighed the insult to Japan. Despite having signed the bill, he continued to insist: "If the exclusion principle stood alone, I should disapprove it without hesitation, if sought in this way, at this time."[34]

The 1924 act was a complex piece of legislation, the result of negotiation and compromise both within and between each house of Congress. Davis and the Immigration Bureau finally got overseas consular inspection, as each arriving immigrant was required to have either a visa or a reentry permit from a US Consul. The head tax was raised to eight dollars, with an additional nine dollar visa fee, making the total monetary requirement seventeen dollars while avoiding the constitutional limitation of ten dollars for a head tax.[35] The biggest changes, however, were made to the quotas.

The basis for the quotas as of 1 July 1924 became two percent of the total number of foreign-born from each nationality according to the 1890 census, rather than three percent of the corresponding 1910 figures. This change explicitly favored "desirable" immigrants from Northern and Western Europe, since the 1890 census marked the high point of German, Irish, and Scandinavian immigration.[36] Wives and unmarried children of US citizens, resident aliens returning from a temporary visit abroad and immigrants from Canada or the independent nations of the Western hemisphere, as well as ministers, professors and students over fifteen were all to be considered non-quota immigrants. Within the quotas, preference was given to immediate family members of adult US citizens and to skilled

---

[33] Coolidge, *Talkative President*, 92.

[34] McCoy, *Quiet President*, 232.

[35] Edward P. Hutchinson, *Legislative History of American Immigration Policy, 1798–1965* (Philadelphia: University of Pennsylvania Press, 1981) 187–94, 465.

[36] William S. Rossiter, *Increase of Population in the United States, 1910–1920*, Census Monograph (Washington DC: Government Printing Office, 1922) 115.

agriculturalists (although the latter did not apply to immigrants from countries with a quota under three hundred, thus excluding all non-Europeans).

Beginning 1 July 1927, however, the basis for the quotas was to change to "national origins," a device which apparently originated with John B. Trevor of New York and introduced into the Senate version of the bill by David Reed after the House had rejected it.[37] Reed and Henry Cabot Lodge emphasized to the Senate that with the national origins plan, "there can be no question...of discrimination, because it will treat all races alike on the basis of their actual proportion of the existing population."[38] But in fact it did discriminate against Asians, who were completely excluded. The new quotas were to be in the same ratio to 150,000 as the number of inhabitants having that national origin were to the number of inhabitants in continental United States in 1920, not counting Indians, African Americans, non-quota immigrants and Asian Americans. The Secretaries of State, Commerce, and Labor were to prepare estimates of the national origins of all White citizens of European origin, based on the census returns and the official immigration and emigration statistics, not by tracing individual family trees. Still, it was an impossible task, even for confident social scientists. Legislators appear to have approved the national origins section without knowing exactly what those quotas would look like—an oversight which would later cost several their seats in Congress.

Charles Evans Hughes, Herbert Hoover and James J. Davis formed the first quota committee, consisting of two representatives from each department and chaired by Dr. Joseph A. Hill, assistant to the director of the Census, to work out the immigration allotments.[39] The first set, based on the 1890 census, were easy to calculate. The 1890 census marked the high point of German, Irish, and Scandinavian immigration, and the assigned quotas

---

[37] Divine, *American Immigration Policy*, 26; John Higham, *Strangers in the Land: Patterns of American Nativism, 1860– 1925*, 2nd ed. (New Brunswick: Rutgers University Press, 1988) 314–15, 319–22. Higham suggests that Trevor and Reed came up with the idea simultaneously.

[38] *Congressional Record*, 68th Cong., 1st sess., 1924, 5568; and Hutchinson, *Legislative History*, 190.

[39] The members of the first Quota Board were Col. Lawrence Martin (Geographic Section, Division of Political Information) and J. P. Doughten (Visa Office) from the Department of State, Hill and Dr. Alba Edwards (Division of Population, Census Bureau) from the Department of Commerce, and Ethelbert Stewart (Commissioner of Labor Statistics) and Albert E. Reitzel (assistant solicitor) from the Department of Labor.

reflected that fact. The annual German quota would be 51,227, with 34,007 admitted from Great Britain, 28,567 from the Irish Free State, 9,561 from Sweden and 6,453 from Norway. Countries which had contributed the greatest number of immigrants to the United States in the past three decades had dramatically reduced quotas: 3,845 a year from Italy, 5,982 from Poland and 2,248 from Russia. The majority of the Austro-Hungarian total was assigned to Czechoslovakia (3,073), with Austria, Hungary, and Yugoslavia receiving quotas under one thousand each. The minimum quotas were assigned to countries within the "Asiatic Barred Zone," but were explicitly reserved for aliens eligible for citizenship (i.e., European expatriates).[40]

Hill also chaired the second quota committee that determined the national origins quotas following the work of the first such committee. The task that he and his "Quota Board" faced was immense—and thankless.[41] The daunting process of determining the national origins of all White citizens was complicated by incomplete records, numerous boundary changes and the existence of transnational groups such as the Jews. Samuel W. Boggs prepared a memorandum explaining the Quota Board's methods and assumptions in some detail[42]. Beginning with the total population of the continental United States as recorded in the 1920 census, African Americans, Indians, Asians and immigrants from the Western Hemisphere, along with their descendants, were subtracted, leaving a European-American population of roughly 90,000,000.[43] Thus the quotas were calculated at the ratio of 150,000 to 90,000,000. The ninety million had to be further broken down between "original native stock" (those present in 1790 and their descendants) and "immigrant stock," a task made difficult by the absence of records. The first year in which annual records of immigration were kept

---

[40] Joseph A. Hill to Charles Evans Hughes, Herbert Hoover and James J. Davis, 19 June 1924, in Herbert Hoover Papers, Commerce, Container 289, Herbert Hoover Presidential Library, West Branch IA.

[41] The members of the second Quota Board were R. W. Flournoy, Jr. and S. W. Boggs from the Department of State, Hill and Leon Truesdell from the Department of Commerce, and William Walter Husband (Commissioner of Immigration) and Stewart from the Department of Labor.

[42] S.W. Boggs, "Memorandum Regarding the Processes Employed by the Quota Board in Determining the Provisional Immigration Quotas on the Basis of Nationality of Origin of the Population of the United States," 10 February 1927, Hoover Papers, Commerce, Container 289, Hoover Library. This paragraph and the following two are based on Boggs' memorandum. See also Divine, *American Immigration Policy*, 28-33.

[43] Actually 89,332,158.

was 1820. The 1850 census was the first one to count the foreign-born by their country of origin, while the children of the foreign-born were not distinguished in the census until 1890. Linguistic breakdowns between immigrant population groups began only with the 1910 census. Clearly, the board members would need to make some large quantitative assumptions in their "statistical" analysis of the immigrant populations.

The assumptions the Quota Board ultimately made, while arguably reasonable, skewed the results in favor of British Americans. The first was that immigration between 1790 and 1820 was too negligible to matter for the final quotas. They divided the "immigrant stock" (1820–1920) into three groups: people born overseas, their children, and their grandchildren and later descendants. The foreign-born totals were simply taken from the 1920 census, already reflecting most of the postwar boundary changes in Europe. The children of the foreign-born were likewise taken from the most recent census, although here boundary changes had to be taken into account. Half of the children with one foreign-born and one native-born parent were counted. Grandchildren and later generations were extrapolated from earlier census figures, with the earliest decades weighted more heavily as having probably produced more offspring.

The "original native stock" was calculated at 41,000,000 by working backwards from the correlation of age, nativity, and race made in the 1890, 1900, 1910 and 1920 censuses.[44] These forty-one million were considered to be the descendants of the native White population enumerated in the 1790 census. That population's "national origins" had been calculated on the basis of last names in the 1909 census monograph *A Century of Population Growth*, accepted at face value by the Board. In response to the furor over their preliminary report, however, the Quota Board accepted the assistance of immigration historian Marcus Hansen and genealogist Howard Barker, commissioned by the American Council of Learned Societies to review and correct the 1909 estimates. Hansen and Barker revised the estimate of British population in 1790 from eighty-two percent down to sixty percent, citing the anglicization of names. In its final 1928 report, the Quota Board nevertheless reduced its estimate of the 1790 British population by only

---

[44] Interestingly, William Rossiter's census monograph calculated it as 47,330,000 (p. 97), and this figure was used in Niles Carpenter's census monograph *Immigrants and Their Children, 1920* (Washington: Government Printing Office: 1927) 4.

10.4%.[45] Since it was impossible to account for intermarriage without researching individual family trees—both impractical and forbidden by the 1924 act—the board simply redistributed the 41,000,000 in the same proportions as they believed existed in 1790.

Several of the board's assumptions doubtlessly led to over-representation of the British element by a considerable margin in the final figures. Nevertheless, it is unfair to criticize the Quota Board too severely. They seemed to have approached their work with no more than the usual bias that any social scientist brings to his work. If they made statistical assumptions that seem dubious in retrospect, it should be kept in mind that they had been given an impossible task. In all probability, given the numbers involved, the errors resulting from their assumptions would have altered the quotas only minimally—a fact Hill emphasized in his testimony before Congress.[46] Any blame for resultant inequities must rather be assigned to the Congress that imposed such an improbable task.

The congressmen and the president alike were slow to realize that the national origins quotas contained political dynamite. Perhaps they assumed that no one could argue with a scientifically derived quota system. Senator Reed of Pennsylvania explained to his colleagues that it was the 1921 Quota Law that had discriminated by disregarding the native-born.[47] But when the preliminary report was issued in January 1927, the unseen dynamite exploded.

The ethnic groups most angered by the national origins quotas were, ironically, the ones the 1924 law was designed to favor. Quotas for Southern and Eastern Europeans remained low, although Italy's rose from 3,845 to 6,091 and Russia's doubled from 2,248 to 4,781. On the other hand, the quotas for Germany, Ireland, and Scandinavia were slashed dramatically. Germany's went from 51,227 to 23,428; Ireland's dropped from 28,567 to 13,682; Sweden's plummeted from 9,561 to 3,259; Norway's plunged from

---

[45] American Council of Learned Societies, "Report of the Committee on Linguistic and National Studies in the Population of the United States," *Annual Report of the American Historical Association*, 1931 (Washington, 1932), 1:107–108; and Divine, *American Immigration Policy*, 32. The Quota Board did additional calculations based on language groups for the territories which were not yet a part of the United States in 1790, and distributed the results among the modern-day countries which spoke the same tongue.

[46] Senate Committee on Immigration, *National Origins Provision of the Immigration Law*, 70th Cong., 1st sess., S. Doc. 65, 17; and Divine, *American Immigration Policy*, 39.

[47] *Congressional Record*, 68th Cong., 2d sess., 1924, 5461.

6,453 to 2,267. The big winners were the British, whose quota soared from 34,007 to 73,039.[48] The changes were due to counting all Whites, not just immigrants, and shifting to the 1920 census as a basis, which meant more Italians and Russians but fewer Germans, Irish and Scandinavians. Congress all along had made clear its real, discriminatory purpose in setting the quotas. The results of the national origins provision made it seem that "Nordics" were the new target of this legislative discrimination. With the memory of persecution during World War I still fresh in the minds of these populations, they denounced the new quotas as motivated by lingering Anglophilia and hostility toward those opposed to America's involvement in the war on the side of the Allies.[49]

The way in which the preliminary figures were delivered to Congress added to the controversy. The original draft of the report by Secretary of State Frank Kellogg, Secretary of Commerce Herbert Hoover and Secretary of Labor James J. Davis to the president offered no comment on the quotas. A letter from Hoover to Kellogg on 15 December 1926 indicated no concern over the matter. By 30 December, however, Hoover had become quite concerned and wrote to the Secretary of State: "I have again considered the racial origin report. I should like to emphasize the fact that I consider the whole statistical foundation under this performance entirely inadequate for correct conclusions, and that I cannot take any responsibility in putting forward this report."[50] The final version of the secretaries' report to Coolidge on 3 January 1927 stated: "We wish to state that in our opinion the statistical and historical information available raises grave doubts as to the whole value of these computations as a basis for the purposes intended. We therefore can not assume responsibility for such conclusions under these circumstances."[51]

The report Coolidge submitted to Congress on 7 January was edited at the White House. This section containing the secretaries' "grave doubts" was replaced by the following caveat: "It may be stated that the statistical

---

[48] US Senate, *National Origin Provision of the Immigration Act of 1924: Message from the President of the United States*, 69th Cong., 2d sess., S. Doc. 190, Hoover Papers, Commerce, Container 289, Hoover Library.

[49] On the debate over national origins, see Divine, *American Immigration Policy*, 31–51.

[50] Herbert Hoover to Frank Kellogg, 15 December 1926; and Hoover to Kellogg, 30 December 1926; Hoover Papers, Commerce, Container 289, Hoover Library.

[51] Frank Kellogg, Herbert Hoover, and James J. Davis to Calvin Coolidge, 3 January 1927, ibid.

and historical information available from which these computations were made is not entirely satisfactory. Assuming, however, that the issuance of the proclamation…is mandatory and that Congress will neither repeal nor amend said act on or before April 1, 1927, the attached list shows substantially the quota allotments for use in said proclamation."[52] Three days later Coolidge sent an amended version containing the secretaries' original wording to Congress, causing an uproar as the timing of the revision's submission suggested the president and secretaries were backtracking due to public pressure. The New York *Herald-Tribune* commented: "The [amended] report…is taken to mean that the president will either not proclaim the national origin quotas or that Congress will repeal the national origins provision.…It was said today that Secretaries Kellogg and Hoover objected to the form in which the subcommittee's letter of transmittal went to the Senate, although Secretary Davis approved it."[53]

Boggs' memorandum explaining the Quota Board's process of calculating its figures also proved quite controversial. The memorandum's title indicates that it was given to the three secretaries along with the Board's preliminary report on 15 December 1926. Hill and Hoover later denied receiving it.[54] As controversy over the national origins quotas raged, the Senate passed a resolution in 1927 requesting this document from the Quota Board. When Hoover was asked by Coolidge to draft a response, he prepared several versions, each with a different story.[55] Davis wrote Hoover on 26 February 1927 to say that Ethelbert Stewart informed him that the memo was never submitted to nor approved by the Quota Board, and that only Hill would really know how the figures were arrived at since all the calculations were done by the Census Bureau.[56] Coolidge's official response to the Senate was that "no such memorandum was prepared by the six statistical experts," which was technically correct (only Boggs had prepared

---

[52] US Senate, *National Origin Provision of the Immigration Act of 1924*.

[53] New York *Herald Tribune*, 11 January 1927, clipping in Hoover Papers, Commerce, Container 289, Hoover Library. See also Divine, *American Immigration Policy*, 30–31. It is not clear why the incorrect version was sent; however, the language used in the 7 January 1927 letter is not found in any of the drafts in the Hoover papers, which indicates that the changes were undoubtedly made at the White House.

[54] Joseph A. Hill to George Akerson, 24 February 1927, Hoover Papers, Commerce, Container 289, Hoover Library.

[55] Everett Sanders to Herbert Hoover, 1 March 1927; and Hoover to Sanders, 1 March 1927; Ibid.

[56] James J. Davis to Herbert Hoover, 26 February 1927, ibid.

it) but hardly honest. Senator Matthew M. Neely of West Virginia and Senator Frank Willis of Ohio insisted that they had seen the memo. Neely produced it and read it into the *Congressional Record*, making special note of the original title (which Hill had tried to change). Neely accused Hoover of trying to subvert the national origins quotas to win the foreign-born vote in a possible presidential run the following year, an accusation which probably struck close to home.[57]

Congressmen, under fire for the quotas, were looking for scapegoats. Preliminary national origins quotas had been given to Congress in June 1924, shortly after the act was passed, but apparently few senators and representatives had paid attention. Senator Irvine Lenroot wrote Coolidge after losing his Wisconsin seat in the 1926 election, largely over the quotas: "I was ill and not in the Senate at the time this act was passed, but find there was very little debate on Section II and I doubt if many members of either House knew just what the effect of the Section would be."[58] Albert Johnson had figured it out by August 1926, however, and summoned Hoover and Davis to meet with him in Seattle. After securing their agreement, Johnson wired Coolidge on 25 August: "My opinion is that a pronouncement by you in plenty of time before [the] general elections will save our party not less than twenty districts in states where German, Irish and Scandinavian people are disturbed over possible further restriction under National Origins Selection." The politician from Washington State also urged the president to talk to Trevor, the originator of the National Origins system, who was warning that after 1930 there would be great pressure placed on Congress to use that year's census, further increasing quotas for new immigrants.[59]

Despite Johnson's plea, Coolidge remained silent about the national origins scheme, although the New York *Times* reported that he was displeased with the new quotas.[60] No doubt he had little interest in saving Republican Congressmen after the shabby way they had treated him in passing the law. Besides, it would have been hypocritical for him to come out suddenly against a law for which he had been taking credit. In the 1924

---

[57] *Congressional Record*, 69th Cong. 3d sess., 1927, 5948–951.

[58] Irvine Lenroot to Calvin Coolidge, 15 November 1926, copy in Hoover Papers, Commerce, Container 289, Hoover Library; and McCoy, *Quiet President*, 312.

[59] Albert Johnson telegram to Herbert Hoover, 18 August 1926; Johnson telegram to Calvin Coolidge, 25 August 1926, copy in Hoover Papers, Commerce, Container 289; Divine, *American Immigration Policy*, 31; and McCoy, *Quiet President*, 312.

[60] New York *Times*, 2 January 1927, 1; ibid., 5 January 1927, 24; ibid., 11 January 1927, 21; and Divine, *American Immigration Policy*, 32.

campaign he had told labor leaders: "We want the people who live in America, no matter what their origin, to be able to continue in the enjoyment of their present unprecedented advantages. This opportunity would certainly be destroyed by the tremendous influx of foreign peoples, if immigration were not restricted."[61] Coolidge understood that economic prosperity was the basis of his popularity, and he had no intentions of jeopardizing it.

Coolidge deflected criticism of the new immigration law's discriminatory nature by focusing on the "economic necessity" of restriction. Addressing a delegation of foreign-born citizens at the White House on 16 October 1924, Coolidge pointed out that the United States would be unable to support too large an influx of immigration. Appealing to his audience's most intimate concerns for those of like national origins, he predicted: "The first sufferers would be the most recent immigrants, unaccustomed to our life and language and industrial methods." He further insisted that the new quotas were "not a reflection on any race or creed."[62] Of course, they *were* a negative reflection on several races, cultures and even religious creeds. The president, however, chose to believe immigration restriction was needed to maintain the era of "Coolidge prosperity"—therefore, at least in this case, it appears he also believed the ends justified the means.

Prejudice was very much an issue in the 1924 campaign due to the resurgence of the Ku Klux Klan, drawing most of its support in the 1920s from Northern cities and focusing most of its wrath on Catholic and Jewish immigrants. Coolidge kept silent about the group, believing that the burden was on Democrats to break their historic connection to the Klan. He refused a request from Corinne Roosevelt Robinson, Theodore Roosevelt's sister, that he openly attack the Klan.[63] Despite earlier criticism of his message to the Knights of Columbus shortly after taking office, Coolidge reviewed and addressed the parade of 100,000 members of the Holy Name Society in Washington in the fall of 1924, thereby signaling as clearly as he could without actually saying so that he disagreed with the Klan.[64]

---

[61] Coolidge, *Foundations of the Republic*, 83.

[62] Ibid., 162.

[63] Corinne Roosevelt Robinson to Calvin Coolidge, 28 October 1924; and Coolidge to Robinson, 1 November 1924; in Coolidge Papers, PPF 683.

[64] "Cardinal Enthusiastic Over Holy Name Demonstration," Boston *Sunday Herald*, 12 October 1924, clipping in ibid., PPF 548; and Lynn Dumenil, "The Tribal Twenties: 'Assimilated' Catholics' Response to Anti-Catholicism in the 1920s," *Journal of American Ethnic History*, 11/1 (Fall 1991): 21, 35–36.

Coolidge thus continued his practice of courting immigrant Catholic voters. Like Harding, however, Coolidge denied that the United States should be an asylum for all Europeans. While discrimination violated his ideal of universal brotherhood, he rationalized restriction by pointing out that brotherhood begins at home and that America had no obligation to accept everyone who wanted to enter. Indeed, unrestricted immigration in his view heightened racial and ethnic tensions, so restricting the flow could even work to foster brotherhood and assimilation. Such rationalization was made easier for Coolidge as he had no relatives who were denied admittance to the United States.

Coolidge did not receive much support from foreign-born voters in the 1924 election. German and Scandinavian-American voters overwhelmingly supported the Progressive candidate, Wisconsin Senator Robert LaFollette, who won more than four million votes. The senator ran well in the north-central states, outdoing New York Democrat John W. Davis in twelve of them and winning his home state outright. Coolidge nevertheless exceeded the combined Democratic and Progressive totals by two and a half million votes. While he received over four hundred thousand fewer votes than Harding had in 1920, Coolidge did better than his predecessor in New England and the middle Atlantic and Pacific coast states, regions with large numbers of foreign-born voters.[65]

In his inaugural address in March 1925, Coolidge, like McKinley and Harding, linked immigration restriction and the protective tariff as economic necessities. Coolidge proclaimed, restrictive immigration and protective tariffs resulted in high employment, good pay rates, and a general contentment among workers as seldom before seen in the country. But he also spoke of the need for toleration: "It would be well if we could replace much that is only a false and ignorant prejudice with a true and enlightened pride of race…. The fundamental precept of liberty is toleration."[66] Coolidge thus sought to distinguish between immigration restriction and nativism. The ideal of asylum was fading, but the president continued to extol the virtues of the melting pot.

---

[65] Allan J. Lichtman, *Prejudice and the Old Politics: The Presidential Election of 1928* (Chapel Hill: University of North Carolina Press, 1979) 104–107; and Edgar Eugene Robinson, *The Presidential Vote, 1896–1932* (Palo Alto: Stanford University Press, 1934) 21–24.

[66] Coolidge, *Foundations of the Republic*, 203, 204.

He also continued to reach out to ethnic voters. Perhaps attempting to head off Scandinavian-American unrest over the new quotas, Coolidge journeyed to the Norwegian Centennial Celebration at the Minnesota State Fairgrounds in June 1925. He praised Norwegian Americans as "representatives of a stalwart race, men and women of fixed determination, enduring courage and high character...well worthy to follow in the wake of the Pilgrim and Cavalier."[67] The president also expressed appreciation for all ethnic groups in the United States. Americans used to fear "that from such a melting pot of diverse elements we could never draw the tested, tempered metal that is the only substance for national character," Coolidge said. The American experience had instead "demonstrated conclusively that there is a spiritual quality shared by all races and conditions of men which is their universal heritage and common nature."[68] The melting pot was creating Coolidge's ideal of universal brotherhood; it just needed time to yield its positive results.

Coolidge clearly wanted to preach toleration and national unity now that the election was won and European immigration had all but ceased. He agreed with those who said that immigration needed to be curtailed to give America a chance to assimilate the more recently arrived foreign-born. But he abhorred the nativists' racism, and he attacked it as un-American, a violation of the republic's ideals. On 6 October 1925 Coolidge took a sizable political risk by lecturing the American Legion convention in Omaha on the need for "Toleration and Liberalism." The Legion campaigned for a temporary halt to all immigrants, even after the passage of the 1924 law, because of the threat posed by "alien slackers" living in "un-American enclaves," who imported Communism and took jobs away from native-born Americans. They had also lobbied for the abrogation of the Gentlemen's Agreement with Japan and the total exclusion of Japanese immigrants. On the other hand, the Legion secured an amendment to the Johnson Act in 1925 that allowed alien veterans of the American armed forces living abroad to return to the United States with their families regardless of the quotas, and relaxed the standard for naturalization for them. The veterans' organization also sponsored close to 1,800 citizenship schools in the inter-war years, as

---

[67] Ibid., 247.
[68] Ibid., 248–50.

well as naturalization ceremonies that impressed new citizens with their responsibilities to uphold American ideals.[69]

As governor of Massachusetts, Coolidge had cooperated with the American Legion. He allowed them to set up their headquarters in the State House, take over the state employment bureau for veterans, and gave them a seven-hundred-dollar weekly subsidy.[70] As president, however, Coolidge criticized the Legion's nativism. He conceded that wartime intolerance had been a natural reaction, but nevertheless called it "a disturbing product of war psychology. He insisted further, "There should be an intellectual demobilization as well as a military demobilization."[71] Coolidge had assisted that demobilization by pardoning or commuting the sentences of all the remaining alien Wobblies by 1925. His new attorney general, Harlan Fiske Stone, terminated the Justice Department's anti-radical division with its domestic espionage and unlawful searches and seizures.[72]

Coolidge understood the spirit at work in the slogan demands, "America First" and "One-Hundred Percent Americanism." He admonished the nativist American Legion, however, that intolerance and bigotry were un-American, while insisting diversity in a patriotically loyal population was actually a source of national strength. The president informed the former servicemen that "Divine Providence has not bestowed upon any race a monopoly of patriotism and character."[73] The United States could best fulfill its own destiny and serve the world by being a shining example of toleration, a city set on a hill of brotherly love between all races and nationalities. "We can only make America first in the true sense, which means by cultivating a spirit of friendship and good will, by the exercise of the virtues of patience and forbearance, by being 'plenteous in mercy'…standing as an example of real service to humanity."[74]

Assimilation did not mean the abandonment of one's culture and language to Coolidge. It did mean the adoption of American ideals and the English language, which best expressed them. Dedicating a Washington DC statue of the Swedish-American engineer John Ericsson in May 1926,

---

[69] William Pencak, *For God and Country: The American Legion, 1919–1941* (Boston: Northeastern University Press, 1989) 256–62, 290–91.

[70] Ibid., 67.

[71] Coolidge, *Foundations of the Republic*, 295–96.

[72] William Preston, Jr., *Aliens and Radicals: Federal Suppression of Radicals, 1903–1933* (Cambridge: Harvard University Press, 1963) 242–43, 261–62.

[73] Coolidge, *Foundations of the Republic*, 298–99.

[74] Ibid., 300.

Coolidge declared that America was the place where artificial distinctions between persons—race, lineage, social rank—were cast aside. He was careful to add, however, that "this is not done by discarding the teachings and beliefs or the character which have contributed to the strength and progress of the peoples from which our various strains derived their origins, but rather from the acceptance of all their good qualities and their adaptation to the requirements of our institutions."[75] Coolidge declared John Ericsson should not be honored simply as "a great son of Sweden," but rather as "a preeminent example of the superb contribution which has been made by many different nationalities to the cause of our country."[76]

Other administration officials joined Coolidge's efforts to encourage assimilation and downplay ethnic tensions. The Bureau of Immigration tried to stress the positive results of the National Origins Act rather than its obvious racist intent. Commissioner General William Walter Husband's 1925 annual report declared: "In no previous year has so even and regular a volume of immigrant travel come to our ports nor has such travel ever before been so carefully and consistently inspected by Government officers." The former secretary of the Dillingham Commission called the 1924 act "a law with a heart" because it ended overcrowding and rejection at Ellis Island. Husband did not seem to recognize that overcrowding was eased in large part because the new quotas shifted the burden to the land borders, especially the one with Mexico. A total of 706,896 immigrants arrived in 1924, but fewer than half of them (315,587) entered through Ellis Island.[77] New York's long reign as the primary entry point for immigrants was over. With the establishment of overseas consular inspection and harshly restrictive quotas, Ellis Island would become primarily a detention center for aliens awaiting deportation.

Further restrictive efforts failed in 1926. Albert Johnson introduced a constitutional amendment to deny citizenship to the native-born children of Asian immigrants, but it was rejected by Congress. The House passed a bill that year which greatly expanded the grounds for deportation and extended the time limits, but the Senate failed to act on it. Meanwhile, Congress did pass two laws that year which gave non-quota status to alien veterans of the US army in World War I and their families, and to Spanish citizens who

---

[75] Ibid., 415.

[76] Ibid., 416.

[77] Thomas M. Pitkin, *Keepers of the Gate: A History of Ellis Island* (New York: New York University Press, 1975) 153–55.

were residents of Puerto Rico when the United States conquered it in 1898. The final national origins quotas were delayed for one year in 1927 to give the Quota Board time to secure more acceptable figures. The quotas were postponed again in 1928, as neither party wanted to deal with such a volatile issue in the campaign that year.[78]

During the decade following World War I, the debate shifted from the question of whether immigration restriction was legitimate to what form restriction should take. President Coolidge, like many of his fellow Americans in the 1920s, believed that the American national interest required a period of restricted immigration to enable assimilation and unification to take place and to continue economic prosperity. He argued that the national origins quotas—whatever Congress' racist intent—did not violate the egalitarian ideals of the United States because they were based on impartial science. Since the loudest complaints came from Germans, Irish and Scandinavians—alleging their own racial superiority as an argument against the quotas—it was easy for Coolidge to dismiss such criticism as self-interest. Like Harding, Coolidge disavowed the ideal of asylum; overseas consular inspection and restrictive quotas had all but ended that role for the United States. It would remain for Herbert Hoover, however, to declare officially the end of asylum.

---

[78] Hutchinson, *Legislative History*, 197–201.

CHAPTER 8

HERBERT HOOVER
AND THE END OF ASYLUM

Herbert Hoover, like his predecessors Warren Harding and Calvin Coolidge, came from a middle-class, rural background. Unlike them, he had never previously served as an elected official, and his political inexperience severely hampered his presidency. Although he was an active administrator as US Secretary of Commerce in the Harding and Coolidge Administrations, he had not spent much time lobbying Congress to secure legislation. His experience with the Quota Boards, moreover, taught him to be wary of immigration restriction. Like his predecessors, Hoover publicly declared his faith in the melting pot concept. He also consistently called for repeal of the national origins quotas and a return to the two percent quotas based on the 1890 census. But in the face of the Great Depression, Hoover moved to cut off all immigration by executive order. In the process, he declared the end of America's role as an asylum.

Hoover was born in West Branch, Iowa, a Quaker farming community in the eastern section of the state. His father's family had emigrated from Switzerland to the Palatinate in the 1700s, and thence to the United States. His mother was a Canadian immigrant, although her ancestors had originally settled in the United States before moving to Ontario. Unlike most immigrants, she had an easy cultural transition. Hoover's father died when he was six and his mother passed away two years later. Hoover eventually wound up living with his maternal aunt and uncle in Newburg, Oregon. He also spent one summer with another uncle, Laban Miles, who was the agent on the Osage Indian Reservation in Oklahoma.[1]

---

[1] Herbert Hoover, *The Memoirs of Herbert Hoover*, 3 vols. (New York: Macmillan, 1951) 1:1–15; David Burner, *Herbert Hoover: A Public Life* (New York: Alfred A. Knopf, 1979) 3–16; and George H. Nash, *The Life of Herbert Hoover: The Engineer, 1874–1914* (New York: W. W. Norton & Co., 1983) 1–25.

After graduating as part of the first class at Stanford University, Hoover spent most of the next twenty years overseas as a mining engineer with Bewick, Moreing and Company, a large British firm. Wherever he went, he was known for his American patriotism: British acquaintances called him "Star-Spangled Hoover," while Australians knew him as "Hail Columbia Hoover."[2] In addition to seeing more of the world than either Harding or Coolidge, Hoover also had first-hand experience in employing immigrant labor. As superintendent of the Sons of Gwalia mine in Western Australia, Hoover introduced Italian immigrants to the labor force, telling his superiors that they were "in every way superior workers to the men we formerly employed." In an article in the *Engineering and Mining Journal* in December 1898, Hoover praised the Italians for accomplishing half-again as much work as the Australians, although he admitted that they possessed "certain disqualifications," no doubt referring to their lack of English language skills.[3] In 1904, a public outcry against the use of these Italian workers prompted an investigation by the governor of Western Australia. When Bewick, Moreing and Company dismissed all employees incapable of speaking English, Hoover was in England and made no public comment.[4]

Hoover's experiences in Australia and later in China, where he and his wife were living during the Boxer Rebellion, caused him to view Asians negatively. His 1909 book, *Principles of Mining*, expressed racist disdain for both Asians and Blacks. "Much observation and experience in working Asiatics and negroes as well as Americans and Australians," he wrote, "leads the writer to the conclusion that, averaging actual results, one white man equals from two to three of the colored races, even in the simplest forms of mine work such as shoveling or tramming." He also denied the claim that such "cheap labor" lowered the cost of production, because the costly errors committed by workers of "low mental order" offset any payroll savings. He concluded there was no "industrial yellow peril" to the West because the "Chinese workman cannot be made as efficient as the European."[5] This stand was contrary to that of most advocates of Asian exclusion, such as Woodrow Wilson, who argued that Asian workers were

---

[2] Nash, *The Engineer*, 502.

[3] Burner, *A Public Life*, 29–31; and Nash, *The Engineer*, 72–73.

[4] Burner, *A Public Life*, 50–51; and Nash, *The Engineer*, 329–33.

[5] Herbert Hoover, *Principles of Mining* (New York: Hill Publishing Co., 1909), 163–65; Hoover, *Memoirs,* 1:87; Burner, *A Public Life*, 197; and Nash, *The Engineer*, 505–06.

too efficient in competition with Whites. Hoover did agree with the exclusionists that the Asian and Caucasian races did not mix well, however, writing in the *Principles of Mining* that the good qualities of both races were lost in the offspring.

In a passage of his *Memoirs* written in 1915–1916, Hoover softened his views by expressing an "abiding admiration" for the Chinese people, acknowledging their patience and hard work in the face of grinding poverty. But he continued to describe them as incapable of meeting Western standards of democracy, administrative efficiency and skilled technological work.[6] As he sought to build a political base in California following his return to the United States, he conformed easily to the prevailing anti-Asian prejudice of the Pacific coast. Writing to California Congressman John Raker in 1924 Hoover said, "Ever since I have been able to think and talk I have strongly supported restriction of Asiatic immigration to the United States."[7]

Hoover also moderated his opinion of immigrants from Europe. During and after World War I he organized relief efforts to feed starving Europeans. This humanitarian service exposed him to poverty and suffering, teaching him greater sympathy for the new immigrants, although racism gave way only to paternalism. Hoover also joined the general condemnation of hyphenism during the postwar Red Scare, telling a 1919 Polish-American audience in Buffalo, "Your first and primary duty is to the country of your adoption."[8]

Although he had an upper-class disdain for the foreign-born working class, Hoover did not embrace anti-Semitism, as did many of his contemporaries. Having worked closely with Jewish relief agencies during World War I, he had come to respect and admire the dedication and tireless work of that community. In 1922 he wrote to Alexander Brin, editor of the *Jewish Advocate* of Boston, "I have found a high spirit of Americanism amongst the Jews engaged in this work and a desire to extend the things that America stands for amongst their race abroad."[9] Hoover also lent his support

---

[6] Hoover, *Memoirs*, 1:65–72.

[7] Herbert Hoover to John E. Raker, 19 February 1924, Hoover Papers, Commerce, Container 289, Herbert Hoover Presidential Library, West Branch IA.

[8] Herbert Hoover, "Address Before Polish Conference," Buffalo, 12 November 1919, in Hoover, "Public Statements," scrapbook in Hoover Library; and Burner, *A Public Life*, 197.

[9] Herbert Hoover to Alexander Brin, 15 September 1922, Hoover Papers, Commerce, Container 350, Hoover Library.

to the effort to create a Jewish homeland in Palestine, writing to the editor of the New York *Jewish Tribune* in 1922 that he supported Palestine "as an asylum for the less fortunate masses of Jewish people." Nevertheless, he expressed the hope that leading Jewish Americans like Oscar Straus, Marshall Schiff, Louis Brandeis and Henry Morgenthau would not forsake America for Palestine, since they could not "attain such service and usefulness to the world in general in any place except the United States."[10]

Unlike Calvin Coolidge, Hoover did not believe in the ideal of universal brotherhood. Instead, he championed American individualism because he believed that the individual geniuses who truly make societal progress possible must be free to soar above the plodding masses. "We in America have had too much experience of life to fool ourselves into pretending that all men are equal in ability, in character, in intelligence, in ambition," he wrote in 1922, attributing such "claptrap" to the French Revolution rather than the American Revolution. Instead, he argued, "Our social, economic, and intellectual progress is almost solely dependent upon the creative minds of those individuals with imaginative and administrative intelligence who create or who carry discoveries to widespread application.[11] With very few exceptions, Hoover believed that such individuals, like himself, were of European origins.

When Warren Harding named him Secretary of Commerce in 1921; Hoover probably did not expect to confront immigration issues directly. The 1924 National Origins Act, however, thrust him into the center of the debate by making him jointly responsible, along with the Secretaries of State and Labor, for devising the quotas. Hoover consistently supported the use of the quotas based on the 1890 census rather than the national origins quotas, although he did not view the issue as a major one. By supporting restriction while opposing the national origins quotas, he pleased the German, Irish and Scandinavian immigrants who made up the largest group of foreign-born voters without alienating the nativists too much. In his California speech accepting the Republican presidential nomination at Palo Alto on 11 August 1928, Hoover called for repeal of the national origins quotas. The two percent quotas were based on the same essential principle as those derived

---

[10] Herbert Hoover to Nehemiah Mosessohn, 25 August 1922, ibid.

[11] Herbert Hoover, *American Individualism* (Garden City NY: Doubleday, Page & Co., 1922) 19, 22.

by the national origins mechanism   and worked just as well.[12] The core
principle was, of course, racial discrimination in favor of Northern and
Western Europeans.

Like his immediately past Republican predecessors, Hoover linked the
restriction of immigration to the protective tariff. "The Republican Party has
ever been the exponent of protection to all our people from competition with
lower standards of living abroad," the presidential candidate declared. "We
have always fought for tariffs designed to establish this protection from
imported goods. We also have enacted restrictions upon immigration for the
protection of labor from the inflow of workers faster than we can absorb
them without breaking down our wage levels." He was careful to point out,
as Coolidge had, that immigration restriction was not discrimination because
it protected the foreign-born from economic abuse as well as ensured fair
wages for the native-born worker.[13]

In St. Louis on 2 November 1928, Hoover again called for the repeal of
the national origins clause, a politically astute move in a city with a large
German-American population. Charles Nagel, President Taft's Secretary of
Commerce and Labor, joined Hoover on the platform and blasted the
national origins quotas as a remnant of "war prejudice."[14] But elsewhere,
Hoover avoided any mention of national origins, speaking only of his
support of restricted immigration. In Newark on 17 September, speaking to a
largely working-class audience, Hoover was careful to acknowledge the
merit of immigrants, stating that they brought "many elements of great value
in our cultural development." Rather than calling for a continuation of the
1890 census as the basis for quotas, Hoover simply stated his opposition to
any increase in immigration.[15]

On 6 October at Elizabethton, Tennessee, Hoover stated: "I do not
favor any increase in immigration. Restriction protects the American home
from widespread unemployment. At the same time we must humanize the
laws, but only within the present quotas."[16] By referring to the "present
quotas," Hoover deliberately obscured his meaning, since the audience could

---

[12] Herbert Hoover, *Public Papers of the Presidents of the United States: Herbert
Hoover*, 4 vols. (Washington DC: Government Printing Office, 1974–77) 1:508.

[13] Ibid.

[14] Newspaper clipping in Calvin Coolidge Papers, President's Personal Files (PPF)
871, Forbes Library, Northampton MA. For Hoover's speech, see Hoover, *Public Papers,*
1:599–600.

[15] Hoover, *Public Papers*, 1:534.

[16] Ibid., 552.

not be sure if he meant the 1890 census quotas, still in effect, or the national origins quotas, twice-postponed but due to take effect the following year. Such obfuscation was designed to attract voters in the South, where nativism held sway, as well as placate labor. It definitely succeeded in the latter goal. William Green, president of the American Federation of Labor, issued a statement in response to the Elizabethton speech that called Hoover's remarks on immigration "most welcome indeed."[17]

His opponent, New York Governor Alfred Smith, was even more vague on the issue of immigration restriction. In his speech accepting the Democratic nomination, Smith supported the use of a more recent census than the 1890 one. M. G. Fitzpatrick, chairman of the New York State Republican Editors' Committee, believed that Smith's statement may have cost him support among German and Irish-Americans because the 1920 census base would lower their homelands' quotas. Smith later claimed to be in complete agreement with Hoover on the issue, and he endorsed the principle of immigration restriction both north and south of the Mason-Dixon line. The New York governor told a Louisville, Kentucky audience that the Democrats were responsible for first restricting immigration with the 1917 Act. Commissioner General Harry E. Hull issued a statement denying that the Democrats could take credit because it was the war rather than the literacy test which halted immigration.[18]

The impact of immigration restriction as an issue for foreign-born voters in the 1928 election is obscured by the countervailing issues of Prohibition and Smith's Catholicism. Lincoln Hutchinson, one of the leaders of the Republican National Committee's Division for Foreign Language Publicity and Advertising, reported that the single biggest issue costing Hoover votes among the immigrants was not the quotas, but rather his

---

[17] Statement enclosed in E. E. Hunt to Hoover, 15 October 1928, Hoover Papers, Campaign & Transition, Container 30, Hoover Library.

[18] Hoover-Curtis Campaign Committee, New York City, press release, n.d. [17 September 1928] and Republican National Committee, Washington DC, press release, n.d. [15 October 1928], ibid., Container 200, Hoover Library; Alfred E. Smith, *The Campaign Addresses of Governor Alfred E. Smith, Democratic Candidate for President, 1928* (Washington DC: Democratic National Committee, 1929) 25, 102–103, 147–48, 156, 267, 291; and Allan J. Lichtman, *Prejudice and the Old Politics: The Presidential Election of 1928* (Chapel Hill: University of North Carolina Press, 1979) 110. Hoover, in his *Memoirs* 2:199, listed immigration restriction as one of the issues on which "there was no great difference" between himself and Smith.

support for the Volstead Act.[19] Governor Smith was a well-known opponent of Prohibition, and as a Tammany Democrat, he was a presumed friend of the foreign-born. Immigrants and their children, however, were only slightly more likely than their native-born counterparts to vote Democratic in 1928. Many Protestant immigrants who disliked Hoover's support for Prohibition voted for him anyway on religious grounds. For example, while the majority of German Americans voted for Smith, they did not support him as strongly as they had Robert LaFollette in 1924 or Franklin D. Roosevelt in 1932. Many German Lutherans probably could not bring themselves to vote for a Roman Catholic, even to make beer-drinking legal once more.[20]

The Republicans' Division for Foreign Language Publicity and Advertising worked hard to secure the immigrant vote in 1928, sending news bulletins and articles to over six hundred forty foreign-language newspapers representing twenty-one languages. Coverage of Hoover in all foreign-language newspapers was tracked weekly and rated as favorable, neutral, or unfavorable.[21] A survey by the Foreign Language Information Service indicated that ninety-eight foreign-language newspapers endorsed Hoover, while one hundred fifteen supported Smith, forty-six supported Socialist Norman Thomas, and an additional twenty-six supported either the Socialist Labor or Communist candidates. Democratic newspaper publisher William Randolph Hearst opined in June that Hoover would be a formidable candidate because European immigrants "had not forgotten his relief work in the World War." The Polish National Alliance endorsed Hoover because he was the "alms distributor" of Europe who had fed starving Poles.[22]

In the end, Hoover won the election in the largest landslide in American political history up to that time. The total vote increased by eight million over 1924—nearly double that of 1916 and triple that of 1896, elections in which women had not participated. Hoover carried forty states and won over five and a half million more votes than Coolidge. Smith was victorious in two immigrant-heavy states, Massachusetts and Rhode Island, in addition to six Southern states. He did carry eight more counties in the middle Atlantic states, twenty-three more in the west North-central states

---

[19] Lincoln Hutchinson to Herbert Hoover, 6 October 1928, Hoover Papers, Campaign & Transition, Container 37.

[20] Lichtman, *Prejudice and the Old Politics*, 94–95, 107–08, 116.

[21] Frank Little, "Report of the Division for Foreign Language Publicity and Advertising," Hoover Papers, Campaign & Transition, Container 37.

[22] Lichtman, *Prejudice and the Old Politics*, 113–14.

and six more on the Pacific coast than Davis had in 1924, showing more strength in areas with large foreign-born populations. The election of 1928 halted the shift of immigrant support away from the Democrats which had begun in 1916. Four years later the Democrats regained the support of the overwhelming majority of immigrant voters.[23]

President Hoover's commitment to keeping the 1890 census-based quotas was put to the test as soon as he took office. Congress twice postponed enforcement of the national origins quotas, but they were scheduled to take effect on 1 July 1929. Having gone on record as opposed to the new quotas in the 1928 campaign, Hoover tried to prevent them from becoming law. Furthermore, pressure was being put on him by both business and ethnic interests. North Dakota Senator Gerald Nye presented a massive petition to Hoover on 7 March, asking for repeal of national origins. Nye stated that he had discussed the matter with many colleagues in the Senate and House, where sentiment was turning toward repeal of the national origins immigration legislation. The consensus was that the president was not obligated to issue the proclamation on 1 April because (1) if it were automatic, there would be no need for a proclamation; and (2) the 1924 law made provision for the case that the president did not issue it. Nye further reminded Hoover that his stand against the national origins quota scheme won him "thousands of friends" in the campaign.[24]

One of Hoover's first official acts as president was to request his Attorney General, William DeWitt Mitchell, for an opinion as to whether he was required to issue the proclamation which would set forth the new quotas. At issue was the clause in the 1924 law to which Nye referred, specifying that the quotas would not take effect if the president failed to issue the proclamation by the deadline. Mitchell's opinion argued that this clause was only intended to provide for extra time should the Quota Board prove unable to complete its work by the deadline; it could not be construed as giving Hoover discretionary power to issue the proclamation. Since the quotas had been postponed and revised twice, there was less doubt regarding the accuracy of the quota assessment figures. Furthermore, Congress could not delegate legislative power to the executive branch under the Constitution

---

[23] Edgar Eugene Robinson, *The Presidential Vote, 1896–1932* (Palo Alto: Stanford University Press, 1934) 24–27; and Lichtman, *Prejudice and the Old Politics*, 94–96, 107–108.

[24] Gerald Nye to Herbert Hoover, 7 March 1929; Hoover Papers, Presidential, Container 174.

even if it wanted to do so. Therefore, Mitchell concluded, Hoover had no choice but to issue the proclamation.[25]

On 22 March 1929, Hoover handed a mimeographed sheet to reporters at a press conference. The announcement stated that since the Attorney General had advised him that he was legally required to issue the proclamation by the April 1 deadline, he was doing so. "While I am strongly in favor of restricted and selected immigration," it went on to say, "I have opposed the national origins basis. I, therefore, naturally dislike the duty of issuing the proclamation and installing the new basis, but the President of the United States must be the first to obey the law." The final version of the National Origins Quotas Act differed only slightly from the original 1927 version. The British quota was reduced to 65,721, while the German quota was increased to 25,957 and the Irish quota to 17,853. Other changes were minimal.[26]

Hoover did not passively accept the new quotas. He sent a message to Congress on 16 April requesting the repeal of the national origins provisions of the 1924 law before the new quotas took effect on 1 July. The House of Representatives was willing to do this, but by the rules of the special session, the repeal had to be initiated by the Senate where David Reed had organized stiff opposition. On 13 June, Nye's attempt to force the bill suspending the national origins provisions out of the Senate Immigration Committee was defeated, 37–43, and so the new quotas finally went into effect two and one-half weeks later.[27]

Despite this defeat, Hoover continued to speak out against the national origins quotas. He allowed Immigration Commissioner Harry Hull to speak at a dinner of the National Historical Society, a group formed by the various German, Irish, and Scandinavian American societies and fraternal orders to lobby for the repeal of the National Origins law. Hoover personally sent a telegram to the meeting, reassuring the delegates, "I have not altered my views as to the character of the immigration legislation which I believe is

---

[25] George Akerson to William D. Mitchell, 9 March 1929; and Mitchell to Herbert Hoover, n.d. [22 March 1929]; ibid.

[26] Hoover, *Public Papers*, 1:33–34; and William Starr Myers and Walter H. Newton, *The Hoover Administration: A Documented Narrative* (New York: Charles Scribner's Sons, 1936) 376. A useful comparison table is found in Robert A. Divine, *American Immigration Policy, 1924–1952* (New Haven: Yale University Press, 1957) 30.

[27] Hoover, *Public Papers*, 1:80–81; Myers and Newton, *Hoover Administration*, 380–81, 393; and "Editorial," *New York World*, 25 April 1929, Hoover Papers, Presidential, Container 174.

needed by this country."[28] Hoover's stance also won praise from many restrictionists. Although eugenicists like Harry Laughlin and Madison Grant supported the national origins quotas, other nativists agreed with Hoover that the quotas based on the 1890 census were better. Charles H. Davis, Commander General of the Patriotic Order Sons of America, sent Hoover a resolution in April 1929 commending the president for his stand against the new quotas since the 1890 census quotas admitted "less undesirable aliens."[29]

The Great Depression, of course, pushed the debate over the quotas into the background. In the spring of 1930, Hoover, Davis, and Acting Secretary of State Joseph Cotton urged Albert Johnson and other Congressional leaders to pass a law that would temporarily cut all quotas in half and set up preferences within the quotas for certain skilled workers whom the Secretary of Labor determined could not be found in the United States. Johnson, however, wanted to ban all immigration and many others in Congress desired to add quotas for countries in the Western Hemisphere, especially Mexico. The Senate passed the Harris Bill on 13 May, which took Mexico off the list of non-quota Western Hemisphere countries enumerated in the 1924 Act. But an amendment to suspend all immigration (except for relatives of citizens) for five years, offered by Hugo Black, was narrowly defeated, 37–29.[30]

The State Department strongly opposed quotas for Western Hemisphere countries. Cotton argued that establishing quotas for Mexico and Canada would unnecessarily offend the sister republics, undermining Ambassador Dwight Morrow's hard work in rebuilding relations between the United States and Mexico, and potentially threatening negotiations with Canada over the creation of Hoover's pet project, the St. Lawrence Seaway. Besides, Cotton argued, the real issue was illegal immigration, and the solution was a stronger border patrol.[31] Johnson offered a substitute for the

---

[28] George W. Angerstein to George Akerson, 19 September 1930; Herbert Hoover telegram to Angerstein, 30 September 1930; and Angerstein to Akerson, with enclosed program, 1 October 1930; Hoover Papers, PPF 178.

[29] Charles H. Davis to Herbert Hoover, 27 April 1929, Hoover Papers, Presidential, Container 174.

[30] US Senate, *An Act to Amend Subdivision (c) of Section 4 of the Immigration Act of 1924, as Amended*, 71st Cong., 2d sess., S. 51; *Congressional Record*, 71st Cong., 2d sess., 1930, 7329; and Divine, *American Immigration Policy*, 78.

[31] Joseph Cotton to Robert Lamont, 30 January 1930, Hoover Papers, Presidential, Container 174.

Harris Bill in the House which would have temporarily limited the issuance of visas to the exempted and preferred classes of immigrants. Cotton and Johnson discussed the issue and finally agreed that no immigration legislation would pass, although the *New York Times* reported that it simply got tied up in an "eleventh-hour jam of legislation at the end of the last session of Congress."[32]

Frustrated in his attempts to shape Congressional legislation, Hoover turned to administrative action, a field in which he felt far more comfortable. The State Department began in March 1930 to use the "likely to become a public charge" clause to exclude virtually all Mexican immigrants. The Supreme Court ruled in 1915 in the case of *Gegiow v. Uhl* that the Bureau of Immigration could not use that clause to keep out immigrants on the basis of labor conditions at the port of entry.[33] But the federal courts consistently upheld the State Department's discretionary authority in issuing visas. Finding that the method worked wonderfully, Hoover consulted with State and Labor Department officials about the possibility of extending this creative use of the "likely to become a public charge" clause to all immigrants. Erwin Griswold, an attorney in the Solicitor General's office, prepared a memorandum on 5 September which suggested that the Supreme Court's decision in *Gegiow v. Uhl* could be avoided by simply not giving a sweeping order to the consuls. Rather than ordering them to exclude all aliens, Hoover and Secretary of State Henry L. Stimson told them that they had the discretion to interpret "likely" as "possible" rather than "probable."[34]

Hoover announced at a press conference on 9 September that the "likely to become a public charge" clause would be used to exclude most immigrants. Hoover later explained in his *Memoirs*: "In view of the large amount of unemployment at the time, I concluded that directly or indirectly all immigrants were a public charge at the moment—either they themselves went on relief as soon as they landed, or, if they did get jobs, they forced others onto relief."[35] Since the *Gegiow v. Uhl* ruling, the number of aliens

---

[32] Albert Johnson to Walter H. Newton, 26 May 1930; Newton memo, 28 June 1930; and "Labor Immigration Halted Temporarily at Hoover's Order," *New York Times*, 10 September 1930; ibid.

[33] *Gegiow v. Uhl*, 239 US 3 (1915).

[34] Divine, *American Immigration Policy*, 78–79; and Patricia Russell Evans, "'Likely to Become a Public Charge': Immigration in the Backwaters of Administrative Law, 1882–1933" (Ph.D. dissertation, George Washington University, 1987) 219–22.

[35] Hoover, *Public Papers*, 2:363–65; Myers and Newton, *Hoover Administration*, 44–45; "President Moves to Restrict Aliens As Aid for Jobless," *New York Herald*

excluded as likely to become a public charge had dropped dramatically: fifty-one percent of all exclusions between 1911–1920 were based on the clause, but only twenty percent of exclusions were based on it between 1921–1930. With the consuls given the discretion to use it as a basis for denying visas, it once again became the primary means of exclusion. Within five months, European immigration had decreased by ninety percent, although much of that decline was due to the dismal economic conditions in the United States.[36]

Congress wanted the credit that Hoover was taking for immigration restriction, so the debate continued over restricting or eliminating Mexican immigration by statutes. In 1929 Paul Shoup, president of the Southern Pacific Railroad Company, urged Hoover to create a commission to study the Mexican issue. The railroad executive argued that Mexican labor was essential now that Asian labor was unavailable.[37] Labor Secretary Davis opposed Shoup's call for a commission to study Mexican problem, noting that endless studies and investigations had already been conducted. He warned that such a commission would be widely perceived as just another politically-driven delaying tactic. Davis argued that Congress was obviously determined to put Mexican immigration on a quota basis, and that any attempt to delay that might stir an effort to stop immigration completely. He asked Hoover to support instead a bill drafted by Davis and introduced by Senator James Watson of Indiana which created an immigration quota of ten percent of the Mexican-American population in 1890. It also allowed the Secretary of Labor to admit up to an additional 10,000 persons annually for seasonal or emergency labor, provided that unemployed labor of a like kind could not be found in the region to which these laborers were to be admitted.[38]

Tribune, 10 September 1930; and "Labor Immigration Halted Temporarily at Hoover's Order," *New York Times*, 10 September 1930; Hoover Papers, Presidential, Container 174; and Hoover, *Memoirs*, 3:47–48.

[36] "Statement on Government Policies to Reduce Immigration," Hoover Papers, Presidential, Container 174; Hoover, *Public Papers*, 3:158–62; and Evans, "Likely to Become a Public Charge," 220, 231. Between 1892–1900, sixty-seven percent of all exclusions had been based on the "likely to become a public charge" clause, and between 1901–1910 fifty-nine percent were based on that clause.

[37] Paul Shoup to Herbert Hoover, 10 April 1929, Hoover Papers, Presidential, Container 174.

[38] James J. Davis to Hoover, 24 April 1929, ibid. For the debate in Congress, see Divine, *American Immigration Policy*, 52–68.

Davis once again argued for a selective immigration policy. But the basis for selection was no longer eugenics, but needed labor skills. He called for an immigration policy that would "select the people who can come to this country according to its needs."[39] Hoover agreed. As the former Secretary of Commerce, he understood that companies wanted the freedom to hire immigrant labor; as the president, he understood that the demand for immigration restriction during the Depression was overwhelming. The solution was a flexible policy that would grant the Department of Labor discretion to admit immigrant workers as needed.

In his first annual message to Congress, Hoover asked Congress to devise a better system of selecting the right kind of immigrants while limiting their numbers. Asserting that immigration restriction was a "sound national policy," he argued that the "pressing problem is to formulate a method by which the limited number of immigrants whom we do welcome shall be adopted to our national setting and national need." Hoover called this goal "our real national objective," and explained what he had in mind: to evaluate the "fitness of the immigrant as to physique, character, training, and our need of service. Perhaps some system of priorities within the quotas could produce these results and at the same time enable some hardships in the present system to be cleared up."[40]

What Hoover wanted was a flexible system to grant preferences within the quotas to immigrants with special skills not readily available in the United States. To the engineer, this was the perfect, practical solution: focusing on labor needs rather than discriminating on the basis of countries of origin. Furthermore, if the decision-making power was held by impartial bureaucrats in the Commerce and Labor Departments, the blatant racism of Congress pandering to their constituents could be avoided.

By focusing on job skills, Hoover rejected eugenics as a means of scientifically selecting immigrants with superior genetic qualities. He had no quarrel with Social Darwinism, as had Theodore Roosevelt and Calvin Coolidge. When Leon Whitney, the executive secretary of the American Eugenics Society, wrote to Hoover in December 1929 asking him if he had considered immigration from a "biological point of view," the president replied evasively, talking about a confusion in defining terms and asking eugenicists to make clear their proposals. Whitney responded that a "biological view" meant the use of mental testing, a ban on all Mexican

---

[39] Ibid.
[40] Hoover, *Public Papers*, 1:429–430.

immigration, and the deportation of as many aliens as possible. There is no record of a response to this letter.[41] But Immigration Commissioner Harry Hull made it clear in a *Detroit Times* article in November 1930 that the eugenic component of selective immigration had not been eliminated. He wrote about the advantages of selecting "our own great grandchildren," and explained that Chinese "coolies" would not be admitted, not only because they were "able to work and thrive on a wage at which the American laborer will starve," but also because "Mendel's law renders the admixture of white and yellow blood an unhappy blending."[42]

Hoover continued to call for the selection of immigrants based on job skills even after he moved to virtually end immigration by executive order, and he repeatedly urged Congress to translate his administrative actions into law. On 25 November 1930 he told reporters that he fully agreed with Senator David Reed, the author of the national origins system, "as to the need for revision of the immigration laws, to give them more selectivity and flexibility." He pointed out that the State Department's restriction of visas had reduced immigration from 24,000 to 6,000 a month and commented, "That in itself indicates the great desirability of more flexibility in the immigration laws: It is a little difficult to make such restriction truly departmental. It needs to be based on actual statutory provisions."[43] His desire for legislation indicates his uneasiness with administrative discretion. Hoover feared a large government bureaucracy with few restrictions as a threat to individual liberty, as his later hostility to the New Deal amply illustrates.

The president reiterated his request for legislation in his State of the Union speech on 2 December 1930. In addition he called for stronger deportation laws. Hoover argued that it was necessary to deport the thousands of illegal aliens living in the United States to protect American workers from unfair competition and legal immigrants from the backlash caused by resentment.[44] Diverting attention to the problem of illegal immigration served to take the focus off of the quotas, and allowed all

---

[41] Leon Whitney to Herbert Hoover, 24 December 1929; Hoover to Whitney, 27 December 1929; and Whitney to Hoover, 6 January 1930; Hoover Papers, Presidential, Container 174.

[42] Harry E. Hull, "Our Immigration Policy Shaping New Type of US Citizen," *Detroit Times*, 23 November 1930, clipping in ibid.

[43] Hoover, *Public Papers*, 2:500.

[44] Ibid., 520–21.

Americans of European origin to unite in racist antipathy toward Mexican Americans. James Davis reported that the California Attorney General even went so far as to argue that Mexican immigrants should be excluded as "aliens ineligible to citizenship," although Davis pointed out that determining the amount of "nonwhite blood" in Mexicans would be almost impossible.[45]

Congressman Albert Johnson and Senator David Reed responded to Hoover's annual message by introducing similar bills in their respective houses to suspend all immigration for one year, except for relatives of US residents. The Senate Immigration Committee began to hold hearings on Reed's bill in December 1930. Testifying for the administration, Secretary of State Henry Stimson objected to the proposed exemption for relatives rather than the suspension itself. He pointed out that since the great majority of relatives coming would be from Southern and Eastern Europe, the Reed Bill would undermine the whole premise of the National Origins Act. Stimson proposed instead an across-the-board, ninety percent cut in all immigration. The House quickly adopted Stimson's suggestion on 2 March 1931 over the vehement opposition of Fiorello La Guardia, Samuel Dickstein and other liberal representatives. Senator David I. Walsh of Massachusetts, however, blocked the Senate from considering the House bill before the congressional session ended.[46]

By 1931, Hoover had abandoned any real attempt to end national origins quotas, and instead tried to offer his administration's severe restriction of immigration as proof of his efforts to deal decisively with the Depression. On 26 March he issued a "Statement on Government Policies to Reduce Immigration" that included statistics showing that the number of issued visas had declined by 96,883 during the first five months, or roughly ninety percent of the total possible under the quotas, thus meeting Stimson's proposed goal.[47] At a 15 May press conference he called attention to Acting Secretary of Labor Robe C. White's report that whereas immigration had a net increase of 12,605 per month from April to June 1930, it had a net

---

[45] James J. Davis to Herbert Hoover, 4 December 1929, Hoover Papers, Presidential, Container 174.

[46] Divine, *American Immigration Policy*, 79–83.

[47] "Statement on Government Policies to Reduce Immigration," Hoover Papers, Presidential, Container 174; and Hoover, *Public Papers*, 3:158–62.

decrease of 3,551 per month from January to March 1931.[48] Warren Harding had once boasted that return migration only occurred in lean years of Democratic administrations. Now Herbert Hoover was bragging that his administration was encouraging return migration.

In addition to issuing press releases, Hoover made his case directly to the people. In an address to the Indiana Republican Editorial Association on 15 June, carried on the NBC and CBS radio networks, Hoover discussed the various anti-Depression efforts, including immigration restriction. "We are rigidly excluding immigration until our own people are employed. The departures and deportations today actually exceed arrivals," he boasted.[49] In his 1931 annual message to Congress, the president announced that immigration had decreased by 300,000, and he urged once again that the "immigration restriction now in force under administrative action be placed upon a more definite basis by law." He also endorsed a registration system to protect resident aliens and further strengthening of the deportation laws.[50]

Filipino immigration also became a target of the restrictionists during this period. Republican Senator Samuel Shortridge of California had attempted to amend the Harris Bill in 1930 to exclude all Filipinos for five years, arguing that "to preserve our form of government we must preserve our racial type, the dominant and controlling race within the United States, to guide and direct its destiny." But his amendment was defeated 41–23.[51] In 1932, Filipino leaders negotiated a deal with the American Federation of Labor to work together for an independence bill that would assign a very small immigration quota to the Philippines. California Republican Hiram Johnson amended the bill in the Senate to apply the quota only to people "eligible for citizenship." The conference committee rejected this amendment and stipulated that the Asian exclusion provisions of the 1924 law would apply to the Philippines. Hoover vetoed the legislation in January 1933, but not because of its immigration features; in fact, he called for the

---

[48] Robe C. White to Herbert Hoover, 12 May 1931; White to Hoover, 14 May 1931, Hoover Papers, Presidential, Container 174; and Hoover, *Public Papers*, 3:254–57.

[49] Hoover, *Public Papers*, 3:300.

[50] Ibid., 584, 596; Herbert Hoover, *The State Papers and Other Public Writings of Herbert Hoover*, ed. William Starr Myers, 2 vols. (Garden City NY: Doubleday, Doran & Co., 1934) 2:44, 55; and Myers and Newton, *Hoover Administration*, 148, 151.

[51] *Congressional Record*, 71st Cong., 2d sess., 1930, 7425; ibid., 7510–511, 7529; and Divine, *American Immigration Policy*, 72.

immediate exclusion of all Filipinos in his veto message.[52] Clearly Hoover's opinion of Asians had not improved over the years.

During the Great Depression Hoover was careful to defend the virtual ban on immigration as an economic necessity rather than an attack on immigrants or particular nationalities. He continued to reach out to foreign-born groups and to the foreign-language press, celebrating the success of both the melting pot and assimilation. Congratulating the newspaper *Il Progresso Italo-Americano* on its fiftieth anniversary in 1930, Hoover wrote: "The Americans of Italian origin have brought many contributions to the industries and arts of this country, and these are deeply appreciated." He also thanked the newspaper for its role in Americanizing Italian immigrants, praising its "labors to make easier the transition to the new ideas and loyalties of America."[53] Similarly, he congratulated *Slovake Amerike* on its forty-second anniversary, and said, "The Slovak people in the United States have brought to this new land of their choice many valuable qualities of mind and character that have enriched our national life. Their loyalty to American institutions and ideals is an earnest of continued service of country."[54] In 1931 Hoover used the occasion of Rosh Hashanah to praise Jewish Americans: "In business, the arts, the professions, philanthropy, citizenship and, above all, in the evolution of the spiritual life of mankind, the race has contributed elements of strength, beauty and tolerance which are the common heritage of all men."[55] Like Harding and Coolidge, Hoover used the imagery of the melting pot to soften the blow of race-based restriction, praising the foreigners who were already here while making sure that no more were admitted.

Despite his paeans to the melting pot, Hoover had closed the gates to most immigrants. In the 1932 presidential campaign, he touted his record of virtually eliminating immigration. Trying to raise the old fear of Tammany's friendliness to the foreign-born, the incumbent also pointed out that his opponent, New York Governor Franklin D. Roosevelt, had avoided any mention of the subject.[56] In Indianapolis, Hoover once again called for

---

[52] Ibid., 73–75.

[53] Hoover, *Public Papers*, 2:469.

[54] Ibid., 3:178.

[55] Ibid., 414.

[56] Herbert Hoover, "Radio Address to Women of America," 7 October 1932, ibid., 4:493–94; Hoover, "Address in Indianapolis," 28 October 1932, ibid., 622; and *State Papers*, 2:399.

repeal of the national origins quotas and a return to the two percent quotas based on the 1890 census. He also recommended that "a more humane provision should be made for bringing in the near relatives of our citizens." John B. Trevor, the originator of the national origins quotas, sent him a telegram the next day pointing out that over eighty patriotic societies had voiced support for national origins. He warned Hoover: "Your statement last night that you will persist in seeking a return to the old quota base suggests a revival of a deplorable controversy which will if you do so renew and perpetuate racial animosities."[57] Although Trevor's remark was hypocritical, since racism was perpetuated by the nativists, it was also accurate: Hoover was purposefully "beating a dead horse." Desperate for votes, he was willing to make whatever appeals were needed to gain additional support—no matter where people's sympathies lay.

In extended remarks in Columbus, Ohio, Hoover returned to the familiar Republican theme of restricted immigration as the "handmaiden" of the protective tariff in maintaining the highest standard of living in the world. But in 1932 old slogans like "Republican prosperity" had a bitter, hollow ring for many. Hoover also expressed his faith in the work of the melting pot, stating that "in ordinary times" the United States must "allow a flow of selective [sic] stream of peoples to refresh our population with the ideas and contributions of foreign countries to our civilization." These, however, were certainly not ordinary times.[58]

Most importantly, he rejected the old idea of America as the asylum of the world, both because it was no longer necessary and because it was unfair to Americans in the present economic circumstances. "The United States has received invaluable contributions in its upbuilding, in the growth of its culture from the migration of the various races of Europe. It has held its doors open to those who have fled from persecution, both religious and political," Hoover acknowledged. But he argued that the times and the conditions in Europe had now changed. "With the growth of democracy in foreign countries, political persecution has largely ceased," he claimed. "There is no longer a necessity to provide an asylum for those persecuted because of conscience." Furthermore, he declared, "in times of great crisis

---

[57] Herbert Hoover, "Address in Indianapolis," 28 October 1932, *Public Papers*, 4:622; and John B. Trevor telegram to Herbert Hoover, 29 October 1932, Hoover Papers, Presidential, Container 174.

[58] Herbert Hoover, "Rear Platform Remarks, Columbus, Ohio," 22 October 1932, *Public Papers*, 4:562–63.

like the present where we have millions of unemployed, it is an injustice and inhumanity to our own residents that we should allow the entry of people fleeing from starvation abroad. The obligation remains upon those countries to take care of their own people."[59] Thus the "great humanitarian" turned his back—and America's—on the rest of humanity, slamming shut the nation's gates.

Most Americans in 1932 doubtlessly agreed with the logic of Hoover's words. But a brusque order to European nations to look after their own people sounded strange indeed coming from the man who had fed Europe during and after World War I. His proclamation that asylum was no longer necessary was even more shocking, as it seemed to ignore the fascist regimes of Italy and Eastern Europe, and the brutal repression of Joseph Stalin's Soviet Union. Although they were words uttered in the desperation of a futile campaign, they cannot be dismissed simply as campaign rhetoric. Hoover's announcement of the end of asylum, and his use of administrative action to cut off immigration at the source, had lasting consequences. When Jewish refugees frantically sought to flee the Nazi horror in the 1930s, almost all of them were denied visas due to the interpretation of the "likely to become a public charge" clause that the Hoover administration set up and Franklin D. Roosevelt's State Department maintained.[60]

In the end, of course, Hoover suffered a defeat even greater in magnitude than his 1928 triumph. Franklin D. Roosevelt received 22,809,638 votes, close to one and a half million more than Hoover won in the earlier election. Although Hoover's 15,758,901 votes were over seven hundred thousand more than Alfred Smith had received in 1928, the Iowan carried only six Northeastern states and just three hundred seventy-two counties nationwide. Half of the total number of votes were cast in eight states with heavy immigrant populations: New York, New Jersey, Pennsylvania, Ohio, Indiana, Illinois, Michigan and Wisconsin. Hoover won over eight and a half million votes in those states, which constituted more than half his total. Nevertheless, he carried only two states with large numbers of foreign-born voters: Pennsylvania and Connecticut.[61] Most foreign-born voters, like most Americans generally, voted for the New York governor.

---

[59] Ibid.

[60] Alan M. Kraut, Richard Breitman and Thomas W. Imhoof, "The State Department, the Labor Department, and German Jewish Immigration, 1930–1940," *Journal of American Ethnic History*, 3/2 (Spring 1984): 5–38.

[61] Robinson, *Presidential Vote*, 27–30.

Hoover, like Harding and Coolidge, supported immigration restriction but took only a limited part in shaping that legislation. He and Secretary of Labor James Davis worked unsuccessfully for a more flexible immigration policy which would allow the government to admit foreign workers as needed. He also tried to mitigate the harsh racism evident in Congress by continuing to speak to the American people (and the foreign-born in particular) of the melting pot and the contributions of all Europeans to American culture and society. But this rhetoric of assimilation implicitly excluded Asians and Mexicans. Most importantly, Hoover virtually ended immigration through his interpretation of the "likely to become a public charge" clause and the deportation of illegal immigrants, setting policies that would continue through the 1950s. Grover Cleveland, William Howard Taft and Woodrow Wilson all vetoed the literacy test because it violated the ideal of asylum. Hoover announced from the bully pulpit the end of America's role as an asylum for the oppressed of the world.

CHAPTER 9

THE LEGACY OF THE PROGRESSIVE MELTING POT

All presidents from 1897 to 1933 essentially upheld the progressive version of the melting pot concept. Although expressing support in varying degrees for the restriction of immigration, they rejected the racialist arguments and proposals of nativists and eugenicists. They consistently defined American national identity on the basis of shared political and economic ideals rather than on a common racial ancestry. The presidents praised the cultural contributions of various European immigrant groups to the United States and acknowledged their labor in building the nation. They also called on their fellow native-born Americans to provide the hospitable environment and economic opportunities necessary to welcome and integrate the foreign-born into American society.

In part, the presidents based their support of the melting pot concept on the lingering nineteenth-century confidence in its tenets. Although the frontier was now closed, factories still welcomed newcomers seeking employment. Immigrants from Europe were considered to be assimilated when they accepted the political ideals of democracy, the economic ideals of *laissez-faire* capitalism and committed themselves wholeheartedly to their new country by becoming citizens. The fact that thousands of Europeans wanted to leave the old world reinforced the belief in America's exceptional character and the universality of its ideals. The limits to assimilation were set in the Naturalization Act of 1790, however, which allowed only "free white persons" to naturalize. The 1870 naturalization law extended the privileges of citizenship to Africans and African Americans. Asians, however, were never so accepted. The Chinese Exclusion Act of 1882 began the legal exclusion of working-class Chinese immigrants, although merchants, professionals and students were still welcomed.

The Chinese Exclusion Act and the Immigration Act of the same year marked the beginning of the nativist challenge to the concept of the melting pot. Nativism's three strains—anti-radicalism, anti-Catholicism and Anglo-Saxon racialism—merged and were strengthened in the Gilded Age. The economic dislocations of the late nineteenth century raised fears of immigrant anarchism and communism, particularly in the wake of the Haymarket bombing and the assassination of President William McKinley. The political success of Irish Catholics, and the corruption of the urban political machines some of them ran, renewed concerns about "papists." Meanwhile, the emergence of the United States as a colonial power following its victory in the Spanish-American War renewed racialist notions of Anglo-Saxon supremacy. Ironically, the full panoply of constitutional rights was deliberately withheld from America's colonial subjects. The necessary implication was that in fact all men were not created equal.[1]

As a result, nativists began calling for the restriction of or halting of immigration. Some joined trade unionists in protesting that immigrants took jobs away from native-born Americans. Most informed nativists recognized that such an appeal went against the economic principles of *laissez-faire* capitalism, as well as the interests of wealthy, politically connected industrialists. They focused instead on the "unassimilability" of the new immigrants, contrasting them unfavorably with the old immigrants from the British Isles, the Low Countries, Germany and Scandinavia. They pointed out that Southern and Eastern Europeans often came as temporary "birds of passage," failing to naturalize or learn English, which was surely indicative of a lack of commitment to the United States. Worse yet, some aliens espoused radical political and economic doctrines. This nativist analysis formed the basis for the conclusions reached by the United States Immigration Commission.

The new immigrants failed to assimilate, according to eugenicists, because they were racially inferior. Charles Davenport, Harry H. Laughlin and others argued that physical and character traits were inherited on a simple Mendelian basis, concluding that the negative qualities of Southern and Eastern Europeans were immutable. Davenport wrote in 1914: "The idea of a 'melting pot' belongs to a pre-Mendelian age. Now we recognize that characters are inherited as units and do not readily break up." Eugenicists also appealed to middle-class taxpayers by arguing that the growing burden

---

[1] John Higham, *Strangers in the Land: Patterns in American Nativism, 1860–1925*, rev. ed. (New Brunswick: Rutgers University Press, 1988) 3–11, 53–109.

of providing prisons, asylums, and charitable care could be greatly reduced by excluding "feeble-minded" aliens. Davenport was the leader of his local taxpayers' association, and he railed against the cost of charitable institutions for "defective" immigrants.[2]

Liberal progressive reformers rejected the argument of nativists and eugenicists that efforts to encourage assimilation by improving the housing, workplace conditions and education of immigrants were doomed to failure. The reformers defended the melting pot concept, but in the process they redefined it. Assimilation was no longer viewed as an automatic process. They decided that like other aspects of the economy and society, the melting pot needed to be scientifically managed to create a united American citizenry. Anarchists and those with mental and physical defects had to be excluded because they could not adopt American ideals. While this attitude coincided in part with that of the nativists, anthropologists like Franz Boas opposed eugenics, arguing that differences in character and achievement between groups of people had much more to do with environment than heredity.[3]

While countering bigoted nativist attacks, liberal progressives also rejected the views of cultural pluralists such as Horace Kallen, who agreed with the nativists that nationality was a primordial, "psycho-physical inheritance" that was malleable only on a superficial level. Kallen believed that democracy required, and indeed assumed, that all ethnic groups would maintain their national identities. Instead of a melting pot, Kallen viewed the United States as a federation of nationalities, with each group retaining its own language and customs while using English as the *lingua franca*.[4] Such a

---

[2] Mark H. Haller, *Eugenics: Hereditarian Attitudes in American Thought* (New Brunswick: Rutgers University Press, 1963) 63–94; and Daniel J. Kevles, *In the Name of Eugenics: Genetics and the Uses of Human Heredity* (New York: Alfred A. Knopf, 1985) 44–59, 72–73 (quotation, 47).

[3] Franz Boas, *The Mind of Primitive Man* (New York: Macmillan, 1920); Haller, *Eugenics*, 145–46.

[4] Horace M. Kallen, *Culture and Democracy in the United States: Studies in the Group Psychology of the American Peoples* (New York: Boni & Liveright, 1924) 119–20, 124–25; Nathan Glazer, "Is Assimilation Dead?," *Annals of the American Academy of Political and Social Science,* 530 (Nov. 1993): 123–30; Philip Gleason, *Speaking of Diversity: Language and Ethnicity in Twentieth-Century America* (Baltimore: Johns Hopkins University Press, 1992) 14–20; John Higham, *Send These To Me: Jews and Other Immigrants in Urban America,* 2nd ed. (Baltimore: Johns Hopkins University Press, 1984) 200, 203–208, 212.

concept did not allow for a meaningful American national identity, however, and so most liberal progressives rejected it. Even Randolph Bourne, who also called for a recognition of America's cultural pluralism, saw this as only an acknowledgment that the United States' national identity was more cosmopolitan than Anglo-Saxon racialists wanted it to be.[5] Other liberal progressives, such as Jane Addams and John Dewey, likewise praised the cultural contributions of various European ethnic groups while firmly maintaining that the United States needed to create a common culture and national identity.[6]

The way to create such a common culture and identity was to assimilate immigrants by providing a welcoming, wholesome environment and real opportunities for economic advancement. In particular, liberal progressives advocated three social goals: First, to show affection and appreciation for immigrants while teaching them the English language and American civic ideals; second, to resettle as many immigrants as possible in the wholesome countryside, away from the evils of urban life. Since most immigrants would continue to live in urban areas and work in factories, however, the third goal was to assist workers with minimum wage and compensation laws, workplace regulations and other reforms which would improve their standard of living and quash the appeal of radicalism.

Peter Roberts spoke for many progressives when he wrote in 1912: "I believe in the immigrant. He has in him the making of an American, provided a sympathetic hand guides him and smooths the path which leads to assimilation." He rejected the conclusions of the Dillingham Commission, arguing that the new immigrants did not take jobs away from Americans. Nor did they cause "race suicide," since the birth rate was declining similarly in industrialized Europe. The foreign-born did not "show moral turpitude above the average of civilized men," despite "living under abnormal conditions in industrial centers, and meeting more temptations in a week than they would in a lifetime in rural communities in the

---

[5] Randolph S. Bourne, "Trans-national America," *Atlantic Monthly*, 118/1 (July 1916): 86–97.

[6] Rivka Shpak Lissak, *Pluralism and Progressives: Hull House and the New Immigrants, 1890–1919* (Chicago: University of Chicago Press, 1989) 25–33, 143–54.

homeland"—conditions that were the fault of native-born landlords, businessmen and politicians.[7]

Likewise, Edward Steiner, while acknowledging that there were some "tares in the wheat," insisted that Southern and Eastern Europeans came from "crude, common peasant stock," which was "physically sound" and represented "not the dregs of society, but its basis." Despite their more obvious foreignness, the new immigrants would be assimilated just as rapidly as the old ones. "The things which seem the most ineradicable and written as if by an 'iron pen upon the rock' are in most cases but chalk marks on a blackboard, so easily are they washed away. These things created by long ages of neglect, hunger, persecution and climate, are often lost within one generation."[8]

Presidents Theodore Roosevelt, William Howard Taft and Woodrow Wilson supported this progressive revision of the melting pot concept because it avoided the extremes of nativism and cultural pluralism while preserving America's historic ideal of providing an asylum for the oppressed of Europe. They courted the trade union vote by supporting the exclusion of unworthy immigrants, but they did not share the nativist fears about the unassimilability of all new immigrants. From the bully pulpit they declared that the melting pot was forging a new American nationality, combining the best traits of all the peoples who had come to America. Furthermore, the Progressive Era presidents tried to build coalitions of ethnic voters by insisting that European immigrants could retain their ethnic pride and traditions and still be loyal, patriotic citizens.

Despite his friendship with nativists like Henry Cabot Lodge, Madison Grant, and Owen Wister, Theodore Roosevelt rejected their claims of a superior Anglo-Saxon race, as well as eugenicists' oversimplification of natural selection. "Good Americanism is a matter of heart, of conscience, of lofty aspiration, of sound common sense, but not of birthplace or creed," he declared. Instead, he emphasized the need to judge immigrants on the basis of their individual moral characters, often repeating, "Each must stand on his

---

[7] Peter Roberts, *The New Immigration: A Study of the Industrial and Social Life of Southeastern Europeans in America* (New York: Macmillan, 1912; reprint, New York: Arno Press, 1969) viii, 342, 344–48.

[8] Edward A. Steiner, *On the Trail of the Immigrant* (New York: Fleming H. Revell Co., 1906; reprint, New York: Arno Press, 1969) 75, 294. Steiner was himself an immigrant from Austria-Hungary, but he insisted, "I know no Fatherland but America; for after all, it matters less where one was born, than where one's ideals had their birth" (Ibid., 14). The book was dedicated to Ellis Island Commissioner Robert Watchorn.

own worth as a man and each is entitled to be judged solely thereby."[9] Roosevelt believed that even the most racially different immigrants would eventually blend into the American people. Unlike his successors Taft and Wilson, who concurred with Congress that Asian immigrants were not fit to become American citizens, Roosevelt recommended that upper-class Chinese and Japanese immigrants be accepted and naturalized. He also urged native-born Americans to treat the foreign-born as equals, and thereby encourage them to assimilate and live up to American ideals.

Roosevelt insisted again and again, "We cannot have too much immigration of the right kind, and we should have none at all of the wrong kind."[10] He wanted the Immigration Commission to devise a system which would exclude undesirable immigrants while distributing desirable immigrants throughout the country. He was willing to accept the literacy test as a test of intelligence, although Taft and Wilson rejected it because they believed it was instead a test of opportunity. Roosevelt proposed restriction based on class rather than race because he believed that the middle and upper classes on the whole possessed a higher moral character than the working class. His Gentlemen's Agreement with Japan used class-based restriction to avoid offending that militarily strong empire. In 1912, his Progressive party platform endorsed the revised melting pot concept fully, calling for the education and distribution of immigrants and the provision of greater economic opportunities through the establishment of fair industrial standards for wages, hours, and working conditions.[11]

William Howard Taft likewise supported the progressive version of the melting pot. He believed that the United States' "atmosphere of civil liberty" gave to "every race coming under the stars and stripes an opportunity to flower and manifest its best and most enduring traits."[12] Taft celebrated the cultural gifts brought by the immigrants, and argued that they could maintain their national traditions, language, and literature while pursuing the same political, social and economic ideals as native-born Americans. He rejected the invidious distinctions the Dillingham Commission made between old

---

[9] Theodore Roosevelt, *The Works of Theodore Roosevelt, National Edition*, 20 vols. (New York: Charles Scribner's Sons, 1926) 15:245–46.

[10] Roosevelt, *Works*, 15:175.

[11] Edward P. Hutchinson, *Legislative History of American Immigration Policy, 1798–1965* (Philadelphia: University of Pennsylvania Press, 1981) 631–32.

[12] Taft, "Address to Friendly Sons of St. Patrick Banquet," New York, 17 March 1908, William Howard Taft Presidential Papers, Series 9A, vol. 8, 157 (reel 564), Library of Congress, Washington DC.

and new immigrants, and he opposed the literacy test proposed by the Commission, declaring his "abiding faith in the influence of our institutions upon all who come here, no matter how lacking in education they may be."[13] Taft vetoed the literacy test bill in 1913 because the test judged immigrants on the opportunities afforded to them by their old homelands rather than examining each candidate's individual merit.

Despite earlier negative comments about new immigrants as a scholar, Woodrow Wilson ultimately became a champion of the progressive melting pot concept. Prior to running for president he had been a member of the National Liberal Immigration League, working to distribute immigrants to rural areas and offer them opportunities for education and assimilation. Although he spoke often of the need for national unity, Wilson also argued that the different ethnic groups added vital elements that kept the United States vigorous. He maintained that European immigrants were "all instantly recognizable as Americans and America is enriched with the variety of their gifts."[14]

Like Taft, Wilson also vetoed the literacy test bill, not once but twice. He opposed it because it tested opportunity rather than intelligence; and because its premise was a "radical departure" from the traditional United States policy of offering asylum, a practice "in which our people have conceived the very character of their government to be expressed, the very mission and spirit of the Nation."[15] He expressed the progressive ideal of nationalism perfectly when he told a group of newly naturalized citizens that they had sworn an oath of allegiance not to men, but "to a great ideal, to a great body of principles." Immigrants should bring their cultures and their memories with them, but they had to leave old loyalties behind and reject any class or ethnic group identity. "You cannot become thorough Americans if you think of yourselves in groups. America does not consist of groups," Wilson warned.[16]

---

[13] Taft, "Address at Dedication of Polish College, Cambridge Springs, Penn.," 26 October 1912, ibid., vol. 30, 186–87 (reel 570).

[14] Woodrow Wilson, Thanksgiving Address at Har Sinai Temple, Trenton, 24 November 1910, in *The Papers of Woodrow Wilson*, ed. Arthur S. Link et al., 69 vols. (Princeton: Princeton University Press, 1966–1994) 22:90–91.

[15] Woodrow Wilson, *The New Democracy: Presidential Messages, Addresses, and Other Papers, 1913–1917*, ed. Ray Stannard Baker and William E. Dodd, 2 vols. (New York: Harper & Brothers, 1926) 1:252–54.

[16] Ibid., 318–19.

World War I, however, brought fears of disloyal aliens to the surface of national social politics. The attempts by many immigrants to draw America into this ghastly European conflict on behalf of their former homelands, coupled with the fact that many new immigrants had not become naturalized citizens, convinced millions of Americans—and their representatives in Congress—that too many immigrants had failed to commit themselves wholeheartedly to their new homeland. The United States' entry into the war in 1917 deepened those fears for many Americans. Despite their cautions about fair treatment of loyal immigrants, Roosevelt and Wilson did much to stir nationalist ferment with their attacks on hyphenated Americans.

Just as the chaos of the French Revolutionary Wars had prompted Congress to pass the Alien and Sedition Acts in 1798 out of fear that the aliens in their midst would do irreparable harm to the government and society, so Congress acted during World War I to limit immigration. The literacy test, explicitly designed to exclude most of the new immigrants from Southern and Eastern Europe, was finally passed over Wilson's second veto as a result of the patriotic hysteria of World War I. More stringent deportation laws, including the revived Alien Enemy Act of 1798, were used to round up thousands of alien radicals during the Red Scare of 1919–1920, something which strengthened the traditional association of radicalism with foreigners.

The most significant political result of the wartime xenophobia, however, was its focus on German and Irish Americans. By casting suspicion on the two largest immigrant groups, the Wilson administration muzzled the most politically powerful and vocal opponents of immigration restriction—who, as it happens, were also usually staunch Democrats. The Republicans were thus free to exploit the discontent of the German and Irish Americans, while campaigning simultaneously for "America First" in 1920. The quota laws of the 1920s kept the old immigrant groups fighting over the relative size of their quotas, hampering efforts to unite against the literacy test as they had in 1907, 1913, and 1915. Ethnic group leaders could either risk opprobrium as "disloyal hyphenates" if they opposed the new laws, or argue that the long fight against restriction was over and lobby for the best possible quota. Most chose the latter course because it offered the likeliest opportunity to maintain their status as political power brokers.

The "One-Hundred Percent Americanism" of the war years confused the ideal of the melting pot with the Anglo-exclusivity of the nativists, and the two were never completely untangled afterwards. The demand for national unity and cultural homogeneity did not reflect mere prejudice. People do not try to assimilate those whom they hate and reject as inferior. For example, Southern Whites never advocated the Americanization of Southern Blacks, precisely because they understood that assimilation implies a political and social equality that might culminate in intermarriage. Furthermore, educating the foreign-born to become citizens contradicted the nativists' insistence that the new immigrants were biologically incapable of becoming fully "Anglo-Saxon." Eugenicist Alleyne Ireland wrote in 1918: "Education *can* bring out that which is in a man; it *cannot* put into a man that which is not there. It can impart facts to ignorance...but it cannot make a dullard bright or a fool sagacious."[17]

Nativists and eugenicists achieved restriction in the 1920s because they convinced an overwhelming majority in Congress that attempts at assimilation had failed. Offering civics classes to immigrants could not succeed because "Americanization is not an educational process," Henry Pratt Fairchild explained. Southern and Eastern Europeans could not become Americans, at least not without severe damage to the "racial stock" and corresponding destruction of America's political and social ideals. The "great fallacy of the melting pot," according to Fairchild, was that "nationalities will not mix."[18] Improving the immigrants' home and workplace environment, or replacing it with a rural one, was not enough to overcome the genetic limitations of the new immigrants. Eugenicist Harry H. Laughlin testified to the House Committee on Immigration and Naturalization in 1924 that limited numbers of immigrants were acceptable, but only if the "races to which they belong are compatible with our prevailing races for mate selection and...their family stocks are superior to our existing families."[19]

Progressive reformers responded that it was only the coercive acculturation practiced during wartime that had failed. Beginning in 1918,

---

[17] Alleyne Ireland, "Democracy and the Accepted Facts of Heredity," *Journal of Heredity*, 9 (December 1918): 341.

[18] Henry Pratt Fairchild, *Immigration: A World Movement and Its American Significance*, 2nd ed. (New York: Macmillan, 1928) 412, 419. See also Fairchild, *The Melting-Pot Mistake* (Boston: Little, Brown & Co., 1926).

[19] Congressional Committee on Immigration and Naturalization, *Europe as an Emigrant-Exporting Continent; the United States as an Immigrant-Receiving Nation*, 68th Cong., 1st sess., 1924 (Washington DC: Government Printing Office, 1924) 1295–296; Desmond King, *Making Americans: Immigration, Race, and the Origins of the Diverse Democracy* (Cambridge: Harvard University Press, 2000) 133.

the Carnegie Corporation funded a ten-volume study of Americanization. Based on a progressive definition of the concept, and including immigrants as active participants in the assimilation process, the series stated: "With all our rich heritages, Americanism will develop best through a mutual giving and taking of contributions from both newer and older Americans in the interest of the commonweal."[20] John Palmer Gavit, a former managing editor of the New York *Evening Post*, argued in his volume that the Dillingham Commission created the "legend" of the new immigrants' failure to assimilate because it failed to consider their shorter length of residence in America and poorer economic status. He was glad that World War I's "baptism of blood and suffering, of sacrifice and self-denial" had renewed the commitment of Americans to national unity. The wartime Americanization campaigns, however, took the wrong approach. "You cannot beat love of country into any worthwhile person with a club - or with a law," he observed. In the United States national unity was not based on racial identity but on allegiance to a common set of national ideals—offering asylum to the oppressed of the world, granting individuals freedom and protecting their rights.[21]

Frank V. Thompson, assistant superintendent of schools in Boston, agreed that the war had rightly brought attention to the fact that native-born Americans had neglected to assimilate immigrants. The efforts to assimilate, first begun out of fear, should now be continued "from motives of justice and humanity." He argued that the ideal Americanization program would "submit both the unworthy native and the unknowing immigrant to the same process," since "[m]isunderstanding is the chief obstacle which prevents the fusion process." In particular, the native-born had to give up their notions of racial superiority and treat immigrants as equals because democracy implied racial equality.[22] Similarly, William I. Thomas, Robert E. Park and Herbert A. Miller suggested that the native-born could hasten the assimilation of the

---

[20] John Palmer Gavit, *Americans by Choice*, Americanization Studies: The Acculturation of Immigrant Groups into American Society, ed. Allen T. Burns, 10 vols. (New York: Harper & Brothers, 1922; reprint, Montclair NJ: Patterson Smith, 1971) 8:xxv, xxviii. Theodore Roosevelt had been a member of the advisory committee for the series until his death.

[21] Gavit, *Americans by Choice*, 11–16, 38–39, 197–254, quotations 13, 39.

[22] Frank V. Thompson, *Schooling of the Immigrant*, Americanization Studies: The Acculturation of Immigrant Groups into American Society, ed. Allen T. Burns, 10 vols. (New York: Harper & Brothers, 1920; reprint, Montclair NJ: Patterson Smith, 1971) 1:23, 26–27, 365–70.

foreign-born "[i]f we give the immigrants a favorable milieu, if we tolerate their strangeness during their period of adjustment," and "if we help them to find points of contact" between their old world and new world experiences.[23]

The presidents in the 1920s—Warren G. Harding, Calvin Coolidge, and Herbert Hoover—upheld this progressive version of the melting pot concept in opposition to the nativists and eugenicists. They followed the rhetorical lead of Roosevelt, Taft, and Wilson in urging tolerance and respect for ethnic cultural traditions, while calling on all Americans, native and foreign-born, to unite in patriotic service to the nation. They differed from their pre-war predecessors, however, in strongly supporting immigration restriction. Although Harding, Coolidge, and Hoover opposed bigotry and were embarrassed by the crudeness and cruelty of the immigration quotas, they were all convinced of the economic and political necessity of drastically reducing the influx of foreigners to America. They reconciled this with the melting pot concept by arguing that immigration restriction would insure prosperity for both native and foreign-born, thereby creating a more favorable environment for assimilation of those already present and the few newer arrivals.

The postwar presidents' support for restriction was influenced by their choice of cabinet members. Before the war, liberal Secretaries of Commerce and Labor such as Oscar Straus, Charles Nagel, and William B. Wilson counterbalanced Bureau of Immigration nativists such as William Williams and Anthony Caminetti. The former consistently advised Roosevelt, Taft, and Wilson to oppose restriction. In the 1920s, however, Labor Secretary James J. Davis advanced the agenda of the eugenicists, consequently ensuring that no liberal opposition to the quotas was seriously considered.

Warren Harding, like Gavit and Thompson, believed that World War I had revealed not only the failure of many immigrants to assimilate, but also indifference and neglect on the part of native-born Americans to help new arrivals become a part of the nation's social fabric. While he criticized wartime coercion and the repression of aliens' civil rights, he called for a renewed focus on the melting pot: "In the great crucible we shall burn the dross of indifference and disloyalty and reveal the pure gold of a proud and

---

[23] William I. Thomas, Robert E. Park and Herbert A. Miller, *Old World Traits Transplanted*, Americanization Studies: The Acculturation of Immigrant Groups into American Society, ed. Allen T. Burns, 10 vols. (New York: Harper & Brothers, 1923; reprint, Montclair NJ: Patterson Smith, 1971) 3:308.

loyal American citizenship."[24] Harding endorsed Davis' "selective immigration" proposals, which were based on the ideas of Laughlin. He also established the Federal Council on Citizenship Training in 1923 to coordinate local Americanization efforts, thus rejecting a central eugenicist tenant: that education could not make worthy citizens out of unworthy germ plasm.[25]

Calvin Coolidge also urged his fellow Americans to make immigrants feel welcome and to invest the time, money and effort in teaching them the English language and American ideals. He insisted that all European immigrants had contributions to make to American society, and he urged all Americans to treat each other with toleration and respect. Instead of "crumbling into a chaos of discordant elements" during the war, Coolidge declared, "America proved its truly national unity" and "demonstrated conclusively that there is a spiritual quality shared by all races and conditions of men which is their universal heritage and common nature."[26] He worked to prevent the 1924 Johnson Act from explicitly banning Japanese immigrants, but he defended the national origins quotas as a necessity for maintaining prosperity. Coolidge pointed out to foreign-born citizens that if unrestricted immigration were allowed to bring down wages and the standard of living, "the first sufferers would be the most recent immigrants, unaccustomed to our life and language and industrial methods."[27]

Herbert Hoover followed Coolidge's lead in supporting immigration restriction while celebrating the contributions that all European immigrants made to American society and culture. He fought against the national origins quotas in order to win votes among Irish, German, and Scandinavian Americans, but he supported the principle of restriction as the key to maintaining a high standard of living for native and foreign-born alike: "We welcome our new immigrant citizens and their great contribution to our nation; we seek only to protect them equally with those already here."[28] The Great Depression, however, ended any association between the Republican

---

[24] Warren G. Harding, "Lincoln Club Address," Portland ME, 13 Feb. 1920, Warren G. Harding Papers, Series 5, Box 838 (reel 238), Ohio Historical Society, Columbus OH.

[25] King, *Making Americans*, 107.

[26] Calvin Coolidge, *Foundations of the Republic: Speeches and Addresses* (New York: Charles Scribner's Sons, 1926) 250.

[27] Ibid., 83.

[28] Herbert Hoover, *Public Papers of the Presidents of the United States: Herbert Hoover*, 4 vols. (Washington: Government Printing Office, 1974–1977), 1:508.

party and the "full dinner pail." Hoover responded to the economic crisis by ending the traditional offer of American asylum and using a strict interpretation of the "likely to become a public charge" clause to limit immigration severely.

Harding, Coolidge, and Hoover's task of opposing nativism in the 1920s was made easier because the basic premises of the eugenics movement began to be called into question at the very moment of its triumph. In part this was due to the economic prosperity of those years, which lessened fears of foreign workers stealing jobs from Americans, or prompting Communist revolutions. The second national manifestation of the Ku Klux Klan fell apart as quickly as it had been formed, and Herbert Jennings and other geneticists began to challenge the faulty science of eugenicists like Harry Laughlin and Charles Davenport. Jennings and anthropologist Franz Boas were recruited by Illinois Congressman Emmanuel Celler in his fight against the 1924 National Origins Act, but the full-scale assault on the pseudo-science would not begin until the late 1930s and 1940s, when its ties to the Nazi regime in Germany became clear.[29]

Nativist assertions that the new immigrants were not and could not be assimilated were also challenged. Sociologists affiliated with the University of Chicago, led by Robert E. Park, studied assimilation in the 1920s and concluded that it was a predictable, inevitable process. They described a "race relations" cycle—contact, competition, accommodation and assimilation—that was linked to the "ecological succession" of the cities. The Chicago School sociologists argued that as ethnic groups moved out from the ghettoes into concentric urban and eventually suburban zones, their members became more dispersed and were gradually absorbed into the general American society. While immigrants' desire to retain their culture and the nativists' "ineradicable prejudice" might hamper the process of becoming Americans, there were no inherited racial traits which determined the success or lack of assimilation.[30]

---

[29] Elazar Barkan, *The Retreat of Scientific Racism: Changing Concepts of Race in Britain and the United States Between the World Wars* (Cambridge: Cambridge University Press, 1992) 196–201; Haller, *Eugenics*, 95–123; Higham, *Strangers in the Land*, 324–30; Kevles, *In the Name of Eugenics*, 77–84, 132–35; and Kenneth M. Ludmerer, *Genetics and American Society: A Historical Appraisal* (Baltimore: Johns Hopkins University Press, 1971) 110–13, 121–34.

[30] Robert E. Park and Ernest W. Burgess, *Introduction to the Science of Sociology* (Chicago: University of Chicago Press, 1921); Thomas, Park and Miller, *Old World Traits Transplanted*, 304–305; Gleason, *Speaking of Diversity*, 52–55; and Russell A.

The retreat of nativism continued into the 1930s. President Franklin D. Roosevelt followed the lead of Harding, Coolidge, and Hoover in upholding the progressive version of the American melting pot. Democrat Woodrow Wilson had alienated ethnic Americans by giving in to the prejudiced patriotism of World War I, helping to pave the way for the Republican ascendancy of the 1920s. Not until 1932 did many of those voters return to the Democratic party, although Alfred Smith's 1928 campaign foreshadowed the building of the New Deal's urban, working-class coalition. Of course, given the economic disaster, Franklin Roosevelt likely would have won the 1932 election in any case. Nevertheless, the president built on the idea of the melting pot sustained by his Republican predecessors to forge a powerful political coalition that united the various European ethnic groups and proclaimed them all equally Americans.

Speaking at the fiftieth anniversary of the Statue of Liberty in 1936, Roosevelt became the first president to link that symbol of the American ideal to the millions of immigrants who entered the nation through nearby Ellis Island. "For over three centuries a steady stream of men, women and children followed the beacon of liberty which this light symbolizes," he said, adding that he liked to think of the newly arriving immigrants seeing the statue as their first glimpse of America. He celebrated the contributions which the foreign-born had made, declaring, "They brought to us strength and moral fiber developed in a civilization centuries old but fired anew by the dream of a better life in America." He insisted, however, that the era of immigration had ended and that the various cultures represented among the immigrant population had to be fused into a new, united American nationality. Immigrants might retain affection for "old customs, old language, old friends," but they were nevertheless to embark on being a new people. Roosevelt affirmed that the overwhelming majority of those who came from the old world were "men and women who had the supreme courage to strike out for themselves" in a land prepared by Providence to be "a place of the second chance." He concluded: "Into this continental reservoir there has been poured untold and untapped wealth of human resources. Out of that reservoir, out of the melting pot, the rich promise

Kazal, "Revisiting Assimilation: The Rise, Fall, and Reappraisal of a Concept in American Ethnic History," *American Historical Review*, 100/2 (April 1995): 442–46.

which the New World held out to those who come to it from many lands is finding fulfillment."[31]

Franklin Roosevelt used the rhetoric of the melting pot to build support for his New Deal policies and programs, achieving the improvements to the immigrants' environment that progressive reformers had argued would help assimilate the foreign-born. The Works Progress Administration and other relief agencies provided jobs, and even collected immigrants' stories and songs as part of a conscious effort to lay the foundations of a new American culture. Legislation such as the National Labor Relations Act, the Social Security Act and the Fair Labor Standards Act provided greater economic opportunities and support for a basic standard of living. New Deal programs also took tentative steps toward reaching out to African Americans, who increasingly and overwhelmingly voted for Democratic Party candidates beginning in 1934.[32]

The New Deal not only ameliorated immigrants' lives, but it also built American nationalism on an inclusive basis, unlike the nationalistic exclusivity and racism embraced by Europe's fascist leaders during the early decades of the twentieth century. Assimilation, however, was still limited to European Americans. Asian immigrants remained "aliens ineligible to citizenship" who were barred from entering, although the ban on the Chinese was lifted in 1943 as a gesture of goodwill toward America's ally in the war against the Axis Powers. While World War II led to greater acceptance for the newer immigrants already resident in the United States, it unleashed a barrage of racist propaganda aimed at the Japanese and the internment of over 110,000 Japanese Americans.[33]

Franklin Roosevelt also kept the gates closed to most European immigrants. Like Harding, Coolidge, and Hoover, he supported immigration restriction while also a proponent of the progressive model of the American melting pot. He made no move to overturn the national origins quotas, and despite some misgivings, did not restore the broad-natured American offer of asylum that Hoover had brought to an end. The latter decision proved

---

[31] Franklin D. Roosevelt, *Nothing to Fear: The Selected Addresses of Franklin D. Roosevelt, 1932–1945*, ed. Benjamin D. Zevin (Boston: Houghton Mifflin, 1946) 69–72.

[32] Gary Gerstle, *American Crucible: Race and Nation in the Twentieth Century* (Princeton: Princeton University Press, 2001) 131–55.

[33] See Roger Daniels, *Concentration Camps U. S. A.: Japanese Americans and World War II* (New York: Holt, Rinehart & Winston, 1971); and John Dower, *War Without Mercy: Race and Power in the Pacific War* (New York: Pantheon Books, 1986).

especially tragic as the events surrounding World War II unfolded. Wilbur Carr and Breckenridge Long in the State Department used the interpretation of the "likely to become a public charge" clause—carried over from the Hoover administration—to block the wholesale admission to the United States of Jewish refugees from the Nazi regime.

Roosevelt and Secretary of Labor Frances Perkins did move to admit Jewish refugees who had relatives in the United States, as well as orphaned and handicapped children for whom Jewish agencies had agreed to care. Following *Kristallnacht* in 1938, Roosevelt ordered the State Department to renew indefinitely the travel visas of 15,000 Germans and Austrians visiting the United States. Nevertheless, Perkins was unable to persuade Roosevelt to allow the immediate assignment of the German and Austrian quotas for the next three years to Jewish and other refugees from the Third Reich. Under Secretary of State Sumner Welles rejected the British government's offer to reassign most of its quota to German refugees. In 1938 Roosevelt did invite delegates from thirty-two nations to a conference on the refugee problem in Evian, France, but he explicitly stated that the United States would not change its immigration laws or relax their enforcement.[34]

Despite the tragic failure to offer asylum to more than a handful of Jewish refugees and the inexcusable decision to violate the civil rights of thousands of Japanese Americans, Roosevelt continued to uphold the progressive version of the melting pot ideal fashioned by his predecessors. With most immigrants excluded, native-born Americans no longer felt as threatened by the foreign-born. In the common struggle to survive the Great Depression, the alleged racial and cultural differences of Southern and Eastern Europeans seemed less significant. The great migration of African Americans from Southern farms to Northern cities, along with the influx of Mexican immigrants, also helped Italians, Jews, and Slavs seem similar by

---

[34] Kenneth S. Davis, *F. D. R.: Into the Storm, 1937–1940: A History* (New York: Random House, 1993) 367–72; Robert A. Divine, *American Immigration Policy, 1924–1952* (New Haven: Yale University Press, 1957) 92–104; Frank Freidel, *Franklin D. Roosevelt: A Rendezvous with Destiny* (Boston: Little, Brown & Co., 1990) 296–97; Alan M. Kraut, Richard Breitman and Thomas W. Imhoof, "The State Department, the Labor Department, and German Jewish Immigration, 1930–1940," *Journal of American Ethnic History*, 3/2 (Spring 1984): 5–38; Nathan Miller, *F. D. R.: An Intimate History* (Garden City NY: Doubleday & Co., 1983) 428–29; Frances Perkins, *The Roosevelt I Knew* (New York: Viking, 1946) 348–49; and David Wyman, *Paper Walls: America and the Refugee Crisis, 1938–1941* (Amherst: University of Massachusetts Press, 1968) 46–47, 209.

comparison to the established White majority, and therefore more racially acceptable.[35] Roosevelt rallied workers from all ethnic groups to create a united national culture and pass legislation to provide economic opportunities for all Americans.

Franklin Roosevelt, like his predecessors dating back to William McKinley, praised the contributions European immigrants had made to the United States. He expressed confidence in their worthiness and readiness to assume the mantle of US citizenship. Between 1897–1945, all the American presidents advocated the idea that the nation was a melting pot, welcoming immigrants from Europe and assimilating them on the basis of shared ideals. Although the presidents accepted the need for some immigration restriction, they rejected the racism of nativists and eugenicists. The presidents' desire to unite all Americans, while respecting their rich cultural diversity, is a legacy worth reviving today as the nation again struggles to find the path toward unity—a path that must wind its way between the precipices of militant multiculturalism on the one hand and suffocating xenophobia on the other.

---

[35] Matthew Frye Jacobson, *Whiteness of a Different Color: European Immigrants and the Alchemy of Race* (Cambridge: Harvard University Press, 1998) 91–136.

SELECTED BIBLIOGRAPHY

Presidential Papers

Coolidge, Calvin. Papers. Presidential Manuscripts. Forbes Library, Northampton MA.
———. The Presidential Papers of Calvin Coolidge. Library of Congress, Washington DC.
Harding, Warren G. Papers. Ohio Historical Society, Columbus OH.
Hoover, Herbert. Papers. Herbert Hoover Presidential Library, West Branch IA.
McKinley, William. The Presidential Papers of William McKinley. Library of Congress, Washington DC.
Roosevelt, Theodore. The Presidential Papers of Theodore Roosevelt. Library of Congress, Washington DC.
Taft, William Howard. The Presidential Papers of William Howard Taft. Library of Congress, Washington DC.

Published Presidential Works

Coolidge, Calvin. *The Autobiography of Calvin Coolidge.* New York: Cosmopolitan Book Corp., 1929.
———. *Foundations of the Republic: Speeches and Addresses.* New York: Charles Scribner's Sons, 1926.
———. *Have Faith in Massachusetts: A Collection of Speeches and Messages.* 2d ed. Boston: Houghton Mifflin, 1919.
———. *The Price of Freedom: Speeches and Addresses.* New York: Charles Scribner's Sons, 1924.
———. *The Talkative President: The Off-the-Record Press Conferences of Calvin Coolidge.* Edited by Howard H. Quint and Robert H. Ferrell. Amherst: University of Massachusetts Press, 1964.
———. *Your Son, Calvin Coolidge: A Selection of Letters from Calvin Coolidge to His Father.* Edited by Edward Connery Lathem. Montpelier: Vermont Historical Society, 1968.
Hoover, Herbert. *American Individualism.* Garden City NY: Doubleday, Page & Co., 1922.
———. *The Memoirs of Herbert Hoover.* 3 volumes. New York: Macmillan, 1951–1952.
———. *Public Papers of the Presidents of the United States: Herbert Hoover.* 4 volumes. Washington DC: GPO, 1974-1977.
———. *The State Papers and Other Public Writings of Herbert Hoover.* Edited by William Starr Myers. 2 volumes. Garden City NY: Doubleday, Doran & Co., 1934.
McKinley, William. *Speeches and Addresses of William McKinley, from His Election to Congress to the Present Time.* New York: D. Appleton & Co., 1893.
———. Roosevelt, Theodore. *An Autobiography.* New York: Macmillan, 1913.

————. *The Letters of Theodore Roosevelt*. Edited by Elting E. Morison, John M. Blum and John J. Buckley. 8 volumes. Cambridge: Harvard University Press, 1951–1954.

————. *The Letters of Theodore Roosevelt and Brander Matthews*. Edited by Lawrence J. Oliver. Knoxville: University of Tennessee Press, 1995.

————. *The Works of Theodore Roosevelt, National Edition*. 20 volumes. New York: Charles Scribner's Sons, 1926.

Taft, William Howard. *Collected Editorials, 1917–1921*. Edited by James F. Vivian. New York: Praeger, 1990.

————. *Popular Government: Its Essence, Its Permanence and Its Perils*. New Haven CT: Yale University Press, 1913.

————. *Present Day Problems: A Collection of Addresses Delivered on Various Occasions*. New York: Dodd, Mead & Co., 1908.

Wilson, Woodrow. *A History of the American People*. 5 volumes. New York: Harper & Bros., 1902.

————. *The New Democracy: Presidential Messages, Addresses, and Other Papers, 1913–1917*. Edited by Ray Stannard Baker and William E. Dodd. 2 volumes. New York: Harper & Bros., 1926.

————. *The Papers of Woodrow Wilson*. Edited by Arthur S. Link et al. 69 volumes. Princeton: Princeton University Press, 1966–1994.

Other Primary Sources

Carpenter, Niles. *Immigrants and Their Children, 1920*. Washington DC: GPO, 1927.

Commons, John R. *Races and Immigrants in America*. 2d edition. New York: Macmillan, 1920.

Davis, James J. *Selective Immigration*. St. Paul: Scott-Mitchell, 1925.

Fairchild, Henry Pratt. *Immigration: A World Movement and its American Significance*. 2d edition. New York: Macmillan, 1928.

————. *The Melting-Pot Mistake*. Boston: Little, Brown & Co., 1926.

Gavit, John Palmer. *Americans by Choice*. Volume 8 of *Americanization Studies: The Acculturation of Immigrant Groups into American Society*. Edited by Allen T. Burns. 1922. Reprint, Montclair NJ: Patterson Smith, 1971.

Gompers, Samuel. Seventy Years of Life and Labor: An Autobiography. New York : E.P. Dutton, 1925.

Hall, Prescott F. *Immigration and Its Effects Upon the United States*. New York: Henry Holt, 1906.

Kallen, Horace M. *Culture and Democracy in the United States: Studies in the Group Psychology of the American People*. New York: Boni & Liveright, 1924.

Lodge, Henry Cabot. *Selections from the Correspondence of Theodore Roosevelt and Henry Cabot Lodge, 1884-1918*. New York: Charles Scribner's Sons, 1925.

————. *Speeches and Addresses, 1884-1909*. Boston: Houghton Mifflin, 1909.

Meyers, William Starr and Walter H. Newton. *The Hoover Administration: A Documented Narrative*. New York: Charles Scribner's Sons, 1936.

Powderly, Terence V. *The Path I Trod: The Autobiography of Terence V. Powderly*. Edited by Harry J. Carman, Henry David and Paul N. Guthrie. New York: Columbia University Press, 1940. .

Roberts, Peter. *The New Immigration: A Study of the Industrial and Social Life of Southeastern Europeans in America.* 1912. Reprint, New York: Arno Press, 1970.

Smith, Richmond Mayo. *Emigration and Immigration: A Study in Social Science.* 1890. Reprint, New York: Johnson Reprint Co., 1968.

Steiner, Edward A. *On the Trail of the Immigrant.* 1906. Reprint, New York: Arno Press, 1969.

Thomas, William I., Robert E. Park and Herbert A. Miller. *Old World Traits Transplanted.* Volume 3 of *Americanization Studies: The Acculturation of Immigrant Groups into American Society.* Edited by Allen T. Burns. 1922. Reprint, Montclair NJ: Patterson Smith, 1971.

Thompson, Frank V. *Schooling of the Immigrant.* Volume 1 of *Americanization Studies: The Acculturation of Immigrant Groups into American Society.* Edited by Allen T. Burns. 1922. Reprint, Montclair NJ: Patterson Smith, 1971.

Tumulty, Joseph P. *Woodrow Wilson as I Know Him.* Garden City NY: Doubleday, Page & Co., 1921.

United States Immigration Commission. *Reports of the Immigration Commission.* 42 volumes. Washington DC: GPO, 1911.

United States Industrial Commission. *Report of the Industrial Commission, Volume XV: Report on Immigration and on Education.* Washington DC: GPO, 1901.

Watchorn, Robert. *The Autobiography of Robert Watchorn.* Edited by Herbert Faulkner West. Oklahoma City: The Robert Watchorn Charities, 1958.

Presidential Studies

Anderson, Donald F. *William Howard Taft: A Conservative's Conception of the Presidency.* Ithaca: Cornell University Press, 1968.

Blum, John M. *The Republican Roosevelt.* 2d Edition. Cambridge: Harvard University Press, 1977.

_____. *Joe Tumulty and the Wilson Era.* Boston: Houghton Mifflin, 1951.

Bragdon, Henry W. *Woodrow Wilson: The Academic Years.* Cambridge: Harvard University Press, 1967.

Burner, David. *Herbert Hoover: A Public Life.* New York: Alfred A. Knopf, 1979.

Burton, David H. *The Learned Presidency: Theodore Roosevelt, William Howard Taft, and Woodrow Wilson.* Rutherford: Fairleigh Dickinson University Press, 1988.

Coletta, Paulo E. *The Presidency of William Howard Taft.* Lawrence: University Press of Kansas, 1980.

Cooper, John Milton. *The Warrior and the Priest: Woodrow Wilson and Theodore Roosevelt.* Cambridge: Harvard University Press, 1983.

Downes, Randolph C. *The Rise of Warren Gamaliel Harding, 1865–1920.* Columbus: Ohio State University Press, 1970.

Dyer, Thomas G. *Theodore Roosevelt and the Idea of Race.* Baton Rouge: Louisiana State University Press, 1980.

Ferrell, Robert H. *The Presidency of Calvin Coolidge.* Lawrence: University Press of Kansas, 1998.

Gould, Lewis L. *The Presidency of Theodore Roosevelt.* Lawrence: University Press of Kansas, 1991.

————. *The Presidency of William McKinley*. Lawrence: University Press of Kansas, 1980.

Heckscher, August. *Woodrow Wilson*. New York: Charles Scribner's Sons, 1991.

Leech, Margaret. *In the Days of McKinley*. New York: Harper & Brothers, 1959.

Link, Arthur S. *The Higher Realism of Woodrow Wilson and Other Essays*. Nashville: Vanderbilt University Press, 1971.

————. *Wilson*. 5 volumes. Princeton: Princeton University Press, 1947–1965.

————. *Woodrow Wilson and the Progressive Era*. New York: Harper Row, 1954.

McCoy, Donald R. *Calvin Coolidge: The Quiet President*. Lawrence: University Press of Kansas, 1967.

Miller, Nathan. *Theodore Roosevelt: A Life*. New York: William Morrow & Co., 1992.

Morgan, H. Wayne. *William McKinley and his America*. Syracuse: Syracuse University Press, 1963.

Morris, Edmund. *The Rise of Theodore Roosevelt*. New York: Ballantine, 1979.

Mowry, George E. *The Era of Theodore Roosevelt, 1900–1912*. New York: Harper & Row, 1958.

Murray, Robert K. *The Harding Era: Warren G. Harding and his Administration*. Minneapolis: University of Minnesota Press, 1969.

————. *The Politics of Normalcy: Governmental Theory and Practice in the Harding-Coolidge Era*. New York: W. W. Norton & Co., 1973.

Nash, George. *The Life of Herbert Hoover: The Engineer, 1874–1914*. New York: W. W. Norton & Co., 1983.

Nash, Lee, editor. *Understanding Herbert Hoover: Ten Perspectives*. Stanford: Hoover Institution Press, 1987.

O'Reilly, Kenneth. *Nixon's Piano: Presidents and Racial Politics from Washington to Clinton*. New York: Free Press, 1995.

Russell, Francis. *The Shadow of Blooming Grove: Warren G. Harding in His Times*. New York: McGraw-Hill, 1968.

Sinclair, Andrew. *The Available Man: The Life Behind the Masks of Warren Gamaliel Harding*. New York: MacMillan, 1965.

Sinkler, George. *The Racial Attitudes of American Presidents from Abraham Lincoln to Theodore Roosevelt*. Garden City NY: Doubleday, 1971.

Smith, Richard Norton. *An Uncommon Man: The Triumph of Herbert Hoover*. New York: Simon & Schuster, 1984.

Sobel, Robert. *Coolidge: An American Enigma*. Washington DC: Regnery, 1998.

Traina, Eugene P. and David L. Wilson. *The Presidency of Warren G. Harding*. Lawrence: University Press of Kansas, 1977.

Walworth, Arthur. *Woodrow Wilson*. 2d edition. Boston: Houghton Mifflin, 1965.

Wilson, Joan Hoff. *Herbert Hoover: Forgotten Progressive*. Boston: Little, Brown & Co., 1975.

General Monographs

Asmus, Pamela Katherine. "The Rise and Fall of the Anglo-Saxon Myth in the United States, 1770–1954." Ph.D. dissertation, Brown University, 1987.

Bailey, Thomas A. *Woodrow Wilson and the Great Betrayal*. New York: Macmillan, 1945.

Bennett, Marion T. *American Immigration Policies: A History*. Washington DC: Public Affairs Press, 1963.

Bodnar, John. *The Transplanted: A History of Immigrants in Urban America*. Bloomington: Indiana University Press, 1985.

Briggs, Lawrence John. "For the Welfare of Wage Earners: Immigration Policy and the Labor Department, 1913–1921." Ph.D. dissertation, Syracuse University, 1995.

Chuman, Frank F. *The Bamboo People: The Law and Japanese-Americans*. Del Mar CA: Publisher's Inc., 1976.

Coben, Stanley. *A. Mitchell Palmer: Politician*. New York: Columbia University Press, 1963.

Cuddy, Joseph Edward. *Irish-America and National Isolationism, 1914–1920*. New York: Arno Press, 1976.

Daniels, Roger. *The Politics of Prejudice: The Anti-Japanese Movement in California and the Struggle for Japanese Exclusion*. Berkley: University of California Press, 1962.

DeConde, Alexander. *Ethnicity, Race, and American Foreign Policy: A History*. Boston: Northeastern University Press, 1992.

Divine, Robert A. *American Immigration Policy, 1924–1952*. New Haven: Yale University Press, 1957.

Evans, Patricia Russell. "'Likely to Become a Public Charge': Immigration in the Backwaters of Administrative Law, 1892–1933." Ph.D. dissertation, George Washington University, 1987.

Fuchs, Lawrence H. *The American Kaleidoscope: Race, Ethnicity, and the Civic Culture*. Hanover NH: University Press of New England; Middletown CT: Wesleyan University Press, 1990.

Gerstle, Gary. *American Crucible: Race and Nation in the Twentieth Century*. Princeton: Princeton University Press, 2001.

Gleason, Philip. *Speaking of Diversity: Language and Ethnicity in Twentieth-Century America*. Baltimore: Johns Hopkins University Press, 1992.

Gordon, Milton M. *Assimilation in American Life: The Role of Race, Religion, and National Origins*. New York: Oxford University Press, 1964.

Gyory, Andrew. *Closing the Gate: Race, Politics, and the Chinese Exclusion Act*. Chapel Hill: University of North Carolina Press, 1998.

Haller, Mark H. *Eugenics: Hereditarian Attitudes in American Thought*. New Brunswick: Rutgers University Press, 1963.

Handlin, Oscar. *Race and Nationality in American Life*. Boston: Little, Brown & Co., 1957.

Hershfield, Rachel Leah. "The Immigration Restriction League: A Study of the League's Impact on American Immigration Policy, 1894–1924." M.A. thesis, University of Calgary, 1993.

Higham, John. *Send These to Me: Immigrants in Urban America*. 2d edition. Baltimore: Johns Hopkins University Press, 1984.

————. *Strangers in the Land: Patterns of American Nativism, 1860–1925*. 2d edition. New Brunswick: Rutgers University Press, 1988.

Hofstadter, Richard. *Social Darwinism in American Thought*. 2d edition. New York: George Braziller, 1959.

Hollinger, David A. *Postethnic America: Beyond Multiculturalism*. New York: Basic Books, 1995.

Hutchinson, Edward P. *Legislative History of American Immigration Policy, 1798–1965*. Philadelphia: University of Pennsylvania Press, 1981.

Kevles, Daniel J. *In the Name of Eugenics: Genetics and the Uses of Human Heredity*. New York: Alfred A. Knopf, 1985.

King, Desmond. *Making Americans: Immigration, Race, and the Origins of the Diverse Democracy*. Cambridge: Harvard University Press, 2000.

Lichtman, Allan J. *Prejudice and the Old Politics: The Presidential Election of 1928*. Chapel Hill: University of North Carolina Press, 1979.

Lissak, Riska Shpak. *Pluralism and Progressives: Hull House and the New Immigrants, 1890-1919*. Chicago: University of Chicago Press, 1989.

Ludmerer, Kenneth M. *Genetics and American Society: A Historical Appraisal*. Baltimore: Johns Hopkins University Press, 1972.

Luebke, Frederick C. *Bonds of Loyalty: German-Americans and World War I*. DeKalb IL: Northern Illinois University Press, 1974.

Murray, Robert K. *Red Scare: A Study in National Hysteria, 1919–1920*. Minneapolis: University of Minnesota Press, 1955.

Neuman, Gerald L. *Strangers to the Constitution: Immigrants, Borders, and Fundamental Law*. Princeton: Princeton University Press, 1996.

O'Grady, Joseph P., editor. *The Immigrants' Influence on Wilson's Peace Policies*. Lexington: University of Kentucky Press, 1967.

Pencak, William. *For God and Country: The American Legion, 1919–1941*. Boston: Northeastern University Press, 1989.

Pickens, Donald K. *Eugenics and the Progressives*. Nashville: Vanderbilt University Press, 1968.

Pitkin, Thomas M. *Keepers of the Gate: A History of Ellis Island*. New York: New York University Press, 1975.

Preston, William, Jr. *Aliens and Dissenters: Federal Suppression of Radicals, 1903–1933*. Cambridge: Harvard University Press, 1963. Reprint, New York: Harper & Row, 1966.

Robinson, Edgar Eugene. *The Presidential Vote, 1896–1932*. Palo Alto: Stanford University Press, 1934.

Salins, Peter D. *Assimilation, American Style*. New York: Basic Books, 1997.

Salyer, Lucy E. *Laws Harsh as Tigers: Chinese Immigrants and the Shaping of Modern Immigration Law*. Chapel Hill: University of North Carolina Press, 1995.

Schelsinger, Arthur M., Jr. *The Disuniting of America: Reflections on a Multicultural Society*. New York: W.W. Norton & Co., 1992.

Solomon, Barbara Miller. *Ancestors and Immigrants: A Changing New England Tradition*. Cambridge: Harvard University Press, 1956. Reprint, New York: J. Wiley & Sons, 1965.

Tansill, Charles C. *America and the Fight for Irish Freedom, 1866–1922*. New York: The Devin-Adair Co., 1957.

Vaughn, Stephen. *Holding Fast the Inner Lines: Democracy, Nationalism, and the Committee on Public Safety*. Chapel Hill: University of North Carolina Press, 1980.

Wang, Peter H. *Legislating Normalcy: The Immigration Act of 1924*. San Francisco: R & E Research Associates, 1975.

Zeidel, Robert Fredric. "The Literacy Test for Immigrants: A Question of Progress." Ph.D. dissertation, Marquette University, 1986.

Articles

Barkan, Elliott R. "Race, Religion and Nationality in American Society: A Model of Ethnicity—From Contact to Assimilation." *Journal of American Ethnic History* 14/2 (Winter 1995): 38–75.

Barrett, James R. "Americanization from the Bottom Up: Immigration and the Remaking of the Working Class in the United States, 1880-1930" *Journal of American History* 79/3 (December 1992):996-1020.

Barrett, James R. and David Roediger. "Inbetween Peoples: Race, Nationality and the 'New Immigrant' Working Class." *Journal of American Ethnic History* 16/3 (Spring 1997): 3–44.

Conzen, Kathleen N., David A. Gerber, Ewa Morawska, George E. Pozzetta, and Rudolph J. Vecoli. "The Invention of Ethnicity: A Perspective from the U.S.A." *Journal of American Ethnic History* 12/1 (Fall 1992): 3–41.

Gans, Herbert J. "Symbolic Ethnicity: The Future of Ethnic Groups and Cultures." *Ethnic and Racial Studies* 2 (January 1979): 1–20.

Gerstle, Gary. "Liberty, Coercion, and the Making of Americans." *Journal of American History* 84/2 (September 1997): 524–58.

Gleason, Philip. "American Identity and Americanization." In *Harvard Encyclopedia of American Ethnic Groups*. Edited by Stephan Thernstrom. Cambridge: Harvard University Press, 1980, 31–58.

Jenswold, John R. "Leaving the Door Ajar: Politics and Prejudices in the Making of the 1907 Immigration Law." *Mid-America* 67/1 (January 1985): 3–22.

Kazal, Russell A. "Revisiting Assimilation: The Rise, Fall, and Reappraisal of a Concept in American Ethnic History." *American Historical Review* 100/2 (April 1995): 437–71.

Kerr, Thomas J., IV. "German-Americans and Neutrality in the 1916 Election." *Mid-America* 43/2 (April 1961): 95–105.

Leonard, Henry B. "Louis Marshall and Immigration Restriction, 1906–1924." *American Jewish Archives* 24/1 (1972): 6–26.

Lissak, Riva Shpak. "The National Liberal Immigration League and Immigration Restriction, 1906–1917." *American Jewish Archives* 46/2 (1994): 197–246.

Lund, John M. "Vermont Nativism: William Paul Dillingham and U.S. Immigration Legislation." *Vermont History* 63/1 (Winter 1995): 15–29.

Schlup, Leonard. "William Paul Dillingham: A Vermont Republican in National Politics." *Vermont History* 54/1 (Winter 1986): 20–36.

Zunz, Olivier. "American History and the Changing Meaning of Assimilation." *Journal of American Ethnic History* 4/2 (Spring 1985): 53–72.

INDEX